"A science fiction [novel that] smashes *The Bourne Identity* together with *The End of Eternity* to create a thrilling action rampage that confirms [Jason] Hough as an important new voice in genre fiction."

—*Publishers Weekly* (starred review)

"An enjoyable read . . . expect minor whiplash from the frenetic pace." —*Entertainment Weekly*

"Hough has combined all the ingredients of a first-rate sci-fi thriller." —*Kirkus Reviews*

"One hell of an entertaining read. Hough continues to deliver white-knuckle books anchored by unusual and fascinating characters. *Zero World* is a giant cup of pure badassery that secures his place among the finest sci-fi action writers today."

—Kevin Hearne, *New York Times* bestselling author of The Iron Druid Chronicles

"A high-octane blend of science fiction and mystery, *Zero World* is a thrill ride that shoots you out of a cannon and doesn't let up until the very last page."

—Wesley Chu, author of the Tao series

"Warning: Do not pick up this book if there is anything else you need to do. There is no safe place to rest inside these pages, no lag in the full-throttle action, no moment when you will think, 'Okay, this is a good spot to take a break.' Once you realize how much you don't know—about this world, these characters, this inexplicable ~~~~

way out ~

—Brian Stave~

The Empe~

ALSO AVAILABLE FROM JASON M. HOUGH AND TITAN BOOKS

ZERO WORLD

THE DIRE EARTH CYCLE
The Darwin Elevator
The Exodus Towers
The Plague Forge
Injection Burn

ESCAPE VELOCITY

A DIRE EARTH NOVEL

JASON M. HOUGH

TITAN BOOKS

Escape Velocity
Print edition ISBN: 9781783295302
E-book edition ISBN: 9781783295319

Published by Titan Books
A division of Titan Publishing Group Ltd.
144 Southwark Street, London SE1 0UP

First edition June 2017

1 3 5 7 9 10 8 6 4 2

Jason M. Hough asserts the moral right to be identified as the
author of this work.

This edition published by arrangement with Del Rey, an imprint of The Random
House Publishing Group, a division of Random House, Inc.

A CIP catalogue record for this title is available from the British Library.

Printed and bound in Great Britain by CPI Group Ltd.

For Nathan and Ian

In a far-off place, under the most extreme of circumstances,
he did what he thought best.
For all of us.
—a gravestone in Nightcliff, Australia, A.D. 3911

You seem to forget how utterly alone we were out there. There was no time to plan, no way to even communicate. Can we do this later? I need some time. I need a chance to mourn our dead.

—Dr. Tania Sharma, interrogation transcript, 26.AUG.3911

ESCAPE VELOCITY

1

LOCATION UNKNOWN

He lay at the bottom of a deep hole, in a puddle of filthy water that sizzled as bits of molten metal dripped down from the destruction above.

Skyler Luiken remained motionless for a time, just staring up at the column his arrival had carved. He remembered nothing of the actual crash. Couldn't even remember when exactly he'd lost consciousness, or why. Medically induced, probably. Another gift from Eve. Her last? He called out for her. "Eve?"

No response came. But then she'd said he'd be on his own, hadn't she?

He took a long, shuddering breath and allowed all the sources of his frayed nerves to worm through his mind. He was a thousand light-years from Earth. Alone. His friends were scattered across the gigantic, planet-spanning apparatus of the Scipios, their exact locations and conditions unknown. All of them had been thrown toward the massive collection of alien space stations in the final explosion of Eve, their host. Eve, the only ally they had, the only one who knew what the hell was really going on here. Now gone. *Holy fuck, she's really gone.* The AI had sacrificed herself. Expelled him and the others on precisely calculated trajectories an instant before her destruction in a last-ditch effort to give each of them a chance to accomplish the task at hand.

He found little comfort in that.

Skyler let his breath out, and with it banished the enormity of his task to the edges of his mind. Too much to grapple with, and he wasn't about to lie here and wallow in overwhelmed shock. He'd deal with his immediate predicament now, and damn the rest of it. He had to survive, take stock, find safety. Find his friends.

"Hello?" he called. "Can anyone read me?"

A terrible silence stretched. He fiddled with the comm menu rendered on the inside of his visor. All channels were already on, but it showed no links to anyone else. He bumped the system to maximum broadcast strength.

"This is Skyler. I'm . . . I've no idea where I am. I'm alive. Obviously. I can't hear any of you, but if you can read me . . ."

What? What to tell them?

"Just stay put," he settled on, no better option coming to mind. "I'll report my location once I know where the hell I am, and wait for you all to join me. Keep trying to communicate. We might just be out of range."

Now what? he wondered.

The answer seemed obvious. He had to scavenge.

Now that, *that,* Skyler could wrap his mind around. He glanced around the pool of fluid and debris in the basin of the pit his arrival had created. The pod had burrowed through some kind of multilevel structure. A space station, no doubt. How deep had he gone? Skyler glanced up. The air above, thick with steam and smoke and a fine particulate like snow or ash, obscured the entry wound, but he figured the hole must have been patched by some automated process or else all that crap in the air would have been sucked out into space. Still, what he could see was at least a hundred meters of the shredded remains of a multilevel structure, as if his little craft had dug its way down through a twenty-story building. There were floors every five meters or so, each sprouting mangled pipes and conduits of unknown purpose, though given that most either leaked fluid or rained sparks, it didn't take much imagination to guess. The cavities in between these, though, were truly unknown. In truth it didn't look much different from a cross section of any Earth-based structure.

He shifted his focus to the remains of his escape pod. It lay around him like a cracked egg, with bits of the foamy orange cushion that had surrounded him during the brief flight now melting away into the soup of knee-deep viscous fluids rapidly filling the space around him. He jumped off his toes, just enough to test the gravity without rocketing himself up into the haze above, and judged it to be about three-quarters of Earth normal. What had Eve said about the gravity on Carthage? Pretty damn close to that, if his memory served. So he must be at a pretty low altitude.

As the last of the cushioning melted away, Skyler saw some gray containers floating amid the wreckage. He picked one up and examined it, puzzled at first. It was Builder gear, definitely, but its purpose eluded him. He was about to toss it aside when he realized his suit was telling him the answer. In the bottom corner of his field of view, a display on his visor indicated that this was repair paste for his armored suit. He grinned despite himself and picked another. Ammunition, in the form of six pellets that could be inserted into the right or left shoulder of his suit, powering the beam weapons embedded just above his wrists. Skyler's grin widened. Eve may have sacrificed herself, abandoning him and the others to take on an entire sieged planet by themselves, but at least she'd not left them completely naked and defenseless.

Another case held "nutrients." He almost gagged. This would be the rather nasty food Eve had manufactured for them and never quite gotten around to improving. Skyler decided not to look a gift horse in the mouth, as his stomach growled its desire to be filled with the gritty, overly sweet fare. Last, a self-replenishing container for water, filled by pulling moisture out of the very air around him. This he attached immediately to the receptacle on his lower back and then willed the suit to extend the small tube toward his mouth. He heard the thin whir as the little straw extended, and he drank greedily, ignoring the slightly metallic taste. It was cool and wet and somehow grounded him, putting an almost whiskeylike glow of confidence in his gut. He repeated the process with the food, choking a few gulps down.

Skyler tried the comm again. "Anyone out there? This is Skyler. I'm alive, but I've no idea where the hell I am or what to do. Reply if you can hear me."

No response came. The suit's status indicators still showed no connection to anyone else, nor any Builder equivalent of a network at all. He ground his teeth at that, but decided not to spend any more time worrying about it for now. Maybe it was broken, or maybe the others were simply out of range. He left the comm switched on, and set a recurring timer to remind him every ten minutes to try it again.

Finally, he checked himself for injuries. Bruised and battered, but otherwise he felt good. His suit still had integrity, too.

Fed and hydrated, Skyler turned his focus toward his overall goal.

The enormity of which still boggled his mind, but considered in the simplest terms—that he was here to free the world of Carthage from the Scipios—he figured his first task should be to gather intelligence. How did the Scipios hold this world? What were their society and security structure like? Was his crew truly alone here, or could he perhaps rouse some kind of rebellion from within the metaphorical prison walls? The mental image of a worldwide prison riot was almost enough to make him laugh.

A burst of fire erupted into the cavity just a few meters above him, then quickly receded into a small gas-fueled flame like a welder's torch left on. The sound of it somehow woke Skyler's sense of hearing, and he began to listen as much as see. The dripping water, the slosh of his legs in the now-thigh-deep pool, and something else, too. A new sound, rhythmic, that stuttered even as it rose and fell through sweeps of extreme pitch changes. The noise came from all around him. Instinctively, Skyler sloshed over to one side of the pit, pressing himself against a wall made of charred debris, as the volume grew.

Multicolored light tore through the mists above. Beams of violet and yellow. Skyler knew next to nothing about life beyond Earth, but every fiber of his being came to the simple conclusion instantly: security response. He was an intruder here, an *infection,* and the cavalry had arrived to deal with him.

He raised his weaponized arm and waited, forcing even breaths through his clenched teeth. The one thing he could not afford was a shoot-out. Whatever the population of Scipios here was, it was bound to be far higher than he had ammunition for. No, a subtler approach was the only real option if he was to have any hope of reaching the surface, much less accomplishing what he'd come here to do.

The flashing lights above were joined by others, and then a shadow appeared in the rising steam. The curling white murk spread and swirled around the edges of a teardrop-shaped object maybe two meters tall, with four metallic and heavily segmented tentacles moving in a carefully controlled dance as it lowered itself deeper into the pit.

The sight of it barely registered, for it was what Skyler saw beyond this alien that almost overwhelmed his mind. A brief glimpse through the thick haze, but that was enough.

A night sky, half-obscured by clouds.

He didn't need to get to the surface. He was already there. The realization left him reeling as his assumptions shattered like glass.

Skyler did his best to keep still, tucked in shadow under a curled bit of torn fibrous metal his arrival had peeled from the floor just above. The creature above him bore an obvious resemblance to the Scipio Swarm that had destroyed the *Chameleon,* though it had fewer tentacles and a more streamlined body of much thinner profile. Made for atmospheric use, perhaps, its existence closer to a support apparatus, rather than the swarmers who lived out their lives in that lonely vigil at the edges of this solar system. Those had been dirty things, rugged and scarred. This was sleek in comparison, with a gleaming white skin or hull that looked almost like porcelain on its top half, covering the lower black and gray areas like a tortoise shell.

With a slight bob the Scipio came to a stop. Its four limbs stretched straight outward to where they grasped whatever support they could find with four-fingered mechanical hands. Much more elegant than the spike-tipped monstrosities their space-faring brethren favored, perhaps because to impale every surface they traversed here would be to damage their own home.

For a time it simply hung there, suspended, crying its odd lilting alarm. Skyler remained motionless, too, ready to unleash hell if noticed, happy to remain hidden if possible.

Another shadow appeared as a second Scipio lowered itself into the deep pit. It came to rest a few meters above the first. This one was slightly larger, and had markings along its side, like a bar code made of skewed and curved lines. Abruptly the shrill alarm stopped as the pair of robotic machines or vehicles—Skyler couldn't be quite sure which—settled into position. He stared at those lines, the markings on the side of the recent arrival. They seemed to shimmer, then warp under his gaze. A trick of the light, perhaps, or just his rattled senses, but before he could puzzle it out the situation changed.

A section of the larger one's belly suddenly extended downward, revealing an array of tubes and connective gear. A turret, his brain warned, and he shifted his aim toward it. Before he could shoot, though, the swivel-mounted cannon revealed its purpose. It swung with precision to one side and burped out a white cloud of foam. The material slapped wetly against one of the small fires licking out from a severed pipe on the wall of destruction. The blaze vanished under the thick goop, smothered instantly. Another quick swivel, another blast from the fire extinguisher. Skyler watched, mildly fascinated, as the machine or vehicle systematically doused each open flame. *An alien firefighter,* he thought. When those closest to Skyler, in the basin of his crash-pit, were out, the thing began to climb smoothly back up toward the top. Every meter or so its cannon would cough out more white mucus. Another flame would vanish.

He shifted focus back to the first Scipio to have arrived, the smaller one. It hadn't moved since its big brother had shown up, and as of yet had not revealed its purpose here.

Skyler cursed himself. With everything else going on he hadn't bothered to check his air levels, and if the air here was breathable. He scanned the information splayed across the corners of his visor, the system tracking his eye movements and thought patterns as a means of navigating the interface. He fumbled his way through the menus until he found what he needed: atmospheric analysis. A quick review told him the only thing he really needed to know: breathable to a human. There were indicators for the various gases present and in what quantity, but that meant little to him. Oxygen was the only one listed in orange, the rest green. Nothing red, so he'd count his blessings and worry about the side effects later.

Besides, the suit acted like a giant gill, from what Eve had said. It could pull the ingredients he would need. Already it had replenished his supply to nearly full—enough to last him twenty hours or so, assuming he left the atmosphere and it couldn't pull in anything more. Still, it gave him some small reassurance to know that even in the event his suit tore, he could still breathe. The air, at least, wouldn't be trying to kill him. Probably.

A brilliant light bored into his eyes, forcing his attention back to the visitors. Skyler raised one arm to shield against the sudden flare before his visor recognized the problem and tinted itself to compensate.

The Scipio, the one that had remained near him, had extended a belly pod of its own. Unlike its larger companion, this one screamed "sensor array." Flickering lasers that swept across the ruined crash site in all directions, along with pulsing spotlights that shifted from one area to another. Several converged on him due to the movement of his arm.

"Shit," he said, and fired without really thinking about it. His beam cannon annihilated the small vehicle in a shower of sparks and shrapnel, as if it had no armor at all. Definitely not built like the Swarm that had attacked the *Chameleon,* then.

For a moment Skyler just stood there, surprised at how easily the enemy had been destroyed, and shocked at how quickly he'd fired on it. Some part of him had assessed, in that instant, that his presence had been noticed. And more important, decided that the little Scipio vehicle was likely transmitting everything its flickering scanners saw in real-time back to some control room. He processed this himself only now, but his suit had reacted to the conclusion and his reflexive decision to fire well before he'd even consciously understood the choice himself. *That,* Skyler Luiken thought, *is going to be a problem.* The last thing he needed was this exotic alien armor going all trigger-happy in a moment when his battle-sense needed to be carefully dampened by more strategic needs.

A problem to resolve later when he had a moment to breathe. Right now, he had to get the hell out of here, before this place absolutely crawled with more of these emergency responders or, worse, the Scipio equivalent of a police force.

Back up the way he'd come? Skyler considered that. The air above had closed back in, unnervingly opaque after ten meters, utterly choked now by the smoky outpouring of the fire suppression efforts and the explosion he'd just caused.

No, he thought. *Not up.* As much as he wanted to be outside, to survey his surroundings, he could too easily imagine a whole horde of Scipios up there. This hole he'd made was, at the very least, probably seen as some kind of freak natural disaster. A meteor strike or whatever. They'd be all over it, swarming in to plug the hole and repair the damage.

Sideways, then. Flee the scene, get his bearings, find the others if he could.

Skyler pushed off from the wall and climbed up to the first open cavity above him. The ragged pit his arrival had dug looked like a fist that had punched down through a skyscraper, revealing the interior structure—a very Earth-like stack of floors. Their contents were hidden in darkness, unknowable, but that didn't matter. It was a way to go, nothing more. So he jumped and flung himself into the first cavity, aware of several shadows descending into the pit from above and wanting nothing to do with them. Let the Scipios puzzle out the cause of the calamity if they didn't already know.

With any luck, he'd get a few precious minutes' head start before they realized they had a rat on the loose.

2

LOCATION UNKNOWN

She lay facedown in a puddle of oily fluid, head turned to one side, the black slop leaving weird rainbow patterns as it rose and fell against her helmet's visor.

For a long time Tania Sharma did not move. She just watched the strange pool of oil that obscured half her visor, right up the middle. Gradually the space around her came into focus. It hurt to focus. She blinked a few times, and tears fell away. She could see now. A bit. Grimy walls encircled her. A silo, or tank, perhaps?

Her head pounded. Her legs felt as if a lead blanket had been draped over them. Submerged in the thick goop, she guessed. Slowly Tania brought her arms up and pushed herself onto all fours. The slick fluid rolled off her armor. The drops did not so much splash as merge with the pool below.

Tania rocked back to a sitting position, her legs folded underneath her. She put all her effort into focusing on the display inside her visor.

SUIT INTEGRITY: GREEN. She breathed a sigh of relief.

WATER SUPPLY: 2.4 LITERS. Not great. In fact, very disconcerting.

But she couldn't worry about it just yet.

AIR SUPPLY: BEST BAND EVER. "Argh, Prumble, you wonderful imbecile," she said, the corners of her mouth turning up into a grin despite herself. Why they had let him design the interface she couldn't quite remember. What she did distinctly remember was his solemn promise to take the task seriously.

AIR LEVELS: 40%, but the number ticked up to 41 as she watched. That was good. The suit was pulling in what it needed from the atmosphere in the room. Better still, the outside air, in a worst-case scenario, would be breathable. Cold, thin, and a bit weak oxygen-wise, but breathable. A very good sign.

NUTRITION RESERVES: 4200 KCAL. Only a few days' worth. It could be stretched, of course, but not nearly enough. Tania could not imagine succeeding here in a matter of days. But she'd die of dehydration before she starved, so there was that, at least.

COMMS: NO LINK. Of course not. Tania tried activating it, anyway. The system was already on, it turned out. She just couldn't establish a connection with anyone. Either they were out of range, or something was jamming the signal. Could be a problem, could just be the walls of this . . . What was this place?

Debris lay in the opaque fluid around her. Chunks of orange cushioning from her spherical pod, the edges frothing as they melted away. She tried to recall what it had looked like before climbing into it. Like a . . . black egg, really. The cushioning inside had inflated to secure her from the violence going on all around. There'd been two, actually. Prumble had entered the other. Maybe, just maybe, the others had been similarly expelled.

Inside there'd been something else, too. A small pedestal. Like a miniature aura tower, or a shard cleaved from one of those giant versions she'd seen back on Earth. Tania glanced frantically around, looking for it. Overwhelmed with the need to find it. Water, food, air . . . none of that mattered here if she had no protection from the horrors that the Scipios could infect her with.

There, next to the wall, a lump of blackness concealed in shadow. Tania pushed through the slick goop around her to the device and knelt in front of it. Seemed intact. No obvious damage. But how to know for sure?

The visor, she realized. Had to be. She studied the remaining readouts and saw it, there, at the end.

AURA: ACTIVE.

Tania let out a breath she hadn't realized she was holding. She reached out and gave the little tower a nudge with her finger, watched it glide just above the surface of the oily muck, until it was pressed against the wall of the room. Someday she'd figure out how they did that. The tech still amazed her, after all this time. All that mattered right now, though, was that it worked. She stood, satisfied, and skimmed the rest of the data on her display. The remaining information all concerned her suit's weaponry. A full supply of energy for the beam weapons on her arms. A few mortar rounds. She shook her head at that. At everything. To take on an entire world, with supplies that would last her a day, maybe two if she encountered only a few enemies out of the millions that must live here.

Tania began to pace, her thoughts turning to finding a way out. Her foot brushed against something solid, floating in the pool at her feet. It bobbed and rolled over. She picked it up and waited as the incredibly slick fluid dripped off. The thing was small, about the size of a bunch of bananas, and slightly curved, too. Matte gray in color, in the Builders' style. As she turned it in her hands her visor's display drew a line to it and words appeared. NUTRITION RESUPPLY: 10,800 KCAL.

She went to her knees then, and began to grope through the sludge. Four more of the packages were concealed in the fluid. Water, food, ammo, and fuel. Enough for a week or so now, she thought. "Thank you, Eve," she whispered. Of course, the AI had neglected to provide her with a means to carry the stuff. No, wait. Tania reached behind herself and ran a hand along her back, even as Prumble's description of the suit's full capability set came back to her. There were sockets along the spine, she could feel them. These packages had matching connectors. Tania tried one and sure enough, it snapped into place on its own, as if the two were drawn together by magnets. Which may well be the case, she realized. Instantly her display updated to reflect the change.

Tania attached all four and reviewed her supply levels anew, enjoying the warm confidence the numbers now gave her. Aura shard under one arm, she turned her attention then to finding the others, battling the competing emotions of anticipation and dread.

Her pod had crashed through the ceiling of some kind of storage silo, she discovered. She'd had to burn a bit of fuel to get out, using the thrusters in her boots to power a jump up to the hole at the top that her headlamp had revealed. The gravity was low, about one-third Earth's, making the ten-meter hop that much easier. Tania carefully hoisted herself over the jagged metal edge of the hole in the silo's roof, and crawled out onto it.

The chamber she found herself in was narrow, just wide enough to fit the silo, but very long. Similar vessels were arranged in a long row that curved off to the left at a gentle rate. She turned around and saw a mirror of this sequence going off in the other direction, implying a circular arrangement of silos with, she guessed, a radius of several kilometers. Larger than Eve, in any case, which confirmed what she'd already strongly suspected. The ship had ejected her in that pod. The question was, to where, though Tania felt the conclusion to that was obvious. Still, she had to be sure. She looked up, through the hole in the ceiling of this room. And up, and up. Deck after deck had been tunneled through by her arrival. She saw only the ragged edges of floors, interspersed with bits of dangling, shorn wires and pipes. And beyond, several stars.

Tania had to know. She powered on her boots again and flew up through the tunnel her pod had made. The decks flew past, falling away below her as she rocketed toward the stars. At the last second she let up, willing the suit to slow her ascent. It complied, and as she reached the initial impact point Tania came to a rest, one hand on the fractured edge of some kind of exotic hull plating. Stars, out there. A bluish moon. More important, she saw glimpses of a vast network of space stations, and hints of the space elevator network to which they were attached to the unseen planet she now knew would be below. Carthage, Captain Gloria Tsandi had named it. Home world to the race known as the Creators, now held hostage by the Scipios.

They'd made it, after all.

She pushed herself higher still, intent on going out and looking around, but an invisible barrier seemed to hold her in. *Of course,* she thought. A hull breach like this wouldn't be left unaddressed. There was air around her, after all. Tania lifted one armored hand and pushed at the field. There was no ripple of energy or flickering light. Not even a repelling force, really. Just a subtle vibration that seemed to harden as she pushed against it.

What now? she wondered. Hit it with a mortar and try to push through before the field could reassert itself? Might work. Might not. No way to know, but what did seem certain was the Scipios would notice an explosion like that.

Or would they? She pondered the situation. Despite her arrival having torn a hole one hundred meters deep, she'd seen no sign of a reaction to it. The entry point had been sealed, yes, but from the look of things that was an entirely automated feature of the hull. A sensible one, in truth. Tech she'd wished they'd had on Anchor back home.

But, at least from the perspective of her own species, a severe wound like this to such a structure would have to be investigated, wouldn't it? Repaired? Which meant a response, and soon. Tania wanted to be far away when that happened.

She pushed back down, past ten meters of mangled equipment, until she came to an open floor her arrival had exposed. Tania hauled herself in and flicked on her headlamp, taking in the surroundings.

The room was large, perhaps a hundred square meters and five high. Row upon row of rectangular structures. Silent gray masses that took up the entirety of the floor space. It reminded her of the computer farms on Anchor, only this place was dark, dead.

She turned in place. The hole her arrival had punched was roughly in the center, and while three of the distant walls were identical, one had a wide indented section with lines down the middle. A door. Had to be. She started toward it.

The silence unnerved her. Tania ramped up the audio amplification her suit offered. This only served to increase the distant hum of machinery, a noise she found soothing. It sounded like home. Her home. The hallways and shafts of Anchor Station.

And then a new sound. A distant, sharp clang, and a whirring of motors. In that same instant, she detected movement. Tania dove between two of the hulking silent boxes and waited, breath held, senses strained. Weak light spilled in from the direction of the door, and then more sounds. The whine of electric motors, and the friction of wheels on tiled floor. Not one, but a chorus. The sounds diverged, began to spread around her, as if surrounding her. She felt cornered, at the center of a closing perimeter, yet could not bring herself to move or even to look.

The room had only one exit. No, she thought, that wasn't true. She'd come in through a hole that exposed multiple levels of the station. So go back, or fight her way out? Neither seemed wise, not knowing what approached. She risked a quick glance around the corner of the box, in the direction she'd been going. What she saw reminded her first of a police riot shield. Just a rectangular metal plate moving slowly down the aisle toward her, its surface pitted and scarred from use. There was a band of white near the bottom, with some odd curved bar code–like patterns splashed across one side. She stared at them, baffled as the pattern seemed to shift and twist as if reacting to her gaze. Some kind of strange paint that reacted to being observed?

No, she realized, this was no magical, auto-translating paint. It was just the suit's visor, letting her know she was looking at something it could read. Recognizable English text flashed in the lower corner of the display. Eve must have programmed it to automatically translate Scipio writing into something understandable.

It read: [ERROR] BARRICADE.

Tania leaned back out of sight and considered this. Barricade made sense, it was a moving wall coming toward her, after all. Error, though? What did that mean? Was she the error? A foreign body detected within the Scipio apparatus that they'd come to purge? Or maybe the crash site was considered an error, the mobile wall part of some repair process.

She pushed herself deeper into the grid of machinery, holding her breath, ready to shoot at the first sign of danger and hoping desperately it wouldn't come to that.

Twenty seconds passed before the error-barricade slowly pushed by, working its way down the aisle she herself had been walking along. As it passed she saw a small treaded machine attached to the back of it, electric motor whirring softly. The barricade itself was as thick as her arm, and almost as tall as the space between floor and ceiling. It did not turn to face her, but instead merrily trundled along toward the hole her arrival had made.

She watched in solemn silence for several minutes as a fleet of these mobile walls converged on the hole punched through ceiling and floor of the huge room. Their motions were like a dance, a bit of performance art, as each of the slabs they carried were maneuvered into place. Bands of light seeped between the sections, growing ever smaller. With a staggered series of clangs the segments came together and the light vanished. Tania's world plunged into near total darkness for a moment, sending her heart racing. Then, a dozen brilliant stars erupted before her, sending showers of sparks in all directions, skittering across the tiled floor. Robotic arms with welding torches began to bond the movable barricades together.

"They're sealing it off," she said to herself. "An automated response. They don't know I'm here." It made sense: An orbital superstructure like this would be regularly bombarded by meteors, space junk, and who knows what else. The Scipios had made their prison self-repairing.

The knowledge flooded her with a sudden confidence, and an urge to remain hidden here until the situation changed, if only to gather her wits and think.

But her friends were out there, somewhere. Maybe in similar situations, maybe much worse off. She had to find them, and soon.

Tania slipped out from her hiding place between the towering objects and jogged into the darkness, the way only visible due to the augmented view through her visor. She ran until the door appeared in front of her, closed behind the mobile barricades.

The massive bulkhead, rectangular in shape, had an almost zipperlike joint where the two halves met in the middle. She saw no way to make it open. On a whim, she strode up to stand before it, positioning herself in the center in the hope a camera or another sensor would detect her and let her pass. Nothing happened.

Tania almost gave up, when she heard a thin click. She waited, anxious. Another click. It came from behind, not the door. She whirled, ready to fire, but saw only darkness.

Another click, then another. Then the noises became so frequent they blended together. Suddenly the first row of the gray towers that filled the floor space of the room lit up with multicolored indicators about a meter from their bases. The entire row, stretching off to her left and right for fifty meters, came on in unison, bathing her in their glow.

The second row activated, then the third. With each passing second another row came alive until the whole room was lit by the glowing bases of the machines. Each now hummed with some electric purpose, the lights along their midsection undulating for reasons she could not fathom. Indicators maybe, but of what was anyone's guess. Now the resemblance to the computer grids inside Anchor Station was unmistakable.

In the darkness Tania could just make out the circular arrangement of barricades, wheeled into place evidently to cordon off the damaged area where she'd arrived. An entirely automated process, it seemed, and she was just fine with that. It did beg the question, though: Where were the Scipios themselves? From what information Eve had shared, Tania had imagined this place highly populated. A sprawling city above their captured world. Yet so far, only machines, and very few at that.

There lay the problem with Eve's data. It was old. Very old. Virtually anything could have happened here since the Builders fled, or even since their last attempt to retake their planet. How ironic it would be to come all this way only to find the Scipios, experts in virus design and manufacturing, had succumbed to some disease.

A new sound reached her amplified hearing. A high whir and then, beneath that, a low sustained rumble. She spun where she stood and froze. The giant door behind her had separated in a jigsaw pattern down the middle, and were rolling apart.

So much for the extinction event theory.

Four Scipios moved into the room. Once again Tania concealed herself in the grid of now-humming machinery, her suit illuminated by the twinkling indigo and ruby status displays. She chanced a glance at the approaching aliens, and her breath caught in her throat.

They were upright, but did not walk, instead moving in a sort of fluid hop-and-glide gait unlike anything Tania had ever seen. Perfectly normal, no doubt, for their limb structure and diminutive size, especially in this gravity. To her eye they resembled a chimpanzee crossed with a bat, complete with flappy winglike structures that connected their arms to their torsos. They would hop a meter into the air and then glide several forward, all effortlessly, as natural as humans walking along a promenade. They were dressed, after a fashion, in outfits of varying color, though all four had a large white band around the midsection. Some kind of utility belt, maybe, for there were pockets and other containers all around.

As the Scipios moved across the gigantic room toward the improvised barricade, they chattered to each other. Alien sounds, but unmistakable as language. Like a mixture of birdsong and the clicks and whistles a dolphin made. An instant later, to Tania's surprise and delight, a transcription began to flow across the bottom portion of her visor. Automatic translation was nothing special—humans had been able to do it for centuries. What surprised her was that Eve knew the Scipio language well enough to program it into this suit.

An imperfect knowledge, in truth. Tania understood now the bracketed word *error* translated from the bar coding on the repair machine. It was a substitute for an unknown word. No great surprise, Eve's knowledge of the Scipio tongue would be woefully out of date. Still, she felt grateful. The words told her much.

One was saying, "Examination. Reconfiguration. [error] to be of returned [error] status."

"Copious agreement," the other three said in unison.

Then the group fell silent, continuing their hop-glide march to the site of the incident.

She heard the whir and grating rumble of the door, now sliding closed. Tania slipped back to the main aisle and propelled herself toward it. No time to look through first. Caution lost out to her desire to leave, so she powered through the gap seconds before the door closed. Her momentum took her to a wall on the opposite side of a wide corridor. Bending her legs to absorb the impact of landing, Tania let herself fall back to the floor, dropping to a crouch and twisting left and right. With one arm curled protectively around her aura shard, she raised the other, ready to fire, sure she'd find the area cordoned off by Scipio police, curious Scipio onlookers lining up behind.

What Tania Sharma saw instead brought tears to her eyes.

Standing beside the door she'd just come through, backs against the wall, were two men. They both stared at her, mouths agape.

3

CARTHAGE

A vast unlit room stretched off in every direction, its ceiling supported by elegant pillars that resembled milky hourglasses. Pale spheres, one on the floor and the other above, which had somehow melted until they met in the middle. The floor was some kind of pitted metal, nearly black in color. It gleamed when it caught the wan light spilling in from the hole Skyler's pod had made when it punched through from top to bottom. Above, the ceiling was similarly dark and also strangely elegant despite being more utilitarian, its span crisscrossed with tidy bundles of gently curved cabling and pipes whose purposes he could only guess. A temptation to start cutting those lines just to see what kind of damage it might cause to the Scipios faded as quickly as it had come to him. He had to remember now where he was. This world really belonged to the Creators; he had come to return it to them.

So Skyler pushed into the room, away from his crashed pod. The chamber seemed to have no end, no sides, no beginning. It stretched farther than the light, and its air was filled with the same swirling dusty particulate his entry pit had been. Other than the curvaceous ghostly pillars, the floor was entirely devoted to row after row of nondescript containers, vaguely and unsettlingly reminding him of sarcophagi standing upright. They were all identical, about four meters long, one wide, one tall, with hair-thin filaments connecting them to the conduits and pipes that lined the ceiling above. It resembled some of the data processing facilities he'd scavenged in back on Earth. And much like those abandoned places, this one seemed to be without power. There were no banks of blinking lights indicating electronic traffic, or even the oppressive hum of cooling gear. If this place was indeed a computer center, it was either abandoned or switched off. Of course, it was possible the place was working fine until he'd punched a hundred-meter-deep hole right through its heart.

"Or," he whispered to himself, "it is a bloody crypt."

He forced himself to look at all of it through the lens of what Eve had told them about this world. A once flourishing civilization, now held captive by the Scipios, who mostly lived on the space stations above. This world was like Earth had been just after the Builders came, most of it a wasteland where engineered viruses kept the population subdued. Only, their postapocalyptic state had lasted millennia. Earth had gotten off easy, in comparison.

Millennia.

The word echoed in Skyler's mind. As he walked he looked—really looked—at the pristine surfaces around him. The metal floor, the pearlescent double-teardrop pillars, the containers—all practically gleamed under the wan light spilling in. This in stark contrast to the particulate in the air where he'd landed, which fell heavily enough to coat any floor in a matter of hours, much less years or centuries.

Which meant either this room had been sealed until his arrival, or it had been very, very well maintained. The latter implied a world far from the hellscape Skyler assumed they'd find.

The room seemed to have no end, and Skyler forced himself into a run. The desire to be out under the open sky and out of this tomb suddenly eclipsed all other concerns. He jogged for a long time, a sense of wondrous dread at the sheer size of the place growing with each step, until finally a wall came into view. The surface was smooth, entirely uniform, offering no hint of which way to go. He reached it and turned, at random, to the left, following the edge of the space until finally something doorlike appeared in the darkness.

A massive, almost zipperlike seam running five meters vertically up the wall.

He glanced around for a lever or switch. Nothing obvious presented itself. Skyler sighed. Perhaps this was some kind of vault, the only access being from the outside. He debated retracing his steps to the hole he'd made to get in, but a quick glance over his shoulder made him realize that the breach was either too far away now to be detectable, or the Scipio drones had sealed it off. Without that little patch of light spilling in, he had no way to find it.

"Fine," he said to himself. "I made one hole, I can make another."

He lifted one arm and fired at the zigzagging seam on the wall. He'd expected it to wither and melt under the intensity of the weapon, but what happened was decidedly more final. The energy lanced right through the barrier as if it were made of balsa wood. Fragments exploded into the space beyond, and on this side as well, pelting him and the ground around him. Skyler killed the beam and fumbled through the menus, dialing back the intensity to its lowest setting. This time he got what he'd wanted. A thin, almost surgical line of white-hot energy that required a few seconds in one spot before it could punch through the door or wall or whatever it was. In less than a minute he'd drawn an oval shape on the surface. Skyler stepped forward, kicked, and watched with satisfaction as the chunk fell away and landed with a dull thud on the floor beyond.

The area outside defied explanation. Part hallway, part stairs, the wide passage was tilted at a shallow angle, its floor resembling a wave pattern more than what Skyler would consider steps. The hall was curved as well. Part of a very wide, very large spiral, with doors just like those he'd come through spaced in even intervals on both the inside and outside walls.

Everything here was coated in dust. Creeping vines snaked their way along the surfaces, all black and gnarled. The sight of such decay filled him with a strange nostalgia. Suddenly he was back on Earth, creeping through the ruins of Brisbane or Taipei, Auckland or Phuket. If not for the strange rippled floor this could be any one of a dozen hallways he'd slogged through in the dead cities of Earth.

Go up, he told himself, and moved to his left, picking his way over the undulating surface and the root systems—roots of what, he could not imagine—that sought to reclaim the whole place back to nature. Particulate blew in lazy swirls down the passage, filling his field of view like ash. He glanced at the displays on the visor's interior. The air mixture hadn't changed, but there was a definite breeze here. Skyler amplified the exterior sounds, heard only his own cautious footfalls and the sigh of air pushing past. No more sirens, no hint of air processors or plumbing. None of the telltale signs of a technological civilization. A dead place, then. He felt sure of it. Which meant the breeze came from . . . ?

He saw the opening before he could finish the thought. At the edge of his view of the curved hall, the space expanded into a larger room, one side of which was open to the elements. Leaves, or something like them, swirled in a conical eddy in the center of the room, like a wandering ghost searching for a way out. The sight reminded him of the first time he'd ever seen Ana, dancing in an abandoned courtyard, unaware he was watching. The memory sent a tingle down his spine. He swallowed the pain and regret that thinking of her always brought.

Skyler crept to the end of the hall and crouched in the shadows, watching. Other than the meandering cone of swirling dust and leaves, nothing moved. The far wall of the lobbylike chamber was made up of four massive slabs of filthy but clear material—glass, or something like it—which were attached to huge circular columns so that they could be rotated. They'd been open the last time anyone had actually been here, and left that way.

Beyond lay the ruins of several more buildings. Just shadows, really. It was dusk outside, the system's one star already below the horizon, painting shades of dark red and purple between the dark gaps. Above, through the hazy swirls of the ash-filled air, he saw wisps of clouds and the faint but imposing clusters of hundreds of space stations beyond. Fiery objects—chunks of Eve's wreckage, he had no doubt—streaked across the magnificent view, burning up well before they reached the ground. He'd made it, though. Maybe the others had, too.

With an effort he tore his gaze from the sight and focused on his immediate surroundings. He'd exited into something like a plaza. A long, flat space surrounded by structures of varying height, the tallest being perhaps fifty stories. The bottom floors of each were choked with climbing vines that made odd geometric patterns as they wormed along the existing grooves and panels of the manufactured walls, windows, and doors. But above, where the vines couldn't reach, Skyler caught a glimpse of what had been. Even in this one tiny example of Creator society, their former greatness was evident. He felt like a caveman transported through time to Manhattan or Dubai. All around him were the towering examples of a highly advanced alien culture that prided itself on architecture. No two buildings were alike, and yet they all meshed together as if no one piece had been designed without consideration of the whole. Their profiles curved and intertwined. Soaring bridges connected their highest levels, writ in graceful arcs. Here there were pillars and what must be classical elements, while there stood a monolith of severe edges and cleaved sublevels. And yet it all worked. *Rather, once worked,* thought Skyler, *it's all dead now.*

No lights. No sound but the wind. Not a single face staring down at him from one of those soaring balconies.

No roads, either, Skyler noted. None that he could see.

He walked now, keeping to the shadows, deciding to first circumnavigate the building he'd exited, hoping to find somewhere that offered a better view of the surrounding landscape. If not, he'd go back to the spiral, and climb as far as it would take him, until he found a roof.

A noise made him stop. He ducked behind a triangular pillar and went to one knee on instinct, eyes scanning the vine-choked entryways all around him.

It had been a low grunt. And a crackling sound. He strained his ears, and realized he could let the suit do that for him. Skyler ramped the audio gain to maximum.

"Gnngh," a familiar voice grunted, hazy and yet very close. "Anyone there?"

"Tim?" Skyler asked, baffled.

Only then did he realize it was the comm. It showed a link now, where none had been before. "Tim," he said with more certainty. "Tim, it's Skyler. Where are you?"

"I don't . . . It's dark. I don't know."

"Activate your headlamp."

Silence stretched. Then, "Some kind of machine room. I can't really . . . I don't know what it is."

"Are any of the others with you?"

"No," he said.

"Is there gravity where you are?"

"Huh?"

"Gravity, Tim."

The scientist was likely in shock, and perhaps injured. Skyler took a breath and tried again. "I'm on the planet. Carthage. I'm trying to determine if you're here or—"

"There's very little," Tim said. "Gravity, I mean. I just jumped and went about two meters up."

Skyler jumped himself and barely managed one. "You must be on one of the orbitals."

"Where's Eve?"

"Gone," Skyler said. "Destroyed, I think. We're on our own now."

The other man went quiet. No doubt his mind churned through the same thoughts Skyler's had. "Tim, we have to—"

"Over here," Tim said.

"What?"

No reply.

"I'll be okay," Tim said, after several seconds.

"Uh, good. That's good. Now listen, we—"

But Tim interrupted again. As if he were talking to himself. Or someone else.

"I'll follow you? Nothing. My long range is out, too. Haven't heard from anyone."

Skyler stood there, dumbfounded, then angry. "Tim, are you still receiving me? What the hell are you talking about?"

No reply. Not to Skyler, at least. Tim's conversation went on. He was uninjured. He agreed the air appeared to be breathable, but felt they shouldn't risk it. His pod was also stocked with some supplies—water, food, ammo—and also had a small version of an aura shard.

"Tim," Skyler tried again, asserting as much authority as he could. "Who the fuck are you talking to? Please respond!"

The man went on. It wasn't hard to imagine that Skyler's transmissions weren't actually reaching him, but the fact remained that Tim had specifically said to whomever he spoke, *Nothing. My long range is out, too.* And, worse, *Haven't heard from anyone.*

"Tania?" Skyler tried. "Prumble? Sam? Anyone?"

Tim kept talking, then the conversation went quiet as he and his companion embarked on a plan to "find the others."

Skyler glanced at his visor's display. The comm still showed a link to the bastard. "God fucking dammit, Tim, if you can hear me you'd better explain yourself."

Still, he did not reply. He continued his other conversation, referring to his unseen companion as "Prumble" at one point.

Well, at least there's that, Skyler thought. The big man had made it, after all. If only he could talk to him. No amount of fiddling with the comm interface would allow him to do anything other than talk to Tim, however.

Skyler continued his circuit of the building, but his attention was split between Tim's chatter and his own frustrated navigation of the visor's menu system. He must have accidentally locked himself into a private channel with Tim. Maybe during those hazy moments after the crash. And Tim evidently had taken a nasty knock on the head, because he clearly thought his conversation with Skyler hadn't happened.

Yet the comm seemed in order. Everything did. Just as he'd left it.

No, wait. Eve warned me of this. In the fog of his arrival he'd forgotten, but the memory rushed back now. She'd said only one of the crew would be able to communicate with everyone else. "A necessary precaution," she'd called it, her logic inscrutable, as always. Whatever the reason, she'd evidently given Tim the role of bridge between Skyler and the others, and Tim wasn't playing along.

He stopped dead. He'd almost walked right into them.

Ahead, a veritable fleet of small drones was clustered around the entry wound his arrival had punched through the bottom four floors of the building. The Scipio machines—perhaps vehicles, he couldn't be sure—were all turned in toward the gaping hole, like a rescue team after an earthquake. Or, perhaps, like a squad of police investigating a bombing. Skyler had the presence of mind to flatten himself against the wall and take two slow steps backward. Shielded from view by the curving wall, he leaned out and took in the scene.

The Scipios had arrived in four large aircraft. Bulky things that resembled mechanical whales, their design likely guided by the atmosphere and gravity of Carthage. They were parked in a half-circle some distance off from the impact zone, their cavernous bellies exposed by large ramps that opened from the sides rather than the back, as the *Melville* had.

Smaller dronelike pods swarmed around the place where Skyler's pod had met the building. As he watched, one ducked inside and extended those climbing tentacles he'd seen, suspending itself over the opening. The machine or vehicle trembled slightly, and then puffed a glowing cloud of shiny particulate into the space. The blue-white material coated what little he could see of the interior walls of the pit his escape pod had dug.

More of the Scipios were milling about on the ground level, just a few dozen meters away from his position. These were the actual creatures, not machine augmented like those in the Swarm, but suited, intelligent alien beings. About a meter tall, they resembled upright-walking bats with roundish, flat faces and flaps of leathery skin that stretched from forearm to calf. They wore ugly outfits of grays highlighted in places with patches of color—yellows, blues, and greens. Perhaps an indication of rank or discipline, or merely some element of what passed for Scipio fashion. No way to know. They were huddled around some gear, gesturing to one another and making incomprehensible sounds. Their speech, he felt sure.

None appeared to be armed. Perhaps they were a scientific team, sent to investigate a potential meteor strike or salvage a fallen chunk of one of their massive space stations. They hadn't noticed him, or if they had they made no sign of it. Whatever their purpose here, though, it surely was only a matter of time before they realized the shell of material at the bottom of that pit was not natural or of their own making, and that *something* had walked away from it.

"Likewise," Tim said, so abruptly Skyler thought he'd misheard or missed something. Then came the sounds of relief and hugs. "Any sign of Sam or Vaughn?"

"No," the reply came. From Tania.

"And Skyler?" Tim asked. "Any idea where he is?"

"No," she said again, sounding more distant than she ever had before.

Oh, fuck no. Tim, you son of a bitch . . . Skyler ground his teeth and sent nothing in rebuke this time. These Scipios might have the equipment to sense a transmission. Besides, he could think of nothing to say. Tim had never made much of a secret of his feelings for Tania, and the complication Skyler posed to that equation. The sad bastard saw this whole thing as an opportunity for romance and was taking it.

But then, Skyler recalled Tim's battle prowess during those final moments aboard the *Chameleon*. Perhaps something had awoken in him, there, faced with such a formidable enemy and armed so. Or, maybe, his true nature had finally shown through.

A shrill mechanical sound forced Skyler's attention back to the Scipios. They were fanning out, suddenly. One of the airships lifted vertically into the air on a plume of vectored thrust. It went straight up, then hovered about two hundred meters up. Overwatch position. "Oh shit."

He heard a click. It came from behind, and he knew instantly what had happened. They'd found the door he'd cut through. If they'd been under any illusion this was some meteorite or fallen part of one of their space stations, that had ended there at that clean deliberate cut.

And they'd followed his trail, which led them—

Skyler whirled. Three Scipios stood just five meters behind him. The sound of their movement must have been masked by the liftoff of the airship.

They seemed as surprised to see him as he them. Skyler

raised an arm and fired. The creature took the blast in its chest, staggering backward. The other two hopped away, one gliding back to the ground using flaps of skin that stretched from forearms to calves, the other landing up on the wall, gripping its vine-covered surface and hanging there.

Skyler relented, and to his surprise the one he'd fired on came back to a stand, looking down at its chest. Why hadn't it—*the door.* The door he'd cut through. He'd dialed back the weapon's output. Skyler dove left as the two on either side fired on him. Their weapons sprayed directed plumes of a bluish powdery substance, and he wanted nothing to do with it. He rolled, came to a knee, fired again, this time at increased output. The white-hot rail of energy annihilated the head of the one perched on the wall. It fell and landed in a silent heap. Skyler aimed, fired again. This time the one in the middle did not stagger back. It flew. Arms and legs flung forward like a rag doll, the creature vaulted backward on the power of the beam. Landed five meters away, rolled, came to a sprawled stop, flame and smoke billowing from its chest now.

A blast of blue powder washed over Skyler, forcing him backward onto his rump. He raised his gun arm to shield his visor from the sandlike spray, ignoring the sudden eruption of alerts from his suit. Breaches, everywhere. That was no powder he'd been blasted with; it was like a mist of razors. It filled his vision even as it shredded his protective suit. Thousands of little craters clouded the surface of the visor. He gave up protecting it. He aimed blind, into the torrent of microscopic knives, and swept his beam across the entire space. For good measure he told his mortar to activate and launched eight of its potent bombs in a cluster pattern in a wide circle around his position. He felt the barrel extend from his back and fire—a series of deep *whoomps*. Skyler let the bombs fly and continued to swing his beam across the space in front of him. The powder attack died off. The third Scipio lay on the ground a few meters away, in several smoldering pieces.

Skyler forced himself to his knees and covered his head with his arms.

There was commotion all around him. Alerts and the excited

chittering of Scipio-speak. And then the explosions. Eight, in rapid succession. Shock waves shook the ground and buffeted him like the fists of an angry giant. Skyler screamed and kept his arms clamped over his head, unsure how much his suit would protect him, but knowing he was in the shit like he'd never been before.

Orange-yellow light flickered around the edges of his slammed-shut eyes as the fiery explosions tore up the dead city.

"Move, damn you," he roared at himself, and then he was up. Sprinting away from the shrapnel and falling debris. He could see nothing at all through the fractured glass before his eyes. Angry, he reached up and tore at the panel, but it wouldn't budge. *Fine,* he thought. He leaned forward. He closed his eyes and mouth, then poked two fingers through the surface. The material, once, no doubt, super strong, had been weakened and came apart easily. Skyler moved his fingers around a bit, widening the openings until they met in front of his nose. Soon only a few centimeters of jagged yellow glass remained around the perimeter of the helmet's opening. He looked up, could see again. Cold air bit at his cheeks. Luckily, the readouts Prumble had designed with Eve's help still hovered in the lower left of his vision, though they were blurred now and parts were missing. Legible, but only just. He glanced around.

One of the mortars had exploded into the side of the building he'd been circuiting, ten stories up. Huge chunks of broken wall slammed into the ground where he'd lain. Another piece smashed into the vine-covered walkway in front of him, showering him with debris. Skyler put his trust in his Earth-adapted strength and leapt. Here, on Carthage, he could about double his usual jumping height, and he cleared the lodged section of broken wall with a few centimeters to spare.

Landing, he ran on, unwilling to stop and look at what kind of actual damage his desperate attack had wrought. He needed to get far away from here, and hope they never quite figured out if he'd lived or died in the violence of that assault. With any luck they'd yet to even report an anomalous finding back to whomever they reported back to.

Skyler rounded a corner, surged down a gently curving ramp and through a plaza lined with teardrop-shaped pillars. Air crept in through the punctures in his suit. It felt wonderfully cool on his skin, and smelled of spring rain. He tried not to think about all the alien pathogens flooding his lungs, or the engineered viruses of the Scipios floating like thick dust in the air. He hoped his immunity held on this planet as it had on Earth.

The ground beneath him seemed to tilt. He stumbled, caught himself. Little white dots swam before his eyes. He blinked, hard, but the spots remained. Breathing became a chore.

"It's the air," he wheezed. Oxygen levels had been marked in orange. Too low, or too high, he hadn't bothered to check. Breathable to humans, that had been the extent of his interest. But then the top of Mt. Everest was still technically breathable to humans, wasn't it? Until you died, of course. He slumped against one of the teardrop pillars and put his head between his knees, forcing himself to take long, even breaths. His nose began to run. Skyler swiped at it with his armored sleeve and saw a smear of blood there, black as ink.

Altitude sickness. Had to be. Well, he thought, it didn't *have* to be. "Get moving, then," he muttered, and pushed himself to a shaky stand. He took several long swallows from the water tube in his helmet, hoping he wouldn't regret the draw on his supplies later.

Skyler glanced back the way he'd come. Several small fires burned in the distance, judging by the flickering orange glow that now lit the buildings around him. Of the Scipios he saw nothing at all. Whatever they were doing, however many yet lived, they weren't following him.

He turned and walked now, intent to put as much distance between himself and the crash site as he could. At the far side of the pillared plaza he found an archway that led out into a long, meandering, narrow lane. Circular patches of ground dotted the length of it on either side, and must have once been home to magnificent trees. Now they were choked with tall spikes of sandy-colored grasses, and the trees were nothing more than gray shapes lying on the ground, their long-petrified remains now sprouting smaller plants and wispy vines.

Skyler hardly paid the scene any attention. His gaze was firmly fixed on what lay beyond. The undulating pathway led down to a bay, where foamy water lapped against a rugged shore. Beyond, perhaps two kilometers distant, was another city perched on a headland. The twin of this dead place, only over there the lights were on. Most of the light clustered around the tallest of the buildings there, a majestic shard that vaulted easily a full kilometer into the sky. And where the structure ended the thread continued. A space elevator, like a ribbon, extending straight up and through the clouds.

For a long moment he simply stared, part of his mind convinced that he was back in Darwin. This was Nightcliff he gazed upon, as seen from the water processors on East Point. The geography was remarkably similar, in fact, and he suspected that was no coincidence.

"Tim, are you there?"

He waited. He wasn't sure if his comm even worked anymore. No reply came.

"Listen up, you bastard. I've found a way up. I'm coming. I'm going to find the rest of you, and you're going to have to answer for yourself. Do you understand? So, last chance. I'll give you a pass, if you just pretend right now that you've suddenly made contact with me. Let the others know I'm okay."

Silence, save the water lapping on rocks in the distance, and the wind.

"We can still do what we came here to do, Tim. I know you're a good person. Stop this deception now and no one need ever know."

The link remained silent. Skyler shook his head and took a step forward.

"We're leaving," came the whispered reply. "You won't reach us in time. Finish the mission or not, I don't care, but we're leaving."

"Tim—"

"I have a chance to save the one I love. I have to take it. I say now what I've wanted to say for a long, long time: Piss off, Skyler."

This time the link did close. A barely audible click that somehow was the loudest sound Skyler had ever heard. Alone, then. Betrayed by a self-styled knight in shining armor, a man who no doubt envisioned himself carrying Tania, literally, away from all this with no consideration for what she might want. Oldest mistake there was, and one it seemed some men would continue to make for time eternal.

Skyler rested his chin on his chest and let out a long breath. More blood trickled from his nose. He ignored it. *What now?* he thought. *What now, what now, what now.*

The answer was the same as it had been every time he'd asked the question of himself. The same as it had been when he'd found himself alone when the plague had arrived in the Netherlands. The same when he had crashed the *Melville* in the Outback far from the safety of Darwin: *Press on.*

And that's just what he did.

4

LOCATION UNKNOWN

Tania came to a stand, gazing at her two compatriots. "Well," she said. "How about that."

Prumble crossed to her and pulled her into a soldier's embrace, then held her at arm's length by her shoulders, then enfolded her in another embrace.

"Good to see you, too," she said to him, not bothering to fight her tears. "Both of you."

"Likewise," Tim said, sounding almost sad. He must have thought he'd lost her. The young man came up beside them and awkwardly added himself to the reunion. "Any sign of Sam or Vaughn?"

"No," she admitted.

"And Skyler?" Tim asked. "Any idea where he is?"

Tania shook her head, offered a weak, "No." She was barely able to say the word.

"Vanessa is missing, too," Prumble said.

"A minute ago I thought I was all alone here," Tania said. "That the two of you made it safely gives me hope that we all did. Eve did this on purpose, I'm sure of it."

Tim's face darkened, and he slowly shook his head.

"Tim?" Tania asked. "You disagree?"

"I . . . I'm not sure. About all that, I mean. Eve was headed here, on this trajectory I mean, when she exploded. I think she protected us from that, put us in those escape pods, because the alternative was to just let us die. We simply continued on the path. Textbook orbital mechanics. We couldn't help but come here."

Before Tania could consider that, Prumble voiced his own disagreement. "Somehow I doubt she'd save us unless she knew we'd have a fighting chance to finish the job."

"You think she'd kill us?" Tim asked.

"I think we know too much," Prumble replied. "About how the Builders look for species that can help them. If the Scipios knew what we were tested for, what traits the Builders hoped to find, they'd change their defenses to account for that, would they not?"

Tim said nothing, but the darkness in his expression remained.

"Now," Prumble added. "How about we get out of the open and figure out what we're going to do with our second chance."

The big man led the way. Tania fell in behind him, keeping herself just a few meters back, not wanting some bulkhead door to suddenly clap down and separate them, yet wanting to be close enough to help should Prumble turn a corner and run straight into trouble they all somehow knew would come at any moment. This was an enemy that specialized in viruses, and here was an infection of humans in their body. Of course they would react. The question was when?

Tim trailed behind, too far for Tania's comfort, but he seemed to need some time and solitude to process what had happened. Once she thought she saw him speaking, his mouth moving in silent conversation, comm perhaps malfunctioning. "Repeat?" she asked. "I can't hear you."

"Never mind," he replied, after a few seconds. "I . . . I was talking to myself. Embarrassing, really."

"No need to apologize," she said, only then realizing he hadn't, actually. Tim let that go, and Tania turned back to following

Prumble, feeling slightly embarrassed herself for having brought it up.

The smuggler had found an iris door on the outer wall and pried it open a few centimeters. Machinery in the walls whined as it struggled to outmatch Prumble's suit-augmented strength. A sign above the circular portal read EXTERIOR [ERROR].

"Look through," he said, voice strained.

Tania moved up and peered through the narrow gap. A small cube-shaped chamber waited beyond, with another iris door at the far end. "Airlock, I think," she said.

Prumble grunted. "Help me with this. Tim, get inside and hold it from in there."

Tania positioned herself opposite the man and heaved against two of the door segments. Once a gap large enough had been made, Tim squeezed through and took her place from the inside, placing his miniature aura shard against one wall. Tania followed him in, guiding her own aura shard to rest beside the other, then added her strength so Prumble could join them.

The door hissed closed with a thin clack.

A palpable silence surrounded them.

"Suddenly regretting this," Prumble said. "Feels like a cell all a sudden."

"Or a tomb," Tim added.

"Go back?" Tania asked.

Prumble shook his head. "Let's at least peek outside, shall we? Assuming that's what this is. Be nice to get some sense of the lay of the land."

The technique for opening the door proved surprisingly easy: a simple handle in a slot that moved horizontally, then rotated ninety degrees. The lights in the chamber changed hue once the handle clicked into its open position. Green to orange. Tania heard a hiss as air was pulled from the room, a detail confirmed by the readouts on her visor display. She held her little aura shard under her right arm, left hand resting across it. They each had one. She wondered if Eve had given them to the entire team, or if only those not immune were the recipients.

Air pressure fell, into the unbreathable red zone, then finally to negligible. Almost immediately there came a series of mechanical taps from around the edge of the outer iris door, and the panels rotated apart to reveal a breathtaking view.

The graceful curve of Carthage's horizon, kissed by the red-orange hue of the star it orbited. Space stations stretched away from Tania's viewpoint, bending to match the planet's circumference, vanishing somewhere beyond the rim of the world. An artificial ring system of floating cities, networked together by physical bridges as well as those made of shimmering laser light, connected to the ground in several places by familiar strands of silk. Space elevators. A strange comfort to see them. For all the alienness of this place and its inhabitants, for all the unknowns that lay ahead, space elevators were something she knew. She thought of Darwin. Of her father.

"Look there," Prumble said, and pointed.

She followed his gesture and saw nothing out of the ordinary, at first. Certainly nothing to warrant the surprise in his voice.

Then that all changed. On a station a few kilometers away, there was a large indented section, like an artificial canyon. A rectangular depression. It held things, and some part of her mind recognized them, bubbling up the word at the same moment the explosions began.

Ships, her mind said, as the whole place began to erupt.

5

ABOVE CARTHAGE

Sam drifted in null gravity, gazing numbly at the strange world around her.

An outside observer might think her dead, and until a few seconds ago she'd probably have conceded the point.

Everything ached.

Thoughts came to her like bubbles on a pool of lava, only to burst and sear her mind every time she tried to grasp them. Iconography on her visor occasionally registered. Warnings about injury, and air. Proximity something-or-other. Blah, blah, fucking blah.

A single word nudged her closer to coherent thought. It meant something. Something important. Not a word, actually. No, it was a name. Vaughn.

Her random endless drift brought him into view. Another inanimate object like her, one of thousands that made a lazy path through the impossibly vast chamber. He was curled, fetal, hands over his head. A crash position, wasn't it? She wished she'd thought of it. Not that he seemed any better off.

"Hey," she tried. Came out more like a half-choked gasp. "Hey," she said again, a bit more clearly.

Vaughn stirred. His legs unfolded and stretched out flat. His arms came out as if he were feeling for a wall that wasn't there. Then they went to his stomach, pressing. The kind of movement someone made when they'd been stabbed in the gut.

"Hey yourself," he said. More clear than she. "About time you woke."

She laughed, though it turned into a racking cough. Somehow the action brought feeling back to her limbs. "What the hell happened?"

"My guess? Eve fired us out like a cannonball before she went nuclear. Launched us all the way to our destination."

"Well, goddamn. How thoughtful of her. We're actually here?"

"A guess, I said. But yeah . . . seems so."

Sam searched her mind, piecing the memories together. That desperate battle against the Scipio Swarm. Eve, guiding them so carefully and yet urgently to a specific place within her battered hull. Tricking her and Vaughn into entering some kind of room and then trapping them within.

The question was, had it been Eve's plan all along? Bring her human cargo up to the edge of the Swarm, forcing the enemy ships to get all nice and snuggly close, then detonate her massive bulk and hide her agents in the debris? Sam had little love for the Builder AI, but she could respect a well-played scheme when she saw one. "Effing brilliant, really."

"Except for the part where our ride home exploded," Vaughn observed.

Laughter really did erupt from her then. Sam couldn't help herself.

"The hell's so funny?"

She gestured, wide and slowly, toward the space around them. "Have you not looked at where we are, jackass?"

In truth it had only registered for her an instant before, but the timing only made it more funny. She giggled as if half-drunk.

The room . . . No. Not a room. A room had comprehensible dimensions. This place was something Sam had no word for. She judged the rectangular space to be five hundred meters wide and at least ten kilometers long. One of the long sides was open to vacuum, making the place appear as a trench from one perspective. The other sides were an incomprehensible mess of ductwork, small buildings or containers, and many thousands of gantries that extended out, up, or over to the things the vast space contained.

Spacecraft. She had no doubt about this whatsoever. Inside this . . . dockyard, she supposed . . . were thousands of moored craft of every imaginable size and shape. Some sleek and shiny, others barely more than cobbled together junk with no recognizable front or back. Most were of Scipio design, the cargo ships Eve had shown them, only somehow more refined. Sam supposed that made sense, given how ancient the AI's data had been. But the others! The variety staggered her. The scope of it left her breathless. Eve may have destroyed herself, but she'd sent them right into the heart of a shipyard so big it boggled her mind.

"Looks to me like we can pick any ride home we like."

"I'll give you a minute to figure things out," Vaughn replied, "then you can take the jackass comment back for yourself."

The smug attitude made her want to smack him, but his confidence gave her serious pause. Sam's drift had turned her away from the expanse of the chamber—apparently Eve had crash-landed them at one end of the massive trench-room—forcing her to endure the sight of a wall forty meters away until she'd made a full circle. She studied the moored fleet again.

And saw what Vaughn meant instantly.

Decay. Dismantlement. Scaffolds that absolutely writhed with robotic machines. As Sam watched those closest to her, she saw that the little automatons were not bringing supplies or materials to the ships, but carrying them away. Scrap metal and bits of exotic filament wires, looking very much like they'd been shorn with an old, rusty pair of hair clippers. This was no dock or refueling depot. This was a salvage yard on the grandest possible scale. Rose-colored glasses gone, Sam noted the true state of the ships around her. Some were mere skeletons, like great butchered whales. Many more, those that appeared to be fully intact, were in truth only shells. She could tell because most had at least one gaping hole looking in on empty, ravaged interiors.

"Why the hell are they taking apart so many ships?" she wondered aloud.

"A damn good question," Vaughn replied. "But what I really want to know is why they're ignoring us."

The thought hadn't even occurred to Sam, as if the tactical part of her brain had yet to recover from their turbulent arrival. She twisted about, looking for the actual impact site. Eve had ejected them in a small pod, all inflated orange cushioning on the inside, but until this moment Sam hadn't seen the outside. If not for the cracked-open state of it, she'd have assumed it a random chunk of rock. "Is that what we came here in?"

"Yeah. What's left of it."

It looked like a shard of an asteroid, utterly natural. The kind of thing that drifted in abundance out in a star's Kuiper belt. Which explained why the Scipios hadn't shot them out of the sky. Well, partially explained. It may appear natural, but why let it actually impact? She pulsed the thrusters on her suit to right herself, then flew to the wreckage. Vaughn joined her.

"Supplies," he said, gesturing. "Food, water, something my suit tells me is ammunition for the wrist weapons, and these . . ."

She looked at the objects his finger pointed at. Little blobs, like coals for a barbecue. A bit of text appeared in the lower right of her vision, projected on the inside of her visor. HIGH-EXPLOSIVE MORTAR ROUNDS.

"I feel better already," Samantha said.

Vaughn grunted, amused. "Twenty? Against an entire world?"

"It's a start. What about the others? Heard from them?" She was already deep into the comm menu on her visor when he replied.

"Nope. It seems we're limited to short range only, don't ask me why. It's deliberate, as far as I can tell."

Sam bit back a reply to that. Eve had been like a god and gods had a nasty habit of working in strange ways, didn't they? Maybe she thought they wouldn't fight on if they knew their companions hadn't made it. She turned her focus to Eve's other unexplained gift: the small black pedestal that had been between them inside the capsule. It floated, silent and cold, like some impartial observer. "What about that thing?"

"Beats me," he replied. "Maybe we were supposed to use it to fly away."

"No," Sam said. "First off, Eve wouldn't have let us go that easily. Second, I recognize it. Sort of."

Vaughn waited.

"It's an aura shard," she said. "A small one, granted, but otherwise just like those Skyler found in Brazil. The black material, tapering down to a point. I bet if we were in gravity it would still float." She turned to the man. Her friend, her lover. "You're not immune, Vaughn. She sent this for you. We have to keep it close."

He wrinkled his nose. "It's a boat anchor. I can't fight if I'm lugging that thing around."

"It floats, moron."

"It's *bulky*."

"Well, it's that or the disease."

"My suit will keep their shit out," he countered.

"Until they get a hit on you," Sam replied, thinking of the tentacle that had punctured her own suit at the calf. That Scipio had fled an instant later, as if it had accomplished its goal. Had it tasted her? Discovered her immunity? No way to know. "Might be that we both need it," she said carefully.

"Meaning what?"

"SUBS, back on Earth? That was Eve's approximation of the Scipio virus, and based on her understanding of it from a few thousand years ago. Who knows what variants they have? Fuck, they're probably manufacturing a new version as we speak."

He grimaced. And then his expression changed, his gaze off in the vague middle distance. "Trouble," he said simply. All that needed to be said.

Sam whirled. For the first time she realized another detail about the massive shipyard. Their little pod wasn't the only one to crash here. She counted four other crash sites in their immediate area, hard to see in a room full of semi-dismantled vessels, but entirely obvious now. Deep blackened gouges along the "floor," surrounded by the shredded remains of alien machinery. Sam squinted and, in response, her view zoomed in. A purely digital enhancement, but still quite impressive. Part of her wanted to see Skyler floating beside one of those impact sites. Hell, she'd be happy to see Tania right about now. But somehow she'd known these objects were not pods like hers. They were the remnants of the *Chameleon*. A slab of matte-black hull. There, a surprisingly large chunk of one of the biosphere walls, the segmented glass panels webbed with cracks, but still connected to one another. Sam wondered if Eve had meant to do this. Hide her and Vaughn's arrival in this wreckage. Probably. But it hadn't worked. Vaughn was right. A kilometer away at least, and closing, was a squadron of fast moving craft. Teardrop shaped and white in color, they sped along just a few meters from the floor in a V formation, heading straight toward Sam and Vaughn. As they neared they began to spread out, preparing to surround.

Not today, Sam thought.

Vaughn, as was his way, read her mind, and together they unleashed a salvo of mortars on the incoming Scipio craft. Sam assumed they were Scipio, at least. Seemed reasonable. Under the circumstances she felt entirely justified in a "Shoot first and ask questions later" policy.

The mortars scythed through the air, their trajectories curling with the evasive maneuvers of their targets, and slammed home. Vaughn's was a direct hit. A soundless explosion flashed, followed by a rapidly spreading sphere of debris. He'd be bragging about it at the first opportunity, she knew, because hers somehow missed. The Scipio did a neat little shimmy to the left at the last possible second. The mortar missed by a hair-width, plowing into an array of cylindrical containers secured to the floor by some kind of scaffold. Sam's disappointment gave way to elation as a brilliant flash lit up the room. Fuel containers of some kind, she realized in hindsight, knowing she'd tell Vaughn it had been her plan the whole time. The queer vacuum-hindered fireball flashed out and vanished in little trails of prismatic sparks like a summer firework. The Scipio that had dodged was already twenty meters in front of the explosion when it came. Not far enough to escape damage entirely. It flipped forward, nose scraping the floor in a moment of friction that sent it cartwheeling off.

"Lucky shot!" Vaughn shouted, already moving away to her left to put some distance between them.

"You wish," she replied.

Vaughn fired again at another enemy, but stopped short of a third salvo when Sam urged him to hold fire. "What is it?" he asked.

"Shoot the moorings," she said.

"The what?"

Lead by example, she decided. Sam raised her arms and fired twin beams, spreading out from her position, sweeping slowly with the movement of her arms across two truly gigantic bundles of tubing and filament that held one of the ruined starships in place. Whatever fear she had that the beam would not be up to the challenge melted away as the plasma lance severed the cables like they were made of paper. Vaughn caught the drift and sliced away the two other visible supports holding the ship steady in the bay. Compared with others in the massive chamber, this one was small, but that didn't bother Sam. She wanted a bowling ball, and when the next mortar she fired struck home, she got one.

The explosion nudged the freed ship into movement. The next mortar pushed it even harder. When Vaughn added two more from his position, the derelict craft got up a head of momentum that served the purpose she'd intended. The rapidly approaching Scipios slowed, then stopped. Their focus divided, and then, seconds later, completely consumed by the huge mass of metal and ship's innards that now tumbled through the dockyard with total, directionless abandon.

Sam watched, a smile of childish satisfaction on her face, as the ship slammed into its nearest neighbor. From a distance the crash looked about as violent as two baby strollers bumping into each other. The scale simply defied comprehension. All she wanted was to distract the incoming enemy force.

What she achieved was something altogether more.

"Holy fucking shit," Vaughn whispered.

Later she'd theorize as to just what that second vessel contained that caused such an incredible release of energy. A reactor or, hell, several goddamn reactors. Some cache of missiles too exotic in their makeup to reasonably ponder. In that moment, though, all Sam could do was watch the calamity unfold, her mouth agape the entire time.

Her projectile ship had plowed into its victim—a much larger ship, but much less substantial. Hardly more than a skeleton, really, to Sam's eye. After the first few layers of scaffold were torn asunder, though, her projectile hit something that exploded with a force just short of nuclear. Even her Builder-made visor struggled to dampen the bright flare. Heat washed over her body, no worse than the Darwin sun on the inside, but a dark fear coursed through her at the sudden appearance of a glowing marbleized pattern all across her armor. There was a shuddering sensation as radiation was absorbed and reemitted. The floor, a few meters from her feet, melted, leaving a trail of warped metallic tiles as the energy of the blast pushed her backward.

Seconds passed in a blur as her mind recoiled from the inferno. Sam righted herself with the pulse from the suit's thrusters, grateful the engines still worked. Grateful she hadn't been cooked alive.

"You okay?" Vaughn asked, his voice an island of calm amid the violence.

"I think so."

"Jesus, Sam, look what you started."

She blinked, willed enough concentration to take in the vastness and insanity spread out before her. Her plan had been to set a ship loose, hoping it would knock a few others around and force the Scipios to alter their priorities. Those Scipios were utterly gone. Vapor, or a smear of black on the gaping wound the accidental bomb had left on the shipyard. When it went, it annihilated the four other ships around it. But even *that* wasn't what left Samantha Rinn utterly without words.

It was the vessels farther away that her eyes now struggled to track. Dozens of them, propelled on the wave of high-energy particles that had slammed into them. Flickering secondary explosions boiled across their surfaces, adding even more chaos to their movement, and causing the support filaments that held them in place to snap. It all reminded her of a billiards table, the cue ball, hard struck, sending the rest into a riot of unpredictable movement. Only this was in three dimensions. And on a truly massive scale, rife with catastrophic explosions. "Time to bail," Sam said.

"Amen," Vaughn replied.

"Get the . . . shard," she said, gesturing toward the meter-tall object that had been at the core of their escape pod. However much it resembled an aura shard, shard seemed more appropriate. Vaughn knew exactly what she meant and propelled himself toward the object.

She led the way, knowing he would fall obediently in behind her and for once his puppy-dog loyalty didn't bother her. Sam decided to do the counterintuitive thing and get outside, rather than heading for the shelter of the space station's interior. She aimed herself out toward the open edge of the dockyard and triggered her thrusters on full burn for a few seconds, gaining speed through space full of glowing-hot debris that streaked across her vision. Crossing the distance took only a few seconds, giving her just enough time to take one last glance at the drama she'd unleashed. The ships were falling like dominoes, either loosed from their moorings or simply being pelted by the truly astonishing amount of debris now flying about the room. A chunk of indefinable gear sailed past Sam's own head and out into space. She followed it.

Another, smaller piece smacked into her thigh. She felt the armor harden up and down her entire leg a fraction of a second before the blow arrived. The impact sent her spinning, and despite the suit she still felt a pain across her thigh as if she'd been kicked.

Sam willed the suit to cancel her errant rotation. It complied, and then she was out, leaving the confines of the vast chamber before immediately turning and firing her thrusters again. She sailed along the outer hull of the space station, Vaughn just a few tens of meters behind, carrying the Builder shard under his arm like a rugby ball.

No pursuit that she could see, and that was just fine with her. She needed time to think. To lay low and make contact with Skyler or, hell, anyone. Racing along just meters away from the curved surface of the space station, Sam had to suppress a laugh. *No plan survives first contact with the enemy.* The age-old phrase came to mind, unbidden. So damn true. Despite all of Eve's careful efforts to find, select, and ultimately recruit humans to help her, and all the scheming and work to get them to her home world, in the end the best the AI could do was throw her champions vaguely in the right direction and hope it all worked out. What a cock-up.

To his credit, Vaughn never questioned the route Sam had taken. He followed, nothing more, the kind of silence Jake the sniper used to afford her when they were out scavenging in the Clear. She'd never really realized just how much confidence Jake's presence gave her, knowing that he had her back no matter how distant his roost was. Only after his death had she felt that peculiar loss, and only now could she wrap her mind around the fact that Vaughn had replaced that missing element. The two men couldn't be more different, of course, but the result was the same. In battle, at least, they complemented her.

Sam turned, flying downward toward the planet below, keeping herself barely an arm's length from the surfaces of the Scipio space station. Fighting a sudden sense of vertigo, she allowed herself a moment to take it all in.

The world down there, Carthage, resembled Earth and yet was clearly not. The colors were just enough different, the landmasses wholly alien. More shocking was the scale of the Scipios' presence up here. The stations that lined the two space elevators back at Earth were pitiful in comparison. Child's play. The one she flew beside alone could probably hold every one of Neil Platz's creations, with room to spare. And this was just one of dozens she could see in her limited patch of sky. Gigantic metastructures, composed of hundreds of smaller sections linked together by curved hallways or support trusses, with only the barest hint of the literal thread that held them all in place. Like Earth, the space elevators were equatorial, or near enough. Unlike Earth, the space stations were not limited to those vertical corridors. Sam could see dozens of smaller—yet still massive—collections of orbiting structures, off in the distance. Each was linked to the other and their bigger siblings by beams of violet energy. Tania would wonder what purpose they served, how they worked, Sam mused.

What Sam wanted to know is what would happen if she turned them off.

After what had happened in the shipyard, she found a certain thirst for playing the role of saboteur. She had some serious firepower at her disposal, after all, and the way her armor absorbed that impact to her leg . . . she felt just shy of invincible. Make a big enough mess here and the Scipios would have to divert more and more resources to dealing with it, perhaps making the others' jobs that much easier. But that assumed they were all alive, and even in a position to continue the mission.

"There," Vaughn said.

She glanced at him, then followed his pointed finger. Their path had taken them along a towering support beam, linking the dock where they'd crash-landed to the station below. Vaughn had spotted another opening, though much smaller than the last and nearly pitch-black inside. Still, even if the alcove was no more than a surface feature of the station, with no way inside, it looked as good a place as any to hide and catch their breath. She shifted a bit and cruised to it, allowing her visor to augment her view in different ways, looking for any signs of the enemy within. It showed nothing more than an empty rectangular depression on the station's surface, though. Large by any standard, provided she forgot about the incredible vastness of the place they'd fled.

Blackness swallowed her, and the visor took a few seconds to find a radiation band that would give her some semblance of vision. An alcove, indeed. Just a cube-shaped pit on the side of a station that served some purpose she'd likely never understand.

"Look at that," Vaughn said, whispering even though they were communicating via the comm.

Sam turned and felt her muscles twitch. Behind them, a cloud of sparking dust soared across her view. The particles within it began to twist and curl even as they spread out, now resembling a school of fish seen from a hundred klicks away. Her mind finally registered the truth: a squadron of distant spacecraft, flying in an organic and ever-changing formation, fanning out as they zeroed in on the giant trenchlike shipyard Sam and Vaughn had just fled.

"The cavalry has arrived," she said, though she thought maybe they were the emergency responders. The entire shipyard roiled in explosions and the ancillary damage of superheated shrapnel.

"Good thing we're not there to meet them."

Sam couldn't quite bring herself to agree. A stand-up fight always beat skulking and sneaking, in her experience. Tania's failed plan to camouflage their way into the system, case in point. Still, even from here, their overwhelming numbers could not be disputed. Fighting a horde like that would be suicide.

"Keep an eye on them," she said, and turned back to the shadows. More details of the surface began to register as her visor composited views from several different EM bands. The joints where hull plating met. A quartet of vents, each no larger than her hand, with carbon scoring on the surfaces around them. And then there was the hexagonal indentation, with a window inset in its center. Darkness waited beyond the tiny porthole.

"We're in luck," Sam said, and ignited the beam on her arm to use as a cutting torch.

"You'd better hurry," Vaughn said urgently.

"Do I want to know why?"

"Something coming this way. Three of them, I think. One has . . . Oh . . . Ah! *Here! Here!*"

Sam couldn't resist. She turned from her cutting efforts to gaze at Vaughn, who waved like a maniac toward an object in the distance. Three objects, she realized, just as he'd said. *Scipios,* her brain said. But then she saw what Vaughn already knew. The shapes were human.

6

ABOVE CARTHAGE

"Prumble," Sam whispered. It was hard to miss the big man's outline.

And who else? she wondered. Almost as an afterthought, she went back to her work, the sense of urgency returned. Heightened. Her beam traced a glowing line around the inside edge of the window. Roughly circular. An artist she was not, but she thought it would get the job done. Eventually, her circuit completed, Sam winked the beam off. She reached down and pushed at the clear surface. It fell away without complaint, swallowed by the still-dark interior. The hole would be wide enough, she thought, and she turned just in time to be swept into a crushing embrace by Prumble. He clapped her on the back several times, and she could feel the joyous laughter that all but overwhelmed him. The next arrival landed beside Vaughn, taking his offered hand for balance. Sam saw the face through the visor: Tania. And then the third, Tim.

Part of her couldn't help but feel disappointed. She thought she hid it pretty well, though.

"Good to see you," Sam said to Prumble. "Why didn't you tell us you were approaching?"

The big man shook his head and pointed at his ear. "No long-range comms," he said. "Eve disabled them for some reason. Local is all we've got."

Sam nodded, understanding the situation, but not the reasons behind it.

"Skyler? Vanessa?" Prumble asked, as if reading her mind. Hoping the same hope she'd held.

Sam could only shake her head. But at least now she could attribute that to a matter of distance, rather than assumptions about their fate. "Let's get inside. We're totally exposed out here."

He offered no objection. Sam nodded at each of them in turn, then hopped feetfirst through the circular hole she'd carved. In the weak gravity of this altitude, her descent took several seconds.

Sam landed in darkness and took a step to one side before turning on her headlamp.

The only one among them with both hands free, Sam took the lead. Each of the others carried the small aura shards. She felt blessed at her lack of such a burden. They looked like toddlers carrying beloved teddy bears, a visual she decided it was best not to share. Something to tease Vaughn with later.

The hole she'd carved led to an airless length of hallway. A wide space, with two grooves of unknown purpose along the floor. She picked a direction at random and walked until they reached a bulkhead door. Sealed, she guessed, as an automatic precaution after the opening she'd made in the hull. Sam opened it to more of the same dull hall, let the others through, and closed it again behind her. Readouts concerning the air began to update on her screen. From vacuum to trace gases to breathable.

"Breathable?" Vaughn asked.

Always in lockstep with me, Sam mused. For better or worse. Another visual to keep to herself.

"Yes," Tania said. "Not an ideal mix, the oxygen level is . . . minimal at best. What worries me is what else is drifting around in this air." She waved one hand through the dusty air to hammer the point home. The particulate formed eddies behind her splayed fingers.

Prumble grunted. "How can these bastards live in this stuff?"

"They are masters of viral engineering. Such cells probably do everything for them," Tim said. "Clean their bodies. Carry messages and data. Cure their ailments or infect those requiring punishment. Surveillance—"

"Okay, okay," Sam said. "It's nasty. We get it. So keep your aura shard close and your visor down, just in case. Unless we're forced to, I vote no one breathes this air at all."

"Our suits will help us there," Tania noted. "Our air supply—"

Prumble giggled.

"—Our air supply is being replenished by scrubbers in the membranes. Mine was at forty percent, now it's up to forty-eight."

The others fell silent, no doubt checking their own status. Sam glanced at hers, ignoring the immature joke Prumble's interface displayed. Fifty-six percent.

"Hmm." It was Vaughn.

She glanced at him, an eyebrow arched.

"Thirteen percent," he said. "Twelve."

Sam went to him, turned him around, and took a knee. The light from her headlamp played through the particulate in the air. There, near the base of his spine, the virus cells were being blown by a leak. A pinprick hole in one of the bulging pockets hidden under the Builder armor. "Eve couldn't throw in a roll of duct tape, eh?"

"Actually," Prumble said, "she did."

Everyone looked at him as he rummaged through his own pack. Eventually he produced a small gray container and held it out. "My visor indicates this is 'repair paste.' Worth a try."

Sam took it and turned it about in her fingers. "I didn't get one of these." From the expressions of those around her, no one else had, either. More of Eve's bizarre logic, she supposed. Still, Prumble was right, it was worth a try.

There were no instructions, so she did the natural thing and simply pressed the object against Vaughn's suit, covering the hole. Almost instantly it began to vibrate in her hand, a hum not unlike a comm's silent alert mode. After a few seconds, the vibration stopped. Sam pulled the container away. It left a shiny circular patch behind, slightly raised compared with the armor around it. As she stared at it, the shine dulled and then vanished completely. Some kind of hardening process.

"Air level is holding," Vaughn said. "Just ticked up a percent."

"Well," Prumble said, "that's handy."

"Too bad we have only one," Sam noted. She turned the container about in her hand again. It felt and looked smaller already. She guessed it would provide only half a dozen uses.

Samantha stood and met her lover's gaze. His expression was questioning. "Relax," she said. "Whatever penetrated your suit, it was small."

Vaughn opened his mouth to reply.

"If you're going for innuendo here," Sam said, "think twice."

He shut his mouth dutifully.

"Can we please get out of the open?" Tim asked.

Sam led them through the empty hallways until they reached a dead end, with another iris door that led into a room full of dusty, forgotten bits of machinery. She'd imagined many things about the Scipios, but never expected such first-order pack rats.

"Someone should stand guard," Vaughn said. When no one objected, and Sam gave him a quick knowing look—*You just volunteered, love*—he remained in the hall and let the door hiss closed.

The others had arranged themselves in a loose circle in the entryway of the chamber. Sam decided to ignore them all for the moment, hopping lightly past them to survey the dark corners of the chamber. The place was filthy. It reminded her of the ramshackle storage shed behind her uncle's vintage automobile repair shop, back in Australia, where weeds poked through the decaying remains of old combustion engines and battery packs. No weeds here, no recognizable parts, either. Just forgotten junk. Sam scanned the ground more than anything, looking for any signs of recent Scipio presence, but there was nothing. She went back to the others. "It's empty. They haven't been here in years, I'd guess."

"Good," Prumble said. "So, now what?"

Before Sam could reply, both Tania and Tim spoke over each other.

"Find the others," Tania said.

Over her, Tim said, "Find a way out of here."

The two options, laid out with absolute simplicity. Sam couldn't help herself. She nodded toward Tim. "Leave? Just like that?"

The young man shifted uncomfortably, wilting under the intensity of Tania's glare. Sam wanted to slap them both. This was no time for awkward romantic bullshit. Eventually he spoke. "We came here to help Eve, and she's gone. We don't have the supplies to survive here for more than a few days, at best." Tim swallowed, confidence building. "We haven't heard from the others."

"Comms are locked to local only," Tania noted.

Sam grunted at that. Both agreeing and bemused at why Eve would have done that. No doubt it made sense to the now-dead AI. Typical Builder crap.

Tim winced. "I know they are. But we all landed near each other. If the others are out there, they'll have to come to us. We don't have the supplies to do anything here other than find a way to leave. Not if we want to survive."

"It's a bit cold, though," Prumble observed. " 'Fuck everyone and run.' As plans go, that's quite frigid, isn't it?"

Tim chewed on his lower lip. "I'm just saying what we all know is true."

"We came here on a mission," Tania said.

Now Tim did look at her. "It ended when Eve blew up. We've done more than enough to try and help them but, let's face it, her plan failed—"

"That was my plan, actually," Tania shot back, not much more than a whisper.

"And it was a good one! The best we could come up with! But it didn't work, Tania."

"Didn't it? We're here, aren't we? Farther than anyone else has made it."

"Without supplies or guidance or even a clue as to where to go next. A good portion of our team is dead."

Tania pointed at him. "We don't know that."

"We do," Tim said. "Some of us are just in a better position to accept it."

"Oy," Sam said. "Enough. I agree helping the Builders is no longer the priority. Survival is. And by survival I mean getting away from this place. Tim's right. Sorry, Tania, but he is, at least with the shit we're in right now. Without a way out of here, nothing else makes sense."

"What do you propose?" Prumble asked.

Sam bit her lip. She said, "I'm suddenly regretting blowing up their entire shipyard."

The blank, astonished stares spoke volumes. Sam winced. "It was an accident."

"Hang on," Vaughn said via the local comm, from outside the door. "Sam, that was a scrapyard. They were dismantling those beasts."

"Yeah? Your point?"

"If we found that, we can find the one where they're storing the good ones. Or the factory they're coming out of."

"We didn't find it, though," Sam said. "We fucking crashed there."

Prumble held up his hands. "Can I make a suggestion?"

The others quieted down.

He went on. "We've all seen that our visors can translate Scipio words."

"Barely," Sam noted.

"Well enough. So we do one of two things, whichever comes first." He had their attention now. "We either find a map, via some terminal or something that can tell us what's where."

"Or?" Sam asked.

"Or," Prumble said, "if you'll pardon the crudeness of the idea, we capture a Scipio, and ever so politely beat it out of them."

7

LOCATION UNKNOWN

A candle in the dark, drifting as if carried by a fearful child, cast a faint red-orange glow on the surrounding walls.

Fire.

An open flame.

Fire burned breathable air. Fire was the most feared enemy inside a spacecraft. That's the first thing they taught her, and never stopped hammering the point home.

Gloria Tsandi blinked. That tiny motion made pain blossom behind her eyes, yet somehow pain felt good here. It meant she was alive to feel it.

The flame remained. But it wasn't being carried, or even drifting. No, it simply leaned, as if being pulled toward . . .

She saw the hull breach a meter away, clogged with random bits of the devastated ship, air still managing to escape through the cracks between debris.

Events began to replay in her mind's eye. It took all the concentration she had to put them in the right order. The severing of the *Wildflower*'s umbilical. Scipios slithering all over the hull, punching their way in. Then the hammer blow. A massive explosion aboard the Builder ship Skyler had renamed the *Chameleon*. Blinding pain, long periods of unconsciousness. Tumbling through space, all systems offline except those installed within her own suit. A dead ship, unable to be righted. Her crew in pain. Herself in pain, unable to help them. Just a captain aboard a wreck.

A wreck wasn't good enough, though. Her charter, her oath, was to leave no trace. The Scipios must not find anything that could give them a clue about how to build their own field cavitation imploders, nor could they learn the location of Earth. A wreck was too much to leave behind.

She remembered giving the order to Xavi. Burn all the fuel. Get us going fast enough to slam into something. Even better, overload the engines.

He'd said something. She couldn't grasp the meaning of the words now. Nor could she then. She'd hit her head, saw stars, slept.

Then came the impact. A jarring thud that woke her briefly. The sound of something scraping against the hull that seemed to go on for days. Finally, quiet, though she couldn't be sure if that was due to the end of the scraping or her own return to the abyss of her mind.

Gloria focused on her body. Listened to her own heartbeat thanks to the anguished pulse in her ears. She twitched a finger, then another. All of them. Next came the toes, which took a bit of cajoling. So she'd kept all her limbs. Small victory.

She opened her eyes again and watched the candle. Over time the flame became more real, more focused. She saw the trail of smoke that seemed to flee as if alive, right toward the hull puncture. Gloria shifted her gaze to the wall beside the fire and saw a familiar bulkhead, which put her near the *Wildflower*'s midsection. The flame was no candle at all. A ruptured pipe behind one of the wall panels, and no suppression system online to extinguish it. As if in control of a puppet, Gloria raised her heavy leg and, panting from the effort, pressed her boot on the little oval of fire. The space plunged into darkness. She pulled her foot away, and the flame did not return.

There, she thought. *I saved us all.* She wanted to laugh, but knew her body was not ready for that kind of exertion yet. Besides, the humor drained as quickly as it had come. The fact that she was alive was a very, very bad thing. The ship had not been destroyed. The ship was a tidy bundle of intelligence waiting to be consumed.

With great effort Gloria turned her head to one side. To her surprise, the blackness was not absolute. A shaft of blue-white light filtered in from the airlock porthole, illuminating the wall opposite. Dust swirled lazily in the beam. But, she noted, no debris drifted. She herself was planted against the hull, too.

So, gravity. Must be.

She heard no roar of engine, felt no vibration through her suit, so it must be actual gravity, and not the cargo hold of some Scipio hauler.

"Where the hell are we?" she whispered to her dead ship, and the ship did not reply. Maybe it never would again. Amber glow at the edge of her vision swirled and phased, until collapsing into recognizable icons and characters.

AIR LEVEL CRITICAL, the display read, with an almost comical skull and crossbones blinking away above it. She swallowed hard. Her mouth tasted like desert sand. Her stomach grumbled, empty. One calf throbbed with pain, something deep. Not broken, she hoped, but certainly badly bruised. She needed the med bay, and then water and a packet of nutrition paste. Also, air. The alert was coming from her own suit, not the ship. She'd almost used up her own supply.

But first, the others.

Propping herself up on one elbow left her shaking, cold sweat slimy against the fabric of her space suit. Gloria spent a minute catching her breath, then rolled the rest of the way onto her knees. Standing seemed too great a challenge just yet, so she crawled toward the tail of the ship, where Beth Lee had been.

The engineer lay at her workstation. She'd somehow had the presence of mind to strap herself into her acceleration couch, and appeared to be sleeping peacefully. Though the ship lay on its side, the gimbaled chair had rotated with the angle. Gloria crawled to it and hauled herself up. She took Beth by the shoulder and shook.

The woman spasmed, bucking against her restraints, an

abbreviated scream escaping her lips as consciousness flowed back in.

"It's okay, it's okay," Gloria whispered.

Beth turned to her, eyes wide with shock. She opened her mouth to say something, but all that came out was a single, sharp cough that flecked blood on the inside of her visor. For a moment Beth just stared at the tiny droplets, studying them.

"Let's get you to the med bay," Gloria said, trying her best to sound upbeat. A bitten tongue would be one thing, internal bleeding something else altogether.

Beth barely managed a nod. She lay placid as Gloria undid the restraints and helped ease the diminutive woman from the chair. Together they staggered, each with one arm over the other's shoulder, over several bulkheads to the medical station.

"What a nightmare," Beth managed, sinking to her knees among the spilled contents of three wall cabinets that had sprung open in the explosion. She swept the items aside with one arm and lay down on her back with a grunt.

"Don't sleep," Gloria said. "Not yet, okay?"

"Will . . . try."

"Goddamn fate," Gloria swore silently as she rummaged through the detritus on the floor. Hundreds of sealed plastic bags, each containing some kind of pill or injector or bandage. The *Wildflower* had been stripped to the bone for this mission. Supplies were the bare minimum, and worse, her medical officer had been left behind. Basic triage had been part of Gloria's training, at least, but right now she could remember precious little of it. She'd have to guess. Each bag had been marked with a bar code, which her visor scanned and displayed the contents as she held them up before her face. She tossed them aside as quickly as she picked them up. Behind her Beth groaned, rolling onto her side. Gloria worked faster, picking up bags with both hands now, not even looking at them, but instead just reading the summary displayed on her visor, scanning for keywords. There. SYMPTOM: INTERNAL BLEEDING. She turned, ripping the bag open in the same motion. Gloria opened a flap on the shoulder of Beth's suit and twisted the injector into the port there. Then she thumbed the base of it and heard the *click-click* as the tiny needle within extended and retracted.

Gloria didn't wait to see if it worked. She whirled and continued her search. Several minutes later she'd stimmed Beth and herself with painkillers, hydration boosts, and shock suppressants. She found emergency air and water containers as well and replenished both of their suits.

"Stay here," she said to Beth. "Going to check on the others."

Beth said nothing. Her eyes were closed, but Gloria could see the bloom and fade of fog on the inside of the woman's mask. *Good, rest. Use less air.*

Xavi and Vanessa had sealed themselves into the bridge with the intruder, Alex Warthen, just before the explosion that expelled them from the alien ship. The bulkhead was still closed, but its locking panel had power. It was an isolated system, relying on nothing but its own internal programming, and backed up by an ultracap that would last for decades. Gloria pressed her palm against it, allowing her suit's glove to sample and pass through a skin cell for DNA verification. It took only two seconds before the light turned green and the emergency closure was rescinded. A clunk echoed through the ship and then the door panels retracted into the surrounding bulkhead.

Darkness greeted her. Biting back her fear and worry, Gloria switched her headlamp on and winced as brilliant white light flooded into the cramped space beyond.

Xavi sat, knees to his chest, one arm around the sleeping form of Vanessa. His other arm was propped on one knee, aiming his pistol at Alex Warthen, who lay opposite them, utterly prone.

"Boss," Xavi muttered.

"Hey there," she said, unable to keep the emotion from her voice.

"What happened?" he asked. "Where are we?"

She fixed him with the best glare she could manage. "I was hoping you'd know."

"Huh?"

"Why are we still alive, Xavi? I gave you an order. Smear us on some rock. Leave no trace. You know the directive."

"I . . ." His voice trailed off. He swallowed, eyes shifting away from her. "I screwed up."

"Meaning?"

A long sigh escaped his lips. "Burned the last of our fuel when we were pointed the wrong way. Slowed us down."

"So instead of crashing, we've landed."

"Seems that way."

Gloria bit back the urge to throttle him. For a moment she just stood there, eyes closed, allowing the past to become just that. "We'll have to find another way, then."

"Seems that way," he repeated. "Seriously, though. Where are we?"

She shrugged, realizing after the fact that she hadn't even bothered to look out the porthole window when she'd walked by to get here. "I'll worry about that next. Status?"

His turn to shrug. "Think I broke my wrist. Vanessa's in shock, asleep now. Warthen . . . hasn't moved in a while. Might be dead."

"I'm not dead," Alex Warthen said, in a surprisingly strong and calm voice. "I'm conserving air. A concept the rest of you might want to familiarize yourselves with."

Xavi grunted, eyes shifting back to Gloria in a "The hits just keep coming" look. "Beth?" he asked.

"Sleeping it off. Same as Vanessa."

The man nodded, let his eyes close for a moment. He must have been watching Alex Warthen like a hawk since waking, unable to do anything about the door without the ship's systems online to let his override open them.

"Are you just going to stand there, or will you find out where we are?"

It was Alex who asked. Gloria studied him for a moment, unsure how to treat him. He'd tried to take the ship, yes, but under the circumstances she couldn't really blame him. "My crew comes first," she said. Not only true, but also allowing her to avoid the decision for a bit longer. She met Xavi's gaze and darted her eyes to the prone newcomer. *Watch him.*

Xavi understood. He always understood.

At the airlock Gloria pulled herself to one of the three windows and took in the view.

It was magnificent.

Blue-gray sand dotted by rocky outcroppings and patches of thin ice, all kissed by pinkish light from the setting star, and the crescent form of a world above. Carthage. She'd studied images of it enough to know it at a glance, and that meant the *Wildflower* had somehow managed to come to rest on one of her moons. Judging by what she knew of the terrain it was likely Mago, the largest and nearest moon of Carthage. How they'd made it so far without being caught by the Swarm she had no idea, but it didn't take much imagination to guess Eve had done something. Shielded them, or masked their fall in-system.

What truly baffled her, though, was how the *Wildflower* had managed to land, but she wasn't quite ready to look that gift horse in the mouth. They were here, they were alive. The real question was—

"What now?" Xavi asked, right on cue.

She hadn't heard him approach. "Alex?" she asked.

"Vanessa's covering him. She's awake enough now."

"Good to hear."

Xavi joined her at the window and let out a long, low whistle. "How the hell did we get here?"

"No idea and not going to worry about it."

"Looks like Mago."

"I thought the same thing."

Xavi shook his head. "Airless rock. We're screwed, boss."

Gloria said nothing. She couldn't. To agree meant resigning herself to the hard truth that her ship was truly dead. That she'd failed in the worst possible way for a captain to fail. Doubly so, since any ship left behind here was supposed to be vaporized.

And Xavi, in his unassuming way, read her perfectly. "You did everything you could."

"And you did even more than me. Do you really expect me to believe you fired our engines while pointed the wrong way?"

His grin infuriated her. "Strong survival instinct," he said, tapping the side of his helmet. "Throw me in the brig if you like."

"If we had one I would."

Xavi laughed. "Look, we're here. Let's plug these leaks and figure out a plan."

"You don't give the orders here. I'm the captain," she replied, and hated herself for it. For the rebuke, for not thanking him for saving all their lives, and for hiding behind her rank.

He placed a hand on her shoulder, calm and strong. "Relax, boss. Not an order, just advice." With that he moved toward the med bay, and knelt beside Beth.

Ten minutes later, after sealing the hull breaches with spray foam, Gloria Tsandi sat cross-legged on the floor of the mess, surrounded by Beth, Xavi, and Vanessa. Alex Warthen was in the med bay one deck below—or rather, one deck over now that the ship lay on its side—sedated and snoring.

They'd eaten and drank, removing their helmets once it was determined that the hull punctures had been plugged successfully. The air tasted like melted plastic, but it felt so good to have the helmets off that no one complained.

"That foam," Gloria said, nodding toward one of the beige, mushroom-shaped bulbs poking down from the ceiling, "is temporary at best."

The others nodded thoughtfully.

"I don't know about the rest of you," Gloria said, "but I don't want to asphyxiate or starve or die of dehydration on this lifeless moon. I don't want to wait for the Swarm to track us down, either. Even if it wasn't my sworn duty to vaporize this ship before letting it fall into Scipio hands, it's still preferable to the alternatives."

Silence filled the tiny space. Gloria waited, but when no one spoke, she went on. "Xavi may have accidentally extended our lives—"

Xavi raised a protein shake in salute. "You're welcome, mates. Cheers."

"—*but* the hard fact is that we must leave nothing for the Scipios to study."

"What about the *Lonesome*?" Beth asked.

The ship they'd come for, the original goal of this escapade. Gloria had all but forgotten her. "What about it?"

"Our mission was to find it, yes? If we destroy ourselves, we fail."

"We did what we could and found no trace of it. I have to assume that they at least completed the task we must now accomplish. Besides, we're in no condition to be worrying about that now, so put it out of your mind."

Beth Lee's gaze fell to the floor. She'd barely eaten or drank anything, while Xavi had a pile of used containers around his lap.

"Can we even do it?" Vanessa asked. "Scuttle the ship, I mean? It's pretty beat up, and I don't think my suit has enough firepower."

Gloria spread her hands. "That's what we need to find out. What I'm proposing here is that we spend our last few hours of air finding a way to do that. The easiest way is to force our reactor to melt down, but that means getting it operational again. Beth, can you look into it?"

It took several seconds, but the slow bob of her head finally happened. An acceptance of fate as much as the task. It was the only answer Gloria would get, but it was enough.

"Xavi, you're the backup plan. Get creative. Figure out a bomb we can rig, or a rock outside we can get to fall on the ship. Anything."

"I can do that, I think."

"Vanessa, I'm hoping you'll do an EVA. These foam seals won't last much longer, and I think your Builder suit has the most air. Perhaps with that . . . cannon on your wrist, you can weld some scrap plating to the holes from the outside."

"I'll handle it," Vanessa said.

"Okay, then. I'm here to help any of you with whatever you need, and in the meantime, I'll keep an eye on our guest."

With that the morbid gathering dispersed. Xavi headed for his navigation bay, probably because it was familiar. Or to say goodbye. The idea brought tears to Gloria's eyes, which she wiped away on her sleeve. Another small benefit to having helmets off.

Gloria took one glance at Alex Warthen and decided the man wasn't going to be up and about any time soon, so she followed Vanessa to the airlock. "I'll handle the doors for you since it's manual or nothing right now."

The woman nodded and stepped into the airlock proper. "Wait, how will we communicate?"

Gloria had forgotten. They'd been using external speakers, as the comms in their respective suits were incompatible. Once she was outside, though, that would no longer work. "I have an idea," Gloria said.

She went to the sleeping compartment and grabbed the one extra helmet they'd brought. Sealed for flight, it had a cap attached to the bottom of it to keep dust and other things from getting inside. Gloria twisted the cap off and stuffed a portable ultracap inside. She connected it and powered the helmet on. Configured it so the helmet would be in emergency mode, as no suit was linked, but that was okay. It had a self-contained comm, and that was all that mattered.

"Here," she said, handing it to Vanessa.

"That's not going to fit my neck ring."

"I know," Gloria said, "but you can hold it against your visor and shout really loud. The vibration should carry through."

Vanessa stared at her dubiously.

"Try it when you're out there."

"I won't be able to hear you."

Gloria nodded. "We'll have to do that part the old-fashioned way. Yes or no questions, I'll give you thumbs-up or -down from this side of the porthole."

Vanessa gave her the kind of look someone might give if handed a beer and a slice of pizza at a formal affair. She took the helmet all the same.

With a small wave Gloria closed and sealed the inner door.

"Okay. I'm going to purge the air and open the outer door. Uh." Vanessa paused, staring at the controls on the wall. "You better walk me through the process."

"Remember," Beth Lee said. She'd come to stand next to Gloria, a blanket wrapped about her shoulders. "She's a lawyer by trade, and a scavenger by necessity. Not to mention more than a thousand years old by our perspective. She's never seen an airlock like that."

Gloria studied her engineer, an apparent expert historian. "I thought you were checking on the reactor."

Beth shrugged. "Nothing to check with the computers offline. Vanessa will be able to confirm from the outside, but my guess is the ship's automatic emergency systems jettisoned the core when the explosion hit."

"Could you rig some emergency power?"

The engineer considered that for a moment. "There're a few

ultracaps in here, I think? They could be rewired. In theory."

Gloria forced herself to remember that this wasn't Beth's ship. She'd been assigned because she knew the imploder tech. It was unreasonable to expect her to be an expert on the rest of the *Wildflower's* systems. "Try," she said.

Beth gave a halfhearted nod and moved off again.

Battling back a wave of fatigue, Gloria shifted all her focus to Vanessa. She explained the process of exiting the vessel and talked the other woman through the process until the moment the air was purged and talking became impossible.

"Testing comms," Vanessa said, the spare helmet pressed to her own. Shouted, really.

Gloria heard the voice only as a tinny garble coming through her earpiece. She gave Vanessa a thumbs-up through the window.

"Well," the woman said, turning about and taking in the scene outside, "the good news is there's plenty of scrap I can use to try and seal these ruptures."

That bad. Gloria swallowed.

"We skidded for about a klick before coming to rest."

Gloria recalled the long scraping sound she'd heard in one of her moments of consciousness after the explosion out in deep space.

"I'm afraid the rest is all bad news. I don't know your ship, but all that seems to be left of it is the main body that you're in right now. The rest is . . . debris."

She turned to look through the porthole, as if for direction. Gloria held up a finger, asking her to wait. Then she activated the screen mounted on her forearm and tapped out some text. She held her arm up to the porthole and waited.

"'Beth wants to know about status of the reactor core,'" Vanessa read. "Describe it for me."

You had small thorium reactors in your time, yes?

"Never saw one personally, but I know what you mean."

Like that, just smaller. A pair of them. The housing is painted yellow.

"Hold on."

Out the porthole, Gloria caught a glimpse of Vanessa's form as she went about her circuit of the ship. The woman crouched and then leapt, jets of gas firing from hidden vents along her legs. The combination powered her upward and out of sight.

There was a groan from the med bay. Warthen's sedation wearing off. Xavi immediately went to check on him, and when he returned he said, "Used a spare bungee to secure him. Besides, there's nowhere to go."

Gloria nodded.

A moment of strange calm passed. No one saying anything. No alarms or fires or panicked voices. Just . . . quiet. Gloria reveled in it. One had to take such chances—

"Yes? I'm here! I read you!" Vanessa said. "I am receiving— hello? Ah shit."

The comm abruptly clicked.

"Vanessa?" Gloria asked. "What's happening? Can you hear me?"

Nothing. Thirty seconds passed. A minute. She was about to suit up and go out after the woman when the connection returned. A second later, Vanessa's face appeared at the porthole again.

"Are you okay?" Gloria asked, knowing she couldn't be heard, but hoping her lip movement got the question across.

"We've got a problem," Vanessa said. There was a terrible shake to her voice.

Come back in.

"It's not that," she replied. "It's Skyler."

Gloria held her breath. The others in the cabin went silent, too.

"He made it," Vanessa said. "Down to the surface of Carthage, I think. I heard him talking with Tim."

This is good, isn't it? Why is this a problem?

"That's not the problem. Something's messing with the comm. I can hear Skyler, and so can Tim. Tim is able to reply to him, but I cannot. I don't think either of them can hear me. They don't react when I talk. Must be too far. But that's not it, either. It's the others. They're with Tim based on what he said, but they seem unaware of any of this."

"A range problem," Xavi said. "Maybe we can boost it somehow—"

Gloria tapped out a paraphrased version.

"No," Vanessa said. "You don't understand. This isn't a malfunction. It's contrived. Eve did this. I never trusted that . . . entity. Is Alex awake? I need to talk to him."

"I'm here," Alex replied. Both to Vanessa and via his speaker, so they could all hear him. Gloria hadn't thought to use him as a conduit to talk with her. She still hadn't decided if he was friend or foe.

Vanessa went on. "Just now, could you hear Skyler, or Tim?"

"No," Alex said. All business, that one.

"I still don't understand what you're upset about," Gloria said. "This is progress, isn't it?"

Alex relayed the message.

"You're right," Vanessa said. "You don't understand. The problem is Tim. In theory, he could relay Skyler's messages to the others. But he isn't doing that. In fact, he just lied to them, said he hadn't heard from Skyler. Instead of relaying the news, he just fucking abandoned him."

As she spoke her voice grew more and more steady. The quavering, a manifestation of shock, congealed into a steady anger. "Skyler has saved my life more times than I can count. We have to help him. Get to him somehow. Contact the others, at least, and let them know Tim is lying."

Gloria moved to Alex Warthen and leaned in close to his face. He understood instantly and enabled his transmitter. "Listen to me," Gloria said into it. "At least we know they're alive. And Xavi's right, perhaps. Maybe both Tim and Skyler will be able to hear you if we can figure out a way to boost your signal. At least then you can let Skyler know we're here, and that if Tim won't help him, we will. Agreed?"

"Agreed," Vanessa said, after a moment's thought.

Gloria Tsandi waited. To see if Vanessa would say more, and if not, to give her time to get control of herself. After five seconds or so, she spoke with all the maternal calm she could muster. "Here's what we're going to do. First priority is survival. Second is finding a way to get a message to the others. Okay? Let them know we're still out here, and let them know what Tim has done. Beyond that, well, you all know what needs to be done. We can't leave the *Wildflower* sitting here all gift wrapped."

For one terrible moment Gloria thought the woman might disagree. That the burden of this knowledge and the slim chances of being able to do anything about it might crush what little spirit remained in her. The reply, when it came, was terse and monotone. "Okay. Okay. Expanding my search radius."

"Understood," Gloria replied. "I can talk to you through Alex."

A minute passed. Then two. Finally, Vanessa spoke again. "Wow."

"What is it?" Gloria asked.

"We're not the only thing that crashed here."

"Do . . ." Gloria swallowed, tried again. "You mean the others? They're here?"

"No, no. This is debris. There're impact sites all over the place."

Xavi cut in. "Debris from the *Chameleon,* probably."

"Or debris from us," Gloria countered. "Vanessa, is any of it intact?"

"It would take days to survey it all. But, my guess? No. Nothing larger than a . . . Hold on. Oh my God."

"What?"

Silence stretched.

"What is it?" Gloria tried again.

"We're not alone on this moon," Vanessa replied.

A lance of electric ice shot up Gloria's spine. She pulled Alex over to the porthole.

"Meaning what?" Xavi asked. Gloria echoed his question.

"I . . ." Vanessa paused. "I see buildings. Lights. A small outpost or something, about six kilometers away."

Gloria felt her stomach tighten. "Scipio?"

Outside the window, Vanessa fell into view, back to the ground. She landed, rolled, and bounded off toward a small outcropping about fifty meters away. Gloria watched, her fists clenched, as the woman crawled up to the peak and peered over. Vanessa whispered now, not that there was any reason to. "Yes. I think so. And there's more. About thirty impact sites between here and there. If I'm not mistaken, the Scipios are searching each."

"Radio silence, everyone," Gloria said. "Vanessa, get back inside."

The captain of the ruined ship glanced left. Beth Lee stood

near the engineering console, her face the very picture of dread. Gloria turned to her right, and saw Alex Warthen beside her. An unknown element. At least he'd stopped shooting at everyone.

Beside him, Xavi, her navigator and trusted companion of many years. For the first time since she'd known him, he looked like a defeated man, resigned to the fate coming for them. A fate incongruous with everything the man believed.

He didn't care about scuttling the ship, Gloria realized. He cared about going down with a fight. Not being a lamb awaiting slaughter. And deep down, Gloria found the same desire within herself, outshining her sworn duty.

"Belay that order, Vanessa," Gloria said.

Xavi studied her, one eyebrow suddenly arched.

"Everyone, get your helmets on," she said. "Pack food and water, and anything that might be useful as a weapon."

Her navigator's eyes widened. "This goes against orders, boss."

"You're damn right it does."

A grin tugged at one corner of his mouth. "What are you thinking?"

"There's a Scipio outpost six klicks away. What I'm thinking is that we make a nuisance of ourselves."

"What does that mean?" Beth asked.

Gloria ignored the question for a moment. She placed a hand on the smooth metal of the bulkhead, trailed her gloved fingers along its length, wishing more than anything that this wouldn't be the last time. "It means," she finally said, and with total calm, "all hands abandon ship."

8

CARTHAGE

Skyler let his feet guide him this way and that. Dark streets and plazas and alleys, all devoid of life, all in various stages of being reclaimed by the plant life of this world. Broad, gnarled root systems that spread wide above ground before plunging into the soil. The plants themselves were a mottled creamy-green hue and translucent. No flowers that he could see, though some had seedlike bulbs, which hung below corkscrewing leafy tendrils that stretched outward in domes vaguely resembling jellyfish.

It should have fascinated him. He knew that on some level. Extraterrestrial plants. An alien city on an alien planet. Tania would have stopped to marvel, even theorize their evolutionary reasons for being shaped so, but he found no thirst for it. Quite the opposite, the thought only made him want to find her that much more. He kept his gaze firmly on the distant wispy thread of the Elevator. The way up, to the others.

A climber had descended through the clouds. At least he thought it to be so. From here, it looked no more than a blob, like a tiny dewdrop trailing along a line of spider silk. Whatever it was it reflected the lights of the city below it. Skyler watched it until it vanished behind the silent monoliths of blackness on this side of the bay.

Two cities, separated by a wide channel open to the frothy ocean. One alive and with a way to reach orbit, and one—the one he'd landed in—dead save for the responders who'd come to investigate his crash.

How well had his instincts served him, back there? he wondered as he hiked ever downward toward the shore. Had the Scipios come from that city? Should he have simply allowed himself to be captured? No, he decided. Too much risk in that. They could just as easily have shot him without a second thought as capture him. And if they'd bound him, what then? What kind of prison would a species like this have waiting for an alien visitor on a world—indeed in a solar system—hell-bent on keeping prying eyes away?

Ahead, the shore came into view. Massive smooth boulders piled into a seawall as old as anything on Earth. Here and there the buildings seemed to reach out from the city, right up to the water's edge. Boathouses? Perhaps, but he couldn't imagine anything working, much less afloat, in this run-down place.

Lights caught his eye. Skyler glanced toward the flaring motion and went still. They were coming from the direction of the city. Spreading out, creating little glowing disks on the milky ocean waves. They were racing toward him.

He turned and began to run, fighting for every breath in the alien air. He found a pocket of shadow between two curving pillars, diving between them just as the fleet of aircraft streaked overhead. They roared past, riding an eerie sound unlike any engine noise he'd ever heard. Crucially, they'd flown right over and kept going. Coming to help their friends, of that he had no doubt. Another response to his presence, and in force this time. No longer a curious inspection, but instead a reaction to a hostile situation. Skyler remained in the shadow, counted off twenty seconds. How long would it be before they figured out they had a killer on the loose? Worse, an agent of their chief enemy.

He was about to move, when the sky exploded.

A crackling sound that came from everywhere assaulted his

ears, as if he'd been suddenly surrounded by a bunch of trigger-happy machine gunners. Little white flashes of light erupted all around him. The small explosions, like firecrackers, died in a rolling echo that went on for many seconds.

Then the snow fell.

Skyler watched, utterly shocked, completely fascinated, as the air as far as he could see was filled by a fine dust that swirled and swarmed. Eddies formed. Vortexes and currents. Great cords of dust that seemed almost intelligent as they flocked, coalescing into snakelike bands that dove out of the sky and vanished into open doorways or down side streets. A blast of warm air hit Skyler and he fell backward. The powder washed over his exposed face and neck. It seemed to crawl through his hair. Somehow Skyler had the presence of mind to keep his mouth and eyes closed. He held his breath, no easy feat in the poor air.

As quickly as it had begun, the assault faded. The grit in the atmosphere danced lazily on the breeze, like winter's first snow, as if it had all just . . . died. Maybe that was exactly the case. Skyler ran a hand over his face and studied the whitish powder. He could swear some of it still moved, jerky and inelegant, as if in death throes.

He just stared at it, wondering if the conclusions his mind reached could possibly be true. Those aircraft had just strafed the entire city with a virus. Trillions upon trillions of tiny . . . what? Detectors? Sensors? Poisons? Looking for him?

Anything foreign, probably. And he'd made a gaping hole in his visor. His fancy armored suit had been shredded. The specks on his hand that still crawled, were they even now transmitting their findings?

Skyler leapt to his feet and bolted, running as fast as the thin atmosphere would let him. His breath came in heaving gulps. Never enough. The exertion left him wobbling, his footfalls unsure. He fell and did a clumsy roll down an embankment of polished stone. A building loomed in front of him, low and squat, just meters from the shore. Above, he heard the growing sounds of the aircraft. Skyler came to his knees, blinked away his disorientation, and studied the building. There, an open doorway, nothing but shadows beyond. He crawled to it and flopped onto the floor just inside, pulling his feet in to his chest at the last second as the aircraft howled overhead. They sounded only a scant few meters off the ground, moving very fast. The strange hum of their engines receded.

For a time Skyler simply lay there. He put all his focus on his breathing, and did not move again until he could dictate mentally the pace and depth at which his lungs drew in the tangy thin air.

Propped against a wall, he let his eyes adjust.

The small chamber, perhaps five meters on a side, reeked of something like vinegar and mold. Along one wall there were bundles of fabric, the colors faded and obscured by years of dust. Skyler stared at that filth for a moment, wondering just how much of it was truly "dust," and how much were the dead or dormant viruses unleashed by the Scipios.

A movement in the shadows across the room. The barest hint of noise, like a sheet being drawn from a bed. A snake? Something had slid back into shadow, the motion smooth and ominously quiet. Skyler sat very still. He held his breath, what little he had, but soon his lungs were screaming and he had to let the air out. He raised one shaking arm up and pointed his wrist toward the inky blackness across from him. Whatever it had been, it had either slinked away into the dark or coiled. He had to be ready for anything. Razor-sharp teeth, or the howling alarm of some terrified vermin. He had to stay awake. This he thought as he found his chin had come to rest against his chest and he could not say how long he'd been that way.

Movement again. A face appeared. The barest hint of one, just gray skin in the void. The outline of cheekbones, and a long chin that protruded down and outward. A large vertical scar, long healed, ran down the length of its face. Two huge eyes like pools of calm water, and a third, smaller eye, higher up on the massive forehead. No nose. The mouth just a line of upper jaw covering the lower. Lips, teeth, all covered if they existed at all.

Skyler stared, transfixed. Terrified. Two translucent eyelids slid slowly out from the center of the creature's face and then, once they reached the edges, whipped back into their recessed position. Then, as if it had been waiting for that to happen, the third central eye up on the forehead blinked very purposefully, almost robotically.

It simply looked at Skyler. He let it, did not move a muscle, though he kept his wrist aimed right between those two huge eyes.

The upper jaw rose, revealing a thin pale lip and the mottled glint of filthy teeth. The lower jaw—no, jaws, for there were two connected by a flap of skin—spread out and down. There came a soft, almost melodic moan. *Hooooon.* The sorrowful noise brought goosebumps to Skyler's arms and up his spine. He fought to control his breathing, to keep himself still.

Again the snakelike motion. Its arm, or perhaps a tail, curled around the side of the creature's face from below and rubbed at a spot under one of its eyes. It was, Skyler realized, very much like a combination of tail and arm. Or rather, the upper arm and elbow of something mammalian with the lower arm able to move with the segmentation of a snake. Near the tip, the serpentine portion of the appendage changed again, separating into several—four, perhaps—fingers. Thin, long, nimble things that appeared able to entwine themselves in such a way as to appear as one solid end, a bit like the rattler of a rattlesnake.

Skyler realized with a start that his fear had subsided, replaced with fascination. He tried to hold on to that. This was, after all, a Creator that sat before him. Diseased, outside whatever aura this place offered, but nevertheless one of the beings he'd come here to help. And here it was, cowering beside him in the dark. Sick and evidently alone. Skyler recalled the words of his sniper, Jake, the time they'd come across a feral hog in the jungles of Thailand. "It's as scared of you as you are it, mate," the Aussie had said, walking calmly past the animal without another glance.

So he raised his hand in a gesture he hoped signaled "Hello, I am unarmed," and splayed his fingers in a sort of wave.

The Creator blinked. Skyler's heart lurched as there was a sudden scraping sound against the floor. The being shifted, moving its feet to better face Skyler. It was in a squatting position, Skyler saw, his eyes now adjusted to the nearly absolute dark. Perhaps it had to run in here when the aircraft had flown over. He wondered if the firecracker barrage of virus spreaders had scared it as much as it had scared him, and what effect that sudden influx of viral dust had on it. His head swam, each new revelation about this world seemed to only unleash a hundred new questions.

That third little eye blinked again. Skyler focused on it, recalling finally some of what Eve had told them of her Creators. Their unique dual-sentience. The low mind, and the high mind, she called it. One to control the body and deal with the day-to-day tasks of survival, the other free to ponder the mysteries of the universe. A Traveler, nothing more, reliant utterly on its host for information and senses. Or something like that. He hadn't really been paying attention, the kind of mistake Sam would give him endless shit for, were she here. In truth he hadn't imagined a scenario where they'd arrive without Eve, and figured the details could wait.

Skyler's breaths were coming a little easier. Each exhalation stirred the powder in the air. "Hello," he said.

A split second later his helmet made an odd, guttural noise.

Skyler's first thought was that his suit was failing, but then he noticed the creature had tilted its head to one side at the sound. Its eyes blinked—the big pair, then the small one. A tremble went through its body. Then it made a short burst of similar vocalizations, its triple-jawed mouth barely moving as if from lack of strength. After that it slumped, as if that tiny little amount of activity had drained the last of its life.

Skyler started to shake his head and wave his hands in front of him, when the faded, broken display in the corner of his vision registered.

IT WISHES TO SAY GREETINGS, TRAVELER, the translation said.

Skyler looked up, mouth hanging open. Of course it made sense. More than anything else here, really. Eve may have poor data to translate the Scipio language, but her own Creators? Of course she could do that. And his suit was vocalizing for him.

Another small wave of hope spread through him. Maybe, just maybe, he wasn't alone here, after all.

With no warning the Creator lunged at him, arms outstretched, strange digits splayed. Skyler scrambled back, almost falling over on his back. He aimed and, at the last instant, held fire. The Creator had stopped. Frozen in place. Its body began to tremble slightly, and then, very slowly, it eased back into its original position.

It spoke again. The translation came an instant later. THE DISEASE. WE FIGHT IT, BUT SOMETIMES . . .

"I understand," Skyler replied. He righted himself and did his best to hide how unsettled he now felt.

The alien went on. It spoke in short bursts. IT WANTS . . . TO KNOW . . . WHY YOU ARE HERE.

"It," Skyler repeated. "Do you mean the disease, or your . . . Passenger? High mind. I do not know your terms, I am sorry."

HIGH MIND.

Skyler started to reply, stopped himself. How much to say? What if the billions of little machine-made cells floating around him could listen, record, and transmit?

YOU FIGHT THE DISEASE, TOO, it said. HARD TO SPEAK, IS . . . The rest was cut off by the jagged glass of the damaged visor.

"I," Skyler replied, then paused again. He'd been about to admit his immunity, but thought better of it. If the Scipios weren't aware of that ability, best not to clue them in should they be listening. "I . . . I only want to find my friends," he said. "I need to get to the space elevator. Can you tell me how to reach it?"

A long silence. Then it said: THERE ARE MANY.

"The one across the bay. Closest to us."

It considered this for several minutes. Twice its body erupted into violent spasms. The war for control left it with a different expression on its face. Skyler did not know for sure—the face was alien, after all—but he thought this must be what anguish looks like. He wondered how long the high mind had been alive, transferred from diseased host to diseased host. Had it taught this host how to talk? Fought through their version of the SUBS virus in order to not be trapped with an animal?

Outside the aircraft circled. Their sounds grew more distant.

TRAVEL BY THE OCEAN.

"A boat? Where?"

The alien spoke, but this time the translation took several seconds to come through. Skyler guessed the system had taken considerable liberties when the text finally appeared. [100 METERS] TOWARD OCEAN, ALIGN LEFT, [50 METERS] STRAIGHT.

I can work with that, he thought. "Come with me," he urged, surprising himself.

The being raised one of its semi-serpentine arms a bit. The serpentine portion undulated slightly. Another expression?

"I don't understand," Skyler said.

Another series of lurching, staggered alien sounds. The text came through. SUCH ACTIVITY NOT POSSIBLE IN THIS . . .

Again the visor blurred, then lost, the final words where the display met the edge of the broken glass. But Skyler thought he understood well enough.

THEY COME FOR ME SOON, it added. YOUR SAFETY . . .

Skyler said, "It's all right. I thank you for the information, and wish you well."

With that the Creator curled back into its sullen form. A posture so pitiful and defeated Skyler lost the will to leave it there. He'd seen many horrible things in his life, and this one broke his heart as much as anything. After a moment he forced himself to stand and move to the door.

BE WELL, TRAVELER, the Creator said.

"And you," he replied, and left.

A set of stairs, barely visible under the centuries of uncontrolled plant growth, led down to a crumbling seawall. He looked back then at the city behind him, lit only by murky light filtering through the contaminated air from its cousin across the bay. A breathtaking place even in its semi-abandoned state. Much as in the old cities of Earth, a variety of architectural styles had been employed. Some with long sweeping curves. Others quite angular and stark. Still more, smaller, with great rows of pillars. Despite the differences, they somehow managed to come together in a skyline that pleased the eye. At least, his eye. Maybe the locals thought it was ugly and had protested against it. He almost chuckled at that. Almost. Part of him still reeled from the sorrow he'd glimpsed in that small dark room. Another part feared the patrolling Scipios, no doubt investigating their dead right now just a few hundred meters back up the hill. He had to get moving. A boat, though, on this empty bay? He'd be visible to anyone who glanced in the general direction, much less to searching aircraft that streaked and circled overhead.

More than all of that, though, was the solitude. He was, as far as he knew, the sole human being on a hostile alien planet. How could he possibly hope to leave with his life, much less free the native species from the tyranny of the Scipios? This was ridiculous.

Press on.

Skyler trudged down the path, numb to it all. Find the others, he told himself. That was all he could do. Whatever happened after that he'd accept if he could just face it at Tania's side. Preferably with Sam at his back, unleashing hell, and Prumble somewhere close, bellowing in his dramatic Kiwi voice. That would be bearable. Flipping some ancient raft and tumbling into waves of unknown and likely poisonous waters? Not so much.

The craft lay before him. Calling it a boat had been generous. At least, he thought, it seemed to float, until he realized it was up on some kind of scaffold. The boathouse itself had not fared as well. Centuries of neglect were not often kind, no matter how advanced the building materials might be. Part of the roof had fallen inward, spilling a vast quantity of dead or dormant virus cells, dust, and dirt into the back half of the building. He could see containers and a table poking out of the mountain of spilled scum. Every surface sported black splotches of mold or fungus. His nose, at least, was used to the stench of decay by now. Skyler sighed. He'd spent years scavenging for useful things in the wilds beyond Darwin's safe zone, and liked to think he'd gotten pretty good at identifying what to salvage and what to ignore. If he'd come across this place in the harbor of Hong Kong, for example, he'd have grunted in disgust and kept moving. Of course, back then he'd always had a list of valuable items from Prumble to seek out. He never truly appreciated, until this moment, how useful that had been. Kept his team focused, working toward a goal.

The raft itself had no obvious means of propulsion. No engine mounted on the back, no oars, no controls of any kind. It was little more than a rectangular platform with a slightly raised edge barely visible under untold years of accumulated "dust." He doubted it would even float, if pushed out into the soupy froth that served as an ocean here.

"What a mess," he muttered.

What alternative was there? He glanced around. The bay was

semicircular, perhaps formed by a crater rim from ages ago. The city he stood in ran along the curved shore for another kilometer or so, then tapered off, giving way to high dunes and then a forest of treelike things. After a few kilometers of that, over on the opposite side across the water, the trees transitioned to small buildings, growing gradually larger as they reached the ocean proper. A long way to walk, and through unknown territory.

To sail straight across, though, he judged to be a bit less than a klick in distance. He could put in among the smooth boulders that lined the shore there, and climb up to the city itself. If they didn't spot him first. If they didn't have guards along the shore, waiting to repel unwanted sub-Creators who might wander too close. That, at least, seemed unlikely, given the state of the one he'd just talked to. But then the enemy would certainly be alert for something, given his dramatic crash here and the subsequent annihilation of the first responders.

His eyes scanned farther along this coast, toward the sea, and he saw what he should have seen right away. This was, of course, the first boathouse among many. "Idiot," he scolded himself, and kept on.

A sound like thunder rolled through the streets and alleys around him. The searching aircraft, distant now. That was good. They seemed to be working on the assumption that he'd move away from their gleaming city across the bay and the precious space elevator within, not toward it.

The road meandered, following the shore in a series of graceful curves lined with buildings almost entirely consumed by unchecked vegetation. More sunlight filtered through the buildings, casting pinkish-orange beams along the broken stone structures and the mottled vines and roots that snaked through them. Skyler heard things scurry about in the undergrowth, fleeing at his approach. Their version of rats, maybe. Everything reeked of decay. Or maybe that was just their ocean air, he decided. Perhaps it was pleasant to the senses the Creators had evolved.

The next two buildings facing the bay were taller, and partially collapsed so that they leaned together ten meters above the sloping alley between them. A massive treelike plant grew straight up through the middle of one, its branches now almost reaching the neighbor. Skyler gave the pair a pass and went on to the next.

Unlike the last two, this place was low and sleek. It was caked with mold and virus-dust, like everything else, but had no obvious damage otherwise. More important, it was long, with the side facing the bay extending out almost all the way to the water. Skyler made a circuit of the place on the three landward sides, looking for a way in. Nothing obvious presented itself, so he scaled a pile of rubble and then a series of interwoven vines until he reached the roof. He kept to the edge, not trusting the center, which had no doubt been rained on and sitting here accumulating shit for untold decades. He had to hand it to the Creators, their construction techniques and materials were pretty damn good to have lasted so long exposed to the elements. This place looked only slightly worse off than Belém had, and that city had been left abandoned only for a fraction of the time.

He walked along the roof's edge toward the water. The building jutted out slightly from the seawall. Milky waves with frothy caps lapped and churned at the coastline. Had it always looked so? he wondered. Or was this the result of centuries of viral snow accumulating across the world?

His hope for an open-ended structure, with a boat nestled within, was banished when he reached the edge of the roof, for it was no edge at all. The structure sloped downward into the waves like a slide. Skyler stood there for a time, confused. Perhaps the alien had actually meant that pitiful raft? Perhaps it had confused its memories. There were several millennia's worth, after all. Sullen, he trudged back to the front of the building, scanning the adjacent structures for a vantage point that would allow him to study the entire row along the rocky shore. He felt terribly exposed up here. This roof offered no cover at all from whatever lurked overhead. Aircraft were one thing. But what, Skyler wondered with a fearful swallow, did the Scipios have in orbit? They must monitor the surface very closely, given their absolute need for the bodies—really the minds—of the native population.

Which begs the question, Skyler thought as he slogged back to the front of the roof, *where is everyone?* Granted he'd explored only a few city blocks of a vast world, but from what Eve had said the Scipios relied on a large population of adolescent Creators to pull from when their designs required it. So where were they?

These questions tumbled about in his head as he reached the city-facing edge of the structure. Skyler froze there, staring down at what should have been obvious to him minutes before when he'd walked the perimeter. He'd been too focused on the building to look at what surrounded it. In the middle distance, a wide avenue ran straight toward the edge he now stood on. About fifty meters away, this road—path, track, whatever—plunged down into a tunnel that ran, quite likely at least, right below the building where Skyler now stood.

He clambered down the vine-laced wall and scaled the pile of rubble below that in three neat hops. Jogging, his breathing fully acclimated now, Skyler moved to the tunnel entrance. He had to round the corner to see for sure. When he came around he saw . . . darkness. Absolute darkness. Feeling like a child staring into the pitch-black maw of a train tunnel, he knew he'd found what the alien had meant for him to find.

Skyler crept down the incline, stepping across wide cracks and over exposed, pale roots. A tree with corkscrewing branches grew right out from one of the sidewalls, its bluish spiny leaves reaching upward like thousands of little upheld arms.

The darkness swallowed him. He didn't want to risk his light just yet, though, so Skyler continued into the tunnel utterly blind. He held a hand out in front of him and swept his foot back and forth before each step. Ten paces, he could handle no more than that, the fear rising in him like bile. He switched on his headlamp.

For a time he only stood there, trapped between two options. The tunnel led downward at a gentle slope as far as his light could penetrate. Its surfaces, both flat floor and semicircular ceiling, were cracked and seeping fluid in places. He weighed his choices. Travel through this dank and utterly black passage, or take the raft where he would be exposed to sky and land?

"Trust your gut," he said in a low voice, "it's gotten you this far." The words echoed down the passage for a long time, mingling with the sounds of dripping water.

Skyler crept deeper into the tunnel.

9

ABOVE CARTHAGE

Tania Sharma feared many things just then. As their party crept in tactical fashion through the bowels of a hostile alien space station, she could imagine any number of horrible outcomes—far too many, in fact. She could picture a myriad of ways their plans might fail. What she did not expect, though, was a total lack of Scipios at a time when they actually wanted to find one.

Sam had taken the lead, Vaughn just behind her, the two of them leapfrogging each other as they moved from one cover position to another. Prumble seemed content to bring up the rear, sometimes lagging well behind, tucked in a shadow or behind some bit of unfathomable tech, to make sure they were not being followed.

And so Tania and Tim were in the center of the group, a situation Tim unrelentingly took advantage of.

"Capture a Scipio. This is never going to work," he'd said under his breath at one point, as if it were not meant for her to hear. And after being ignored, a minute later he added, "We should just get back outside. Much easier to find a ship when you can see for a few thousand kilometers."

"Much easier to be seen, too," Tania noted. "Relax, will you? This is going to work."

He snorted. "This is problematic on many different levels, Tania. Language, for starters—"

"Our suits can handle that. Well, from their language to ours, but I've been poking around in the menus and it looks as if the other direction works, too." To demonstrate she enabled the automatic translation and counted to ten out loud. No sound emitted from her suit, instead a series of symbols appeared on her visor, reversed and enlarged so as to be readable from the outside. Centuries out of date, no doubt, but it stood to reason that the Scipios would have a similar technology and could adjust.

"I just have a bad feeling about this plan of Prumble's."

"Why?"

"Remember what that captain from Earth said? We have two things the Scipios desperately want." He held up a finger. "Earth's location." Then another finger. "Immunes. And yet here we are, with both of those prizes in our possession, and *we're* trying to make contact with *them*. We should be getting as far away from here as possible, Tania. Or are we really willing to sacrifice our own world just to save Eve's?"

The second thing the Scipios wanted was the ability to fold space, but Tania decided not to correct the man. The point still stood. She said, "Of course not. But it's not like we're seeking them out to have a chat. We're doing this only to find out where they keep their spacecraft."

"We know where they keep them. In *space*. Not in some dusty, ugly tomb like this. Besides, and I mean no disrespect, but you and I both know that leaving is the last thing on your mind right now."

"That's not fair."

Tim bit back a retort, weighed his words. "Sorry, you're right."

Tania couldn't leave it at that. "I stood beside Vanessa in Colorado as a friend of ours died. Skyler, as you well know, is a dear friend who has saved my life more than once, a favor I've been privileged enough to return and would do so again. So, fine, you all want to leave and I'm going along with that. But if you think for a second I'm not going to take any opportunity that might arise to find out the fate or whereabouts of our friends, you're not the person I thought you were, Tim."

"Okay, okay. I said you're right."

She caught her breath. "I didn't mean that to sound harsh. I just—"

Tim's upheld hand stopped her. He came to a crouch, eyes cast upward, head tilted slightly. "Listen," he whispered.

Her suit, reacting to brain impulses, amplified the exterior sounds. Tim's foot adjusting slightly on the smooth floor. Prumble, moving up from behind. Of Sam and Vaughn she heard nothing, but they'd scouted well ahead to the end of the corridor. She heard the low, constant hum of air circulation, and beneath that, the sounds of power and fluids and who knew what else being routed from one part of the vast space station to another. All of it came through with perfect fidelity.

There, a new sound. Footfalls, she thought, and a lot of them. Tania tensed. Came to a crouch of her own, coiled and ready. This had to be it. The inevitable security response to this breach.

The sound seeped through the wall to her left, giving only minimal indication of the source's location.

"Too many to fight," Prumble whispered, moving up beside them.

Tania nodded. "We should move. Catch up with Sam."

"I think they're coming to us," Tim noted, his gaze on the hall ahead.

Two lights bounded toward them through the darkness. Sam came into view, Vaughn trailing a few seconds behind, burdened with the extra weight of the aura shard.

"What is it?" Tania asked.

"Scipios," Sam replied. "A lot of them."

"Security?"

She shook her head. "No idea. Considering we just blew up a crap ton of their ships, I'm guessing maybe?"

"Did they see you?" Prumble asked.

Again Sam shook her head. Vaughn spoke for her. "We'd only just cracked open a door. Scipios were pouring in from half a dozen different places."

"It was like they'd just arrived or something," Sam added.

A silence settled. Tania decided to ask the question. "Now what?"

"Grab one," Vaughn answered.

Prumble nodded.

"Just a second," Tim said. "Before we add kidnapping to our list of transgressions, can we think about this?"

"It was your fuckin' idea, mate," Vaughn said.

"Actually it was Prumble's. But let's not point fingers. Look, they had to have come here from somewhere, right? What if a ship just docked?"

"What if one did?"

"I say we take it."

"Wait," Prumble said. "Do you actually think some random alien police bus is going to be capable of getting us all the way back to Earth?"

Tim shook his head, frustrated. "Of course not. But perhaps it could get us to a shipyard. And if it has a pilot, which seems likely, we might learn everything we need about what's where, and get a ride as part of the bargain."

"A lot of 'buts' and 'mights' in that plan," Sam observed. "But you make a good point. For now I say we get out of this hallway. We're not going anywhere with a force of that size milling about."

"Agreed," Prumble said. "I've been checking the rooms we pass. Two doors back, a big . . . machine room, or something. Plenty of space, and places to hide. Defensible, if it comes to that."

"Lead on," Sam said.

They hunkered down in Prumble's machine room, though to Tania it looked rather worryingly like a fuel depot. Rows of huge metal silos, along with a maze of pipes and tubing that snaked across walls, floor, and ceiling alike.

Sounds that could all be lumped into a general "life support" category drowned out all else, and within minutes Tania could see the shifting unease of Sam's and Vaughn's demeanors. This was equal parts a hiding place and a cell. Not exactly the style of the warrior couple. Prumble, meanwhile, had parked himself near the back of the room and lay down, arms around his belly, fingers laced together. Tim just paced. For a while Tania watched him, wondering what had changed. *Assertive* had never been a word she, or anyone else they'd worked together with, might use to describe him, but he'd certainly become that.

She could just ask him. Talk it over. That's what friends do, after all. The thought saddened her, because just now she wanted only to find the others.

Aura shard tucked under one arm, Tania wandered between the silos, wondering what they stored or if that was even their purpose. How easy it was to immediately lay her own preconceptions on what she saw.

At the back corner, her gaze ran up the side of one container, looking for markings her visor might translate. It was a dark, hulking thing, something she would have presumed abandoned if not for the faint sounds it emitted. The Scipios were not big fans of lighting and status indicators, it seemed, though she had to remind herself she'd looked upon only a tiny, tiny fraction of their vast infrastructure. And there was still the planet below. The great unknown.

She saw nothing that might indicate what function the silo served, but she did find something else. "Sam?" she called. Not close enough for the short range, apparently, she moved back toward the doors and tried again. "Sam, come look at this."

It took a moment for Sam to find her in the maze. "What's up?"

"I'm not sure, but I think it might be another way out of here. That might be useful, right?"

Tania led her to the back, and pointed. At the very top of the high wall, some ten meters above, was a large round depression, covered by some kind of grate or netting, total darkness beyond.

"Huh," Sam said, and began to climb and jump her way up to the grate, using the dozens of pipes and support trusses on both wall and adjacent silo to support her. At the top she stood on the roof of the silo and switched on her headlamp, leaning to peer through the slats of the grate.

After a moment she turned and looked down. "Come on up, let's see what's inside."

By now Vaughn had wandered over. Tim, Tania noted, stood several meters away, watching from a distance. Prumble still dozed, presumably.

"I'll go," Vaughn said.

"No," Sam replied with patience. "Tania spotted it, she goes. Besides, if anything goes wrong we'll need some gallant knight to come save us."

"All right, piss off."

"Love you, too. C'mon, Tania."

She climbed, mimicking Samantha's path as best she could, which wasn't nearly as graceful due to having to maneuver the aura shard as well. It was light, almost weightless, but damn if it wasn't awkward to move about. Every little push against it sent it floating away with no sign of slowing down.

At the top, Sam helped her onto the roof of the massive silo. To Tania's surprise, the grate had been opened. Sam must have seen her expression. She said, "Gave it a little push, just to test the strength, and it rotated back."

"Just like that?"

"Just like that." Without anther word, Sam leapt across the two-meter gap between silo and wall.

When she stopped and turned, Tania held the small aura shard before her like some offered gift, then propelled it across. The device floated as if on a cushion of air. Sam adjusted her position, caught it, then waited.

Tania made the jump. Not as hard as it looked in the reduced gravity. She landed beside Sam and took her shard back, holding it aloft in the cupped palm of her hand, a position that made her feel like some kind of sorceress from a fairy tale.

The space appeared to be one end of an umbilical tube, or something like it. The undulating surface curved away from her, bending upward ninety degrees and running off out of sight. Sam wasted no time. She squirmed up into it and then paused to let Tania join her, catching the aura shard, as if Tania had floated her a balloon. When Tania caught up again, Sam gave the device back and continued up into the next elbow of the tube. This continued for four lengths until, finally, they reached a flat section that spanned about five meters, ending at another grated hatch like that through which they'd entered. Shifting light poured in through the horizontal slats, illuminating a fine particulate that drifted lazily in the air. Tania set her aura shard on the floor, and together she and Sam approached the end of the tunnel. Bent at the waist, Tania moved up to the narrow openings and looked through.

A wide hallway ran from her left to right, the far edge of it a railing rather than a wall, though what it looked out on she could not tell. The air was absolutely choked with the thick powdery substance the aliens so loved.

Scipios ambled past, oblivious to the thick haze. Some walked alone, some in quiet conversation with one or two others. They wore a variety of colored bodysuits and headgear.

Across the hall, in the murk beyond the railing, Tania thought she saw shapes flowing downward. The shapes were vague, though the mystery did not take long to resolve itself. As she watched, a Scipio walking in the hallway before her moved to the railing, mounted it like a bird perching on a fence, then leaned forward and fell. Her breath caught in her throat until the creature spread its arms and let the long flaps of skin that connected forearm to calf fill with wind. The creature glided gracefully from view. Those shapes falling through the haze now registered as Scipios, floating downward. A simple and natural mode of transportation for a creature so equipped.

"So many of them," Tania whispered.

"I know."

"They don't look like a security force at all."

"Yeah," Sam said, sounding more than a little embarrassed at her earlier assessment. "You know what they remind me of? Students shuffling around campus between classes."

Tania had little experience with that style of education, but she'd seen enough old sensories to appreciate the analogy. "What do we do? Go back?"

Sam hesitated. "Any idea what's gotten into Tim?" she asked.

Tania glanced at her. "What do you mean?"

"You know what I mean. The bloke kills a few swarmers and suddenly he's trying to tell everyone what to do."

Tania considered the other woman. "I think maybe you just

answered your own question. Anyway, what's the problem? If I recall, you agreed with his suggestion that we leave without Skyler or Vanessa."

"I do agree."

"Then what are you concerned about?"

"Just because I agree doesn't mean I think the idea came from a sound mind."

Tania said nothing.

"My fear," Sam explained, "is that if he's willing to leave some of us behind, perhaps he's willing to leave all of us behind. He seems . . . I don't know, agitated."

The words left Tania speechless. Sam turned back to the vents, studying the Scipios that wandered back and forth, or floated down and out of view.

"You really think we should just leave?" Tania asked, finally. "After everything you and Skyler have been through together?"

Sam shrugged. "The wanker left me for dead on Gateway Station once. Fair's fair, isn't it?"

"You don't really mean that."

"Nah, 'course not." Sam offered a sympathetic smile. "But Tim's got a point. Our commitment to Eve ended when she did. None of us agreed to a suicide mission. So I figure sure, we find a way out of here and in the meantime, we keep our eyes open for our missing friends. Keep our eyes on the friends we've got with us, too. We don't owe that fancy computer bitch or her kind anything now. Yeah?"

"Computer," Tania whispered, Sam's choice of word knocking something loose in her mind.

"Huh?"

Tania turned to Sam. "When Blackfield took over Anchor Station, he started with the computers."

"What are you talking about?"

"We don't need to talk to the Scipios, we need to talk to their systems."

For a split second Sam just stared at her, brow furrowed. Slowly she started to nod. "That's not a bad idea," she said, finally. Then added, thoughtfully, "Seems even less plausible than speaking their language, though."

Tania frowned.

A second later Sam straightened. "So we do both."

"What do you mean?"

The woman grinned. "I bet one of these blokes can show us how to use their tech." She turned to the ventilation grate and settled in to wait.

It didn't take long for their moment to come. A brief sound rolled through the space station, signaling something. An end to rush hour traffic, evidently, and that was all Sam cared about.

After the booming noise finished echoing through the vast hallway and the . . . "fallway," Tania supposed, beyond . . . the foot traffic died out almost completely. It really did have the feel of university. Or maybe it had been a call to the start of their workday. She shook her head. These were aliens. They had their own culture, much of which would be derived from the specifics of their original home system, no doubt. Did they even observe a day-night cycle, physically? Did they educate themselves in the same nonoptimized, tradition-steeped way that humans used to?

Again I project myself onto what I observe, she thought. A trap, in truth, and she vowed then and there to not fall into it. The wrong assumption here could mean the end of everything.

Vaughn joined them, his sudden presence at Tania's shoulder almost giving her a heart attack.

"Don't sneak up on me like that," she whispered.

"Right," Vaughn replied. "Next time I should shout my presence for all to hear?"

"Next time use the suit," Tania snapped. Her pulse began to abate. "Sorry, I'm just—"

"It's all right," he said. He looked to Sam. "Sit-rep?"

Sam rolled her eyes at his clipped military tone. She filled him in on the plan all the same.

"What are we waiting for?" he asked.

Tania shushed them both, her suit picking up a faint sound, reminding her of the noise her parachute had made in Hawaii when Skyler had let it drift away. That soft rustling. The noise grew and, a few seconds later, a Scipio came gliding in through the haze of the fallway. It landed on the railing and deftly hopped down onto the tiled floor of the hall, just a few meters away from Tania. She looked at Sam, who nodded.

"Get ready," Sam whispered.

When the Scipio had done its oddly elegant walk and gone a few steps away, Tania opened the grating and slipped out into the hall. She glanced left, then right. Nobody around save the lone creature. There was always one, wasn't there? Late to class, late to work, late to whatever business the Scipios had here. Tania moved toward it, stepping diagonally to give herself a quick look up into the fallway shaft that the hallway ran alongside. Nothing, just the hazy air. For the first time she welcomed the low visibility, though part of her wondered if the Scipios had a way of seeing through it.

She walked on, rolling her feet. In one smooth motion she lowered her aura shard to the floor and gave it a little shove. The black shape drifted easily along the hall, perfectly aimed toward the lone Scipio's left.

Tania found she had no urge to glance back. Sam would do her part, and do it perfectly, of that there was no doubt in her mind, a fact that flooded her with a sudden cool confidence.

Arms held slightly out so they wouldn't brush against her torso, she did her best to channel Skyler. *Don't think, just act. Let instinct take over.* Tania stood at least twenty centimeters taller than the Scipio, and her legs made up most of that advantage.

The shard caught up to the Scipio. It turned, glanced down. Something like a gasp escaped its lips and it stepped to the right, back now turned perfectly toward the circling Tania.

She closed the distance in three quick steps, threw one arm over the being's shoulder to grab it by the torso, another up under its arm to slap a hand across what she hoped was its mouth, confident the armored suit would protect her against a bite.

The creature thrashed. She hadn't accounted for the parachute-like skin flap, and her hand became tangled in it before she could cover the mouth. The Scipio let out a mewling cry, not terribly loud to her ears. Finally Tania's hand came free. She slapped it across the wide mouth and heaved the alien off its feet. It weighed almost nothing; it was like lifting a child.

JASON M. HOUGH

Tania sidestepped and turned, urging the aura shard back toward Sam with one knee, then jogging after it. She felt the fear coursing through the alien as its flailing limbs and muffled cries became more and more urgent. The very air around them seemed to react to this. As Tania moved, the particulate all around began to turn and dart toward her, like a school of microscopic fish trying to feed. The pale little flecks sped in and then, in a sphere roughly ten meters in diameter, began to drift again. Limp and wandering. She could see it easily, and part of her savored this small victory. She'd learned the protective radius of the aura shards, an incredibly useful bit of knowledge.

At the sight of the deactivated virus clumps, the Scipio became very afraid. It wriggled and heaved, rocked its head backward violently but to no avail. Tania's grip was strong, her mass much greater than the alien's. She pushed it into the ventilation duct—or whatever it actually was—where Vaughn wrapped it up in his waiting arms. Tania continued on into the elbow of the tube, trusting Sam to close the grate behind them. Vaughn, with the alien in his arms, fell backward and down deliberately. The brief journey ended with him on his back, the creature on top, squirming but now, somehow, less urgently. Resigned to its fate, perhaps. Tania pushed herself down after them and landed in front of it. Her form, her red-hued face behind the visor, must have been the most shocking thing the Scipio had ever seen. It went rigid, vibrating with terror.

10

ABOVE CARTHAGE

Prumble hadn't slept through the whole business, after all.

As Sam came back down the silo to the floor of their little hideaway, she found the others huddled around the alien as Prumble put the finishing knot on an improvised binding.

"Cables," he said. "Yanked them from behind a loose panel on the wall."

"Resourceful," Sam noted.

"Sometimes you have to do your scavenging for yourself, right?" He winked at her.

Sam grinned.

"And behold," the big man said, turning about. He'd wrapped some of the wires around himself, lashing his aura shard to his back. Prumble finished his wholly ungraceful twirl and held out his hands, demanding praise.

"The judge from China gives you a nine-point-five," Sam said.

"Ah, very kind."

"Australia? A three-point-one, I'm afraid."

Prumble frowned. "Now that is discrimination. New Zealand objects!"

"Hey!" Tania shouted. She quickly lowered her voice. "Do you two mind? We've got a prisoner here. The poor thing is terrified."

Sam stood by as Tania knelt before the trembling creature. A meter separated them, and the thing had been wrapped in cable until only its head and feet were poking out either end. A shivering, wide-eyed Scipio burrito. Sam kept her wrist weapon primed and pointed in its general direction all the same.

Vaughn positioned his aura shard a few meters from the prisoner. "In case it can somehow use the virus cells," he explained. A wise precaution.

"We need information," Tania said to it. A series of symbols flashed across her visor.

The Scipio did not notice. It had its eyes shut tight, Sam realized, and had probably done the equivalent of pissing itself. She gave it a little kick on the leg. Not hard. Enough to get its attention.

"Relax," Tania said to her.

"I'm quite relaxed," she replied. "It's looking at you now. Try again."

Tania turned and sat on the floor, one ankle tucked under the other. She rested her arms on her knees and spread her hands out. "We need some information."

The symbols flashed on her visor again. Nonsense to Sam, of course, but the Scipio seemed strangely calmed by it. The shivering diminished, then stopped.

It said something—rather, it made a few odd noises with its mouth. Sam's own visor displayed a single word in the lower corner.

REVISE.

"Revise?"

Tania's upheld hand quieted her. "Our suits have centuries-old data on their language, remember. This is going to require some time."

"Time is not exactly on our side here."

Tania waved her off. "Just . . . give me a few minutes, will you? Guard the entrances or something."

Samantha glanced up at Vaughn and shifted her eyes to the back of the room where they'd found the twisting ventilation shaft. He nodded, understanding immediately, and trotted off in that direction. Sam eyed Prumble next, and jerked her head toward the main door.

"What, me? Guard?"

"Yes."

"What are you going to do?"

"Keep an eye on our guest."

The big man wandered toward the door, grumbling to himself. "You look like a Sherpa with that shard lashed to your back," Sam called after him.

Without looking or breaking stride, he raised one hand and extended his middle finger.

Sam shifted her gaze back to Tania, and gave her a nod.

"We wish to know things," Tania tried this time. "If you answer some questions for me, you will not be harmed."

The creature studied her for a moment, then made a sort of circular gesture with its chin.

"You must speak," Tania said. "We do not understand your facial expressions."

It puzzled over this for a time, then made more of its peculiar speech noises. DELIVER YOUR QUERIES, the translation said.

And so it went, back and forth, for what seemed like an hour. Sam stood by, doing her best to seem threatening despite sensing this creature felt no concern at all once the initial shock of being grabbed and hauled through a ventilation shaft by a bunch of armored alien strangers had passed. Give the little bastard some credit, Sam decided. Though, on the other hand, it did appear to be completely rolling over on its own kind. Every question Tania asked it gave an answer to. These were nearly always cryptic or utterly incomprehensible, but Tania remained calm and patient through it all.

In this way much was learned. Sam filed what she considered tactically relevant and left the rest to Tania and Tim, who stood nearby with his arms folded, silent and serious.

Tactically relevant: The Scipios had only a minimal security apparatus, relying on their Swarm Blockade to keep unwanted visitors out, and their ever-present clouds of artificial viruses to attack and subdue anyone not specifically authorized to be wandering around Scipio facilities or the planet below. The fact that these tall aliens standing before it were unaffected by their viruses seemed the source of most of the shock and fear the creature had displayed. This, Sam gathered, was something unprecedented. *Just wait until you learn the word* immunity, *my friend,* she'd thought.

According to the low-level worker on the floor before Tania, even now a response was being prepared for the catastrophic incident aboard the nearby "vessel reprocessing apparatus" earlier that day. The workers had all been told to keep a lookout for anything out of the ordinary. Sam took heart at that. Keeping a lookout for "anything" meant they still weren't quite sure what the hell was going on, and that was good. Very good. Assuming she'd interpreted the awful translation correctly.

"Have there been any other such incidents?" Tania asked it. "Reports of other attacks, or anything like that?"

Sam ground her teeth, unsure of the wisdom in asking that. Granted, they might learn of Skyler or Vanessa's fate, but at the same time she'd basically just hinted—strongly—that there were more aliens just like them running around. Not the wisest move.

NO, the Scipio replied. KNOWLEDGE SPREADS SELECTIVELY.

"It sure does," Sam muttered. She nudged Tania. "We need to know how to get away from here. Before they realize this one's missing."

She nodded, and turned to her subject. "We wish only to leave. To return to our . . . own place. We know you have vessels that cross the vast distances of space. Where can we find one?"

UNKNOWN, came the eventual reply.

"Bullshit," Sam said.

Tania held up a hand, urging patience. "How do you move between your various *apparatus* above this planet?"

A seemingly endless series of misunderstandings and clarifications followed. Sam's thoughts turned to what they should do with the prisoner once—if ever—Tania learned what she hoped to learn. The age-old dilemma, Sam mused. Kill your prisoner and have blood on your hands, let them go and risk them talking, or tie them up and hope someone finds them before they die a very cruel death.

The first option, Sam decided. And she'd had enough of this chatter. She stepped forward.

"Thank you," Tania was saying. "That is very helpful."

Sam hadn't been paying attention. She came to stand beside Tania, her eyes on the almost-mummified prisoner, already tied up. Sam raised her wrist, anyway.

Tania's hand came to rest on her forearm. "Let's discuss this first, please?" She spoke louder, for everyone. "In the corner, over there? All of you, please."

She pushed down on Sam's arm, which Sam resisted, but only for a second. She'd didn't really want to kill this one. It was the risk of not doing so that had convinced her to take that path. A few more minutes can't hurt. Let it make its peace, if they do that. She followed Tania to the corner of the room, about fifteen meters from the Scipio. Prumble and Vaughn followed. Tim came last, walking backward, keeping watch. He remained that way until he reached the loose circle and even then, turned only halfway. One eye on the conversation, one on the prisoner.

"Right, then. What did we learn?" Sam asked.

Tania took a steadying breath. "There is something, a shuttle or buslike vehicle, that moves about the stations autonomously."

"Will we be able to operate it?" Prumble asked.

"Maybe," Tania admitted. "If the controls are marked with translatable words, perhaps, but who knows if that is the case."

"I'll tell you who knows," Sam said. "That one, right over there."

Tania shook her head. "It said it has only ever been a passenger."

"Of course it said that. Wouldn't you?"

Tim joined the conversation fully. "Were I the prisoner, and you were asking me how to pilot a spacecraft, would you assume I knew how? I think it's a stretch to—"

"Oy!" Vaughn shouted. He was off, running toward the captive. Sam whirled in time to see the creature buck wildly despite its bindings. It launched a full meter off the floor, writhing, a fountain of horrific brown liquid erupting from its mouth.

"What the hell?" Sam asked, already moving toward the creature without really thinking it through.

By the time she reached Vaughn, he was holding the Scipio

to the ground, making an utterly futile effort to diagnose the problem. It was already too late. Sam could see that instantly. Its lifeless eyes and still features said everything.

Sam knelt beside Vaughn. She said, loud enough only for him, "I guess that solves that problem."

He nodded grimly.

"What happened?" Prumble asked.

"No way to know," Tim said.

"Sure there is," Tania corrected. She pointed off toward the machinery deeper in the room. "No aura. Vaughn's shard drifted away somehow, allowing access to the virus."

"We all had our backs to it," Sam said. "Except you, Tim. What did you see?"

"Nothing," he said. "It was just lying there. Perhaps when I turned to you all to speak, it managed to nudge the shard."

Sam didn't like that explanation, but the alternative—that one of them had deliberately or even accidentally pushed the shard into motion—appealed even less. She glanced at Vaughn, who was looking right at her, and she knew he was thinking the same thing.

"So it accessed the virus. So what?" Prumble asked. "How is it suddenly dead?"

Tania folded her arms across her chest, as if suddenly cold. "Impossible to know for sure. Given access to the virus, perhaps it committed suicide through some silent command."

"Or they knew this one was missing," Tim offered, "and the viruses were already looking for it."

Tania nodded. Her features were unreadable. "Eve once implied they use the cells to communicate. A bit like our old HocNets."

"If that's the case," Prumble said, "we can't stay here. It could have told them where we are. How many of us there are. That we have a way to disable the virus. Christ, everything."

"Let's find that transport," Sam said. "Right now. No debate."

Nobody argued.

At the exit, Sam took one last glance back at the body on the floor, still wrapped in cabling. She'd taken many lives in her years as a scavenger. Subhumans, mostly, but also those who worked against the success of mankind. Never an innocent, though. Never anything like this.

It did it to itself, a voice in her head tried to explain.

Sam bit her lower lip, sent a silent apology, and left.

They climbed through the ventilation shaft again. The wide hall beyond was still empty.

"Which way, Tania?" Sam asked.

The woman cast her gaze upward. "It said the docking port is at the top. I guess maybe that way they can float down to the deck they need to access upon arriving somewhere."

"Who cares why. Let's move. Vaughn, you've got our backs?"

"'Course."

"Good man."

"I know."

Sam hopped up on the railing and glanced at the space above and below. The central open shaft of the space station vanished into inky black in both directions about fifty meters away. Flakes of Scipio virus cells floated down like snow, stirred here and there by the occasional push of air from the ventilation systems.

No Scipios to be seen.

One last glance back at her companions, and Sam was off. She leapt, powering up the thrusters in her suit at the same time. For a few seconds she just hovered, allowing herself time to get used to the gravity. Then she accelerated, swooping upward, arms held out before her, feeling like a superhero. The white viral snow fell past with growing speed. Sam forced herself to ease off. She glanced down. The others were already out of sight. *Above and below, only darkness and falling snow.*

Sam laughed at her accidental poetry. *What the fuck is wrong with my brain?* She shook her head and tried to clear her thoughts, without success. The line kept echoing through her mind. *Above and below, only darkness and falling snow.* She looked down again, knowing Vaughn was in that darkness, somewhere, making sure the others got off that railing safely. Sam grinned wickedly. She knew exactly what she'd do to clear her head if they got out of this hellhole, and it wasn't poetry.

A reinvigorating thought if there ever was one. Grin still firmly in place, Sam lifted her chin to the unseen ceiling and powered on. She rose past seventeen more decks, all identical save for markings on the wall she didn't bother to stop and "read"— the translator was practically worthless, in her view. Instead of cafeteria it would probably say something like "gut satisfaction." *Not a bad name for a restaurant,* she mused.

She chuckled again. *Seriously, what is wrong with me?*

A blinking orange indicator on her visor finally registered. Sam took her eyes off the snowy dark and scanned the display. Nitrogen levels were way off. "Shit."

The ceiling pushed through the darkness before her like the face of a giant mallet. Giggling inanely, it took every ounce of will Sam could muster to swing her feet up and propel herself to one side. She came so close to collision that she was able to brush her hands along the smooth surface and guide herself to an ungraceful but successful stop, then let her thrusters power down slowly until her feet were back on solid ground. Another hallway with an open railing, only this one at the very top of the space station. She turned and ramped her headlamp to full power.

"Something wrong with my air," Sam said.

Tania floated up through the silolike chamber, at a much less reckless speed. She joined Sam and immediately went to work examining her helmet and suit. Tim and Prumble came up and over the railing almost together.

Vaughn was last. "What's happened? What's wrong?"

Sam laughed.

"Your heat sink is absolutely coated with this viral gunk," Tania said. She wiped furiously at Sam's lower back, sluicing away a small pile of white powdery residue onto the floor. "The suit has a special pad between these two armor plates used purely for thermal management. It seems to be attracting the virus cells."

Prumble had crouched next to her, assisting in the effort. He turned to examine Vaughn's back, finding the same problem. Tim, however, seemed mostly unaffected, with less than half the amount of buildup. Tania and Prumble, too, once everyone had been checked.

"Why only us?" Sam asked no one in particular.

Tania's mouth twisted in concentration. "The two of you have been using your weapons and boosters a lot more than us. More heat to manage."

"Okay," Sam said. "But what does any of that have to do with nitrogen levels?"

The woman thought about that, then gave a small shrug. "I can only assume the suit was forced to use more power than it normally needs in order to cool things while you were under thrust, and that resulted in robbing power from the breathers."

"Well, shit," Sam said. "That's a serious design flaw, isn't it?"

"Relax," Prumble replied. "Easily addressed. This simply means we all need to scratch each other's backs once in a while."

"Lovely."

"Like a monkey picking lice from a troop mate's fur."

"Not helping, mate."

Prumble laughed. "Think of it as a bonding experience."

"Can we keep moving, please?" Tim asked. A sober silence fell over the group. "Where next, Tania?"

Tania studied the doors closest to them. Not immediately finding what the prisoner had told her to look for, she motioned for Sam to lead the way farther along the hall. Sam obliged.

Moving along the wide corridor felt familiar. Not much different than securing a site for scavenging in a hundred different cities back on Earth.

Sam's visor indicated her air mixture had returned to something approaching normal. She still felt a little drunk, and decided not to worry about how long that would take to pass. Right now it was taking the edge off and that was all right by her.

"There," Tania said. She pointed at a door directly across the circular chamber.

"Let's go around," Sam suggested. "Save fuel." *Not to mention I'm still a bit dizzy.*

The others agreed. Sam began to jog, wishing for all the world she'd asked Eve to make her a shotgun instead of this precision beam bullshit. She ran past several more doors, ignoring their markings and the translations that winked across her visor. Fifty meters before the door Tania had indicated, Sam pushed up against a wall and waited for the others to catch up. When they were all in a line, looking at her, she spoke. "Wait here. Just in case our suicidal friend down there has led us to a trap."

"We don't know it was suicide," Tania said.

"The fact remains."

Tania seemed to consider several replies. She settled on, "Fair enough."

Sam made eye contact with Vaughn, who gave his customary nod. She turned and moved to the door, running at a low crouch, one arm held before her, the other aimed at the open circular passage they'd come up through. Five long strides. Ten. She reached the door and activated the opening mechanism.

The panels irised aside. Before her, a hallway of staggering beauty awaited. The walls, angled slightly inward, were little more than a series of connected, expansive windows, the tops of which curved over to become a portion of the narrow ceiling.

Along that ceiling, a series of dim lights offered the only illumination beyond what spilled in through those windows. Sam stepped inside, only distantly aware of her state of awe. Outside those windows, two views seemed in perfect harmony. To her left, the sweeping star-kissed crescent edge of the planet Carthage. To her right, farther away, one of its moons hung luminously against the dark of space. Purple, cratered, mountainous. *Damn beautiful,* Sam thought.

Straight ahead, at the end of the twenty-meter corridor, another door awaited. Sam could see, just, that a long and narrow vessel was docked just beyond, exactly as their captive had advertised.

Sam turned back, stepped into the space station proper, and motioned for the others to join her.

Tania started to move, and in that same moment a sound rolled through the whole place. The lights all shifted hue in unison.

Every door along the wall, and on each of the numerous levels below them, clicked and began to open.

"Run!" Sam shouted. Pointlessly. She was beyond the range their broken comms could handle. It didn't matter, the others understood what was happening. Vaughn reacted first. His boots lit up the floor as he flew forward under full thrust, sweeping his arms around Tania and Tim as he flew. The trio roared along the curve of the hall. Vaughn tilted as he went, thrusters pushing

against floor and wall alike. The wash and heat of their power swept across the opening doors. Sam saw several Scipios fall back in surprise. Prumble followed suit, taking Vaughn's example, a second later. The Scipios, students or low-level workers, Sam still wasn't quite sure, threw arms in front of faces and fell back into their companions as these two sudden blasts of heat poured through the doors opening before them. Sam ducked inside her own as Vaughn barreled around the corner. He took it a bit too fast, turning his shoulder to protect Tania from impacting the transparent wall of the access way. He grunted with the impact, let Tania and Tim go, and tumbled end over end a few times before coming to a stop.

Prumble flew in a second behind him. Sam stifled a delighted laugh as the big man somehow managed to run several steps along the glass wall rather than smear himself across it like Vaughn had. He even managed to hop over his fallen companion before finally reaching a more graceful end to his brief flight.

"Ouch," Vaughn said, pushing himself to a shaky stand. Tania and Tim did the same.

Sam closed the door behind them all. "That was close."

"Did any of them see us?" Prumble asked.

She shrugged. "They saw a couple of fireballs race down the hallway."

"Something worth reporting, surely, but we might have bought ourselves a few minutes." He finally seemed to see the breathtaking corridor they'd hidden in. "Crikey."

"You said it," Vaughn agreed.

Tim seemed to ignore the view. He pointed at the far end of the short hall. "Is that the transport our prisoner spoke of?"

"Time to find out," Sam said, brushing past him. She marched to the sealed bulkhead. Vaughn joined her as she manipulated the latching mechanism. Shoulder to shoulder, they swept inside the craft, by silent agreement each taking a different direction.

"Clear," Vaughn said.

"Ditto." Fist held out before her, Sam took four even steps to the end of the narrow space. The walls were lined with what she presumed were harnesses, though not made for humans, of course. She had to bend at the waist to keep from hitting her

head on the low ceiling. Her headlamp lit the fine particulate in
the air as she pushed to the end of the aisle. A small compartment
there, a dead end. The walls were lined with shelves and cabinets,
all with insignia on them. Sam didn't bother to look at each and
try to puzzle out the translation. Tania or Tim could handle that.
Nothing dangerous, that was all she needed to know.

"Up here," Vaughn said.

She turned and joined him. On his side, an endcap
compartment identical to the one she'd found, only there
were no shelves or cabinets. Instead a series of bizarre controls,
handles, and displays graced every surface.

"Cockpit?" Vaughn asked.

"Seems so. Tania?! Tim?! See if you can make sense of this."

She marched back to the center of the ship as the pair came
inside and swiftly moved to the controls. Prumble ducked in and
sighed. He barely fit in the tiny, Scipio-sized space. "Cozy," he
muttered, and moved aft to give Sam room to shut the door
behind him.

Sam hesitated for a few seconds, staring down the glass-
walled corridor and through the door at the far end. She'd
closed that door, after the others had all made their mad dash
from the station proper. It was open now. Three Scipios stood
there. Innocent bystanders, like the one they'd captured and
interrogated. The one who'd committed suicide at the first
opportunity, or, as Sam suspected, been murdered by some new
order transmitted to the virus. She marveled at how these three,
staring back at her now, their mouths agape, could be simply
going about their business already. How was it that this entire
station was not on police lockdown?

She held her fire. Sam heaved the door closed, only breaking
eye contact with the trio of stupefied Scipios when the airlock
blocked her view. It sealed with a faint inverse hiss.

Almost immediately the little transport craft lurched and
began to move. Sam swayed, grabbed one of the alien harnesses
on the wall to keep her upright. From the cockpit, Tania and Tim
let out a little victorious whoop in unison. Tim poked his head
into the main cabin. "We're away!"

"Good. The question is where—"

Tim's wide, knowing grin stopped her short. Sam arched an eyebrow at him.

"For once something wasn't cryptic even in translation. There's a station, a whole complex of them, marked 'Interstellar Departure.'"

"Fucking A," Vaughn said. "Practically gift wrapped."

Tim beamed. He looked like a kid on Christmas. Tania, Sam noted, remained in the cockpit, her gaze still cast outside, blank expression reflected in the glass.

11
MAGO

Gloria Tsandi had worried about many things in her life, but never footprints. Each step on the moon's blue-gray surface left a perfect impression of her boot. The soft sand—really a mixture of pumicelike rock and grit—compressed in perfect, airless clarity.

"Our boots are telling quite the story here," she said to Xavi.

"We should spread out. Stick to shadows."

They'd been traveling in a line, Vanessa at the lead and Gloria in back, in a path that snaked away from the wreck of the *Wildflower*. Gloria had yet to look back at her ship. She couldn't quite bring herself to do that. Not yet. Not until the moment came when she would have to issue one final, fateful command to her.

Vanessa guided the team on a curved path that kept them roughly at the edge of a wide circle around the distant Scipio facility. The plan was to get away from the *Wildflower* first, then move in, but these footprints . . . Gloria shook her head. They couldn't hop from rock to rock. The gravity may allow it, but not the unseen search parties that lurked all around them. Vanessa said as much when Gloria called a break to raise her concerns.

They had to speak by putting their helmets together. "We just have to hope that by the time they find the wreckage it's just a blackened crater, and all these prints have been wiped away."

Gloria decided the choice of words was not-so-careful diplomacy. What Vanessa had really meant was "by the time you blow up your ship." A small but appreciated bit of thoughtfulness, really.

"But Xavi's right," Vanessa added. "Let's spread out a bit. Use shadows where we can. If I remember right there's a large crater up ahead. Once we're below the rim we can trace the lip in darkness all the way around to the other side. That'll put us well away from the crash."

The others all began to separate, save Xavi and Alex Warthen. Her navigator kept close to him by an order Gloria had delivered with a simple glance, acknowledged by a slight dip of Xavi's chin as they'd exited the ship. He hadn't let Alex get more than five meters from him since. If Alex noticed this, or cared, he made no indication. He seemed to be in shock, and she couldn't blame him. Right side or wrong, the man had been through a lot.

Vanessa had been right about the crater. The hill they'd been slowly climbing turned out to be the outer rim. Near the crest, the immune slowed and began to carefully choose her path between exposed boulders and, at one point, a depression so low she had to crawl on her belly to maintain a low profile. No choice here but for all of them to follow her lead. Gloria held her breath when it came time for Alex to make the crawl. There was a moment's hesitation, and for a second she thought he might have decided he owed nothing to her or any of them, that this entire endeavor was a suicide mission, anyway, and why drag it out? But he dropped to his knees as Beth had, lay down on his stomach, and pulled himself through the fine powder and loose rubble. Xavi didn't wait for him to reach the top, he crawled right behind him. Gloria waited until they were both in the shadow of a cleft in the crater's rim, twenty meters up the slope.

There they waited for her, silhouettes against the stars. Carthage hung high above, filling a quarter of the visible sky, its myriad of equatorial space stations glinting like jewels.

"Coming, boss?" Xavi asked.

"In a second," she replied. "There's something I have to do first."

She turned and looked back toward the *Wildflower*. The ship was hidden from sight by all the boulders and dunes they'd just traversed, but their path, viewed from here, was blindingly obvious. She stared in the direction of her beloved vessel and executed the command they'd rigged way back when they'd first docked with the object that turned out to be Eve. The *Chameleon*, they'd called her ship form.

A bright flash lit up the craggy landscape, followed by a rapidly expanding cloud of powdered rock, boulders, and the unrecognizable chunks of the place that had been her home for so many years. The *Wildflower* joined the *Chameleon* then, in that afterlife for starships that was the memory of their captains.

"Hopefully they'll consider that just another impact," she said, aware of the emotion in her voice and not really caring.

"No," Xavi said, "hopefully they were already there, crawling all over it."

"Amen to that," she replied.

Gloria turned and started her crawl. Halfway there the ground began to vibrate as the broken remains of the *Wildflower* rained back to the surface. She lay there, head turned to one side so she could watch, and waited for the storm to pass. Then she reached up and heaved herself forward, one more length. Then another. Again and again until she felt Xavi's hands under her arms. He helped her to her feet and stared into her eyes for several long seconds before clapping her on the shoulder. "Let's move out," he said.

"Yes," Gloria said, "let's."

The crater was several hundred meters across, more than half of it hidden in shadow as the system's star hung midway to the horizon. It was only partial shadow, the light reflecting off Carthage filling in some of the blackness. Vanessa set off, barely visible until Gloria's eyes adjusted.

"Think this will work?" Xavi asked.

Beth replied before Gloria could. "We're assuming their eyes work like ours, and that they have yet to invent the flashlight. I'd say that's a big assumption."

Xavi grunted. "Better than nothing, mate."

Gloria repeated her call for radio silence. They'd been so sloppy already that it seemed unlikely to matter, but the truth was she craved silence just now. Time to reflect, to mourn, and find within herself what resolve might be left for what may lie ahead. *At least,* she thought, *the Scipios won't learn anything from the* Wildflower. A small consolation if there ever was one, especially considering the *Lonesome* may even now be hidden away in some distant corner of this solar system, being picked apart molecule by molecule for every last scrap of intelligence. She wondered if the Scipios were, at this very moment, assembling a factory to reproduce their own imploder. Her gut churned at the idea they could be on the cusp of folding their way to Earth in force, destroying everything humanity had fought so hard to regain. And here Gloria was, sneaking through this unnamed, unimportant crater to what would probably turn out to be a helium-3 mining station, one of thousands the Scipios likely had strewn about. Even if she managed to damage it, much less destroy it, it would amount to a minor blip on some Scipio spreadsheet, and they'd dispatch an automated construction rig to build a replacement within the day, if they even bothered.

She took another step, though, and the one after that. Because no matter how inconsequential their actions, it was another breath, another heartbeat, another chance that rescue might come.

The hike became a monotonous, quiet affair. She frequently glanced back, but the enemy had yet to show their faces beyond the initial sighting Vanessa made. They were out there, of that Gloria had no doubt, but as of yet they'd found no reason to investigate this particular crater.

Hidden in the last of the shadow, on the lip of the far side, Vanessa stopped and chanced a look over the edge. Almost immediately the woman ducked back down, turned, and gave an urgent hand signal demanding radio silence. The others gathered beneath her, waiting until Gloria caught up. They put their heads together so all their visors were in contact, allowing the vibrations of speech to pass between them.

"We're right on top of it," Vanessa said. "Less than a hundred meters."

"Any kind of security perimeter?" Xavi asked.

121

"Not that I could see. Which is to say, nothing obvious."

Beth Lee spoke up. "It's possible they never expected to need one, this far in from the Swarm Blockade. No one's ever breached that barrier."

"That we know of," Xavi corrected.

Gloria shook her head. "Not exactly true. There's Captain Dawson, and the *Lonesome.*"

"Yeah, but who knows how far they got before the Scipios got them."

"I'm just saying," Gloria amended, "we have to assume the Scipios will be on edge, if for no other reason than the massive impact zone our arrival created so close to this facility. Speaking of, Vanessa, did you see anything that might imply its purpose?"

"No," the immune replied. "Domed buildings, towers, a large warehouse or something near the center, connecting hallways. Plus all the various pipes and conduits and silos you'd expect."

Beth Lee said, "Alien or not, some things are evidently universal."

No one spoke for several seconds, and Gloria soon realized they were all waiting for her. Even Alex Warthen stared at her with the gaze of a soldier awaiting orders.

"What's the plan, boss?" Xavi prompted.

She studied them all. Vanessa was by far the most heavily armed. Alex Warthen had the same armor, but none of the weapons. Never mind that his loyalties were suspect at best. Xavi carried the small pistol all spacecraft were required to have on board in the event of a crew member becoming mentally unstable. It was designed to be able to penetrate a helmet visor, but not hull plating. Beth and Gloria herself carried no weapons at all. Their burden instead was the supplies, the meager quantities of food and water salvaged from the wreck.

"Our goal is to figure out a way to destroy that facility. Given we're somewhat lacking in the armaments department, my hope is we can find some kind of reactor or explosive supply of chemicals, and sabotage. With any luck the secondary explosion will be enough to do the job."

"And what happens to us?" Alex Warthen asked.

Gloria met his gaze and held it. "One-way trip, I'm afraid. We don't have the supplies to wait for rescue, or any way to call for one even if we did."

Warthen held any reaction he had to this in perfect check. He just stared back at her.

Gloria Tsandi sighed. "Xavi?"

"Yeah, boss?"

"If anyone in this group tries to flee or otherwise survive this effort, I'm ordering you to shoot them dead. We cannot leave a survivor for the Scipios to interrogate."

A cold silence fell over the group. "Understood," Xavi managed, and she realized he didn't like this much better than Alex. But there was no other option, and the last thing she wanted to do right now was get into a debate.

"Suppose we can't do it?" Beth asked.

Gloria looked at her, an eyebrow raised.

"Suppose," the engineer went on, "the base, or whatever, is solar powered. Or what if it's a peaceful observatory. I mean, for all we know it's a Scipio orphanage."

Nobody said anything. The words were like a plug pulled from the bathtub, and Gloria could only watch as her vengeance-fueled drive drained away.

"She's got a point," Xavi said. "Okay, maybe not the orphanage thing, but we've really got no idea what we're destroying. Hell, they could be part of some kind of resistance against the Scipios."

The captain cast her navigator a dubious glare. "Doubtful."

"Doubtful doesn't mean impossible."

"I . . ." Gloria allowed herself a long, calming breath. "I know. Okay, fine. I'm revising the plan. We'll poke around first. Good enough?"

"Maybe I should go in and recon the situation," Vanessa offered.

Gloria shook her head. "We can't all sit out here, so no matter what, we're going in. All of us. If we can find a—"

A painfully loud pop interrupted her. Gloria winced as the bright ring of feedback followed the sudden noise. She glanced down at herself, sure she'd been shot despite knowing how ridiculous that was. But there was no pain except for that in her ears. Xavi and Beth reacted similarly, but not, she realized, Vanessa or Alex.

"What is it?" Vanessa asked, barely audible. "What's happened?"

"I don't know," she managed. "I—"

Xavi's hand gripped her arm. He was looking at the ground, at nothing, eyes darting back and forth. "Listen," he said.

Listen? Gloria could barely hear anything. But Xavi's strong grip served to steady her, and the ringing finally faded, leaving other sounds behind. Alien sounds. Muffled vocalizations, indecipherable. And something else, too. A groan of pain, and labored breathing. Both, to Gloria Tsandi's ear, very human sounds.

"What is this?" Beth asked, whispering.

Gloria held up a hand. She listened and at the same time racked her brain to figure out what they could possibly be hearing. They'd all gone on radio silence. And who else was here?

Perhaps it was coming from far away, she thought. Quickly she summoned the comm portion of her suit's interface. And then she saw it. A transmission on the emergency channel, slipping through because that had to be deliberately disabled, a separate action from radio silence. It wasn't this that grabbed Gloria's attention, though, it was the identifier displayed below. CAPT DAWSON.

"Dawson," she whispered, and looked up at Xavi, then Beth.

The groans of pain flowing into Gloria's ears turned into a shrill scream, quickly silenced.

"That's a short-range channel, boss," Xavi said. "Nearby. In that fucking base. What are the damn odds?"

Gloria looked into the eyes of each of them, and saw that, this time, no one needed to be told what the objective was.

12
CARTHAGE

The tunnel descended into darkness, beneath the crushing weight of the bay above.

Skyler forced himself to stroll. Cracks laced the arched ceiling above him, allowing the frothy white ocean water—if it was even water—to bubble through. The mucuslike fluid dripped through and formed gelatinous piles on the sloping ground, making the surface slick and treacherous. Several hours passed before the slope began to even out. Here, the white fluid had begun to pool, and Skyler feared the basin of the tunnel would be completely flooded. He had no intention of submerging himself in whatever this gunk was, especially in a compromised suit. Already the acrid smell of it had begun to sting his eyes and forced him into several bouts of sneezing. His throat itched, and his stomach had started to complain.

He trudged on, his feet sluicing through the stagnant "water," each step leaving little bluish contrails in their wake. It reminded him of pearlescent liquid soap. If only it smelled as good.

The fluid reached his waist when the tunnel finally flattened out completely. He stood for a while, trying to banish images his brain concocted of the entire ceiling collapsing, instantly crushing him under the weight of hundreds of meters of this muck. But as he watched, the depth of the accumulation did not change. Seeping out onto the ocean floor, perhaps, or just draining into some unseen lower chamber of the tunnel. It had been this way for centuries, a fact of which he had to continually remind himself. No reason to think it would suddenly fill up now, or collapse.

Skyler waded farther into the pool. It was too murky to see his legs or feet, too dark in any case. Something bumped his leg and sloshed away, producing a string of frothy bubbles that left blue rings of film on the surface. He steadied himself and took another tentative step, probing with the toe of his armored suit. He stepped again, and shifted his focus to the ceiling, scanning it for any signs of surveillance equipment. His assumption so far had been that the Scipios relied on their viral snow for such things, the tiny cells relaying anything they found that was considered out of place. It made sense to do it that way, given how pervasive the little white flakes of engineered nastiness were. Still, this place had not been built by the Scipios. Surely the original occupants would have used more traditional means of defense and policing. But Skyler saw nothing. No cameras, no sensors. Not here, not in the city he'd fled through, either, though admittedly he'd been in a rush to find cover as he'd traversed those streets and alleys.

Here was only the arched ceiling, made of some kind of slightly glittering poured stone. Concrete laced with diamonds, his imagination decided. It sounded cool, at least. There were pipes as well, whole bundles of them that traced the entire length, eerily human in their design and layout. Skyler chalked that up to the universal obviousness of a round container for withstanding pressures. Still, it seemed strange to look at this place so. There was an implied kinship with the aliens who'd built this place, and the city around it, in a "See, we're not so different after all" kind of way.

As he pushed through the slurry, his thoughts drifted to the state of humankind. Their place in this universe. When first encountering the Key Ship, and Eve, Skyler had felt like a feral child encountering true technology for the first time. He remembered a certain embarrassed feeling, that these advanced beings had been wasting their time with such a messy, petty, nasty people and their fucked-up world. To go from that to the news Gloria Tsandi brought left him reeling. Humans belonged out here now. They were members of the club. Actors perfectly justified to be playing on this grand stage. Even knowing how much time had passed back home, this change in fortunes made him stand a bit taller. He wondered how much the "gifts" Eve had given Earth, in exchange for the help of Skyler and his crew, had assisted in this transformation. Eve had bestowed on Earth a way to probe the memories of all those who had succumbed to the plague, and a few of her incomprehensible time-distortion bubbles, in addition to ending her facsimile of the Scipio virus.

At some point the tunnel had begun to curve upward again, a fact he realized only because he could see his knees now. He'd lost track of time, lost in thought, and now neared his destination. Skyler put his thoughts aside. He would look forward to talking to Gloria Tsandi about how, exactly, humanity had made such an incredible leap, should he ever see her again.

And if he wanted to do that, he had a space elevator to catch.

Skyler gritted his teeth as he waded through the last of the murky fluid. His foot plopped onto solid surface for the first time in hours, and almost slipped out from under him. He paused, let the gunk drip off his feet. His legs had begun to itch where the weird chemical stew had seeped into his shredded suit. He tried not to think of the alien bacteria and parasites that were no doubt now snacking on his legs and feet. They were, quite literally, the least of his worries.

Sounds ahead. The hum of machinery and soft bustle of movement. He killed his helmet light. For a time he stood, motionless, allowing his eyes to adjust. Weak light filtered down from the unseen end of the tunnel, illuminating the gentle fall of viral dust, swirling in and out on currents of air. After a few minutes he could see well enough to mark the debris and piles of dripping ocean goop that lay between here and there. He guessed he could see about three hundred meters before the tunnel curved out of sight. If it ended up there, or merely continued on into the city as part of some underground transportation system, he could not yet tell. He picked his way forward, keeping close to the wall for no reason other than it felt reassuring somehow to have a solid surface at his back.

It occurred to him that by walking upright he was making himself an unnecessarily large target. Skyler got on hands and knees, lowered himself to his belly, and began to crawl like a soldier under razor wire.

A barrier came into view. It looked to be a wall about a meter high, made out of some kind of composite material that reminded him of woven Kevlar. Body armor. It had none of the grime seen everywhere else. A recent addition? Made because they were expecting him?

Skyler stared at the surface for a long time, allowing details to register. The grime of age, and in places the creeping vines that seemed to boil up everywhere on the abandoned side of the city. Here, the growth was pale and thin, barely ten centimeters high. New growth, in comparison, but at least he could assume this barrier had been here for a while.

Movement just beyond the wall caught his eye. Two figures, one at either end, shifted position slightly. Until that moment he'd thought they were just support structures or random junk piled against the barricade. No such luck. They were guards, clearly. Each sat or stood on the other side, staring into the darkness toward him. If they'd heard or seen him, or even suspected his approach, they were hiding it well. Now and then they spoke to each other in low voices, too distant and quiet for his visor to recognize, much less translate.

Skyler remained motionless, weighing options. Going back was out of the question, as far as he was concerned. It would take hours, and put him back where he started. However dangerous continuing might be, he simply could not contemplate the idea of retreating after coming so far. Somewhere up there, past that barrier and the tunnel's exit, amid all those buildings and lights, was a space elevator. A way off this world. He was not going back.

So, forward it was. Skyler stayed put. Forward was to reveal himself. Another battle, more death. Critically, the drawing of attention. As of now the Scipios seemed to have no idea where he was, and that was a situation he intended to hold on to as long as possible.

Idly he wondered what would happen if he simply walked up to the wall, hopped it, and kept going. Would they shoot him? Tackle him? Stare in stunned disbelief? Or what if he gave himself up? Walked forward with his hands raised, demanded an audience with their leader. Demanded a lawyer. Skyler almost laughed aloud at that image. Him in a Scipio courtroom, surrounded by arguing attorneys and a gallery of upset citizens, shaking their appendages so that their gliding flaps swayed beneath.

The ground beneath him began to vibrate, and then a humming noise reached him. Ahead, the two guards perked up, and began to move toward the walls. *What the hell is this?* he wondered, shifting to push himself into the space between floor and wall. More light reached him, from behind now. Behind, the way he'd come. Skyler held his breath and watched, helpless, as the noise and light grew. Something was coming through the tunnel.

A new noise, then. The scrape of stone against stone. Skyler shot a quick glance to the guards and their wall, only to see the wall had changed. A wide gap had opened in the center, perhaps ten meters in length. The two Scipios stood to either side of it now, waiting for whatever approached. They did not seem alarmed. He saw no weapons raised nor heard nervous shouts. Skyler returned his focus to the dark depths, and waited. There was nothing else he could do.

No, that wasn't true. A few meters behind him lay a moldy, decaying length of metallic sheet, like a torn bit of body from a vehicle left behind ages ago. He crawled backward to it and slid his body underneath.

Light played over him, pushing through erosion holes in the metal. The air filled with a deep, thrumming moan that made Skyler's whole body ache. He felt sure at any moment some ground vehicle, a train perhaps, or some kind of tank, would roll over him, leaving nothing but a red smear in this ancient tunnel to mark his visit to this world. Only the knowledge that this chunk of scrap metal over him had been here for countless years eased his mind. If it had survived all this time, a body under it should, too.

The light, the heat, the sound all reached a crescendo. He squeezed his eyes shut and, feeling helpless yet unable to control himself, placed his hands against the underside of the metal sheet as if that would keep him from being crushed.

Whatever it was, it moved past. Over him, in the center of the tunnel. Skyler gave his heart several seconds to stop hammering, then rolled, and watched.

A vehicle slowed to a stop in front of the guarded barrier. It was a bulky thing, not wheeled, but instead riding on a series of humming disks that rippled with heat and fantastic amounts of electrical energy. The setup allowed the transport to hover a half-meter off the tunnel floor. The frothy liquid seeping through the ceiling had been evaporated instantly by the passing of the car, and now rolled away across the ceiling as an oily sort of steam. It smelled terrible, like rotten milk. Skyler switched to breathing through his mouth. He crawled forward on his elbows to get a better look.

The vehicle appeared to be of Scipio design, favoring the functional over the elegant, a direct contrast to the cities the Creators had built. Riding atop the array of lifters was a bulky carriage nestled under a series of tubes, heat sinks, and vents. Heat poured from every surface, making the air shimmer. A series of grimy windows ringed the center of the hull, and Skyler could see several figures moving about within. The two guards approached as the huge car settled onto the ground, its engines winding down.

A hatch popped open on top of the car, and a Scipio pushed up. Words were exchanged between it and the guards. One made a sound like laughter, though Skyler knew such assumptions were dangerous. He focused on the body language of the guards, not that he had a better understanding of that, either. Still, they seemed relaxed. In his mind the conversation was going something like "See anything out there?" "Nah, just the usual wandering diseased." "Okay, then. Good night."

Much better than "Who's that weird creature hiding under the sheet metal back there?" Skyler eased back a bit into the shadow. A few minutes later the transport, or whatever it was, powered up its engines once again and pushed on past the barricade. It drove away, soon out of sight, though its engine noises went on for several minutes, growing quieter all the while. Skyler began to worry the tunnel might go right underneath the city and out the other side.

He lay there for a long time, watching, ignoring his aching limbs and spells of dizziness from breathing this stagnant, alien air. Perhaps he was dying, allowing this foreign atmosphere into his lungs. No way to know, he supposed. Soldier on.

Minutes passed. His body began to shiver uncontrollably despite the warmth in the tunnel. Something would have to give, and soon. Skyler shifted to get one arm forward. He sighted along his wrist, trying to keep one of the guards in his line of fire. A memory came to him, camped with his sniper, Jake, on a hillside during the Purge, sighting down on a village overrun with subhumans. He wondered if Jake ever had to take a shot when his body wouldn't cooperate. Probably, and it probably hadn't mattered. Jake had been born to snipe, he'd said it himself. In his veins. Skyler let his wrist fall to the damp ground with a dull smack, laid his head on his arm, and waited for the buzzing in his body to go away.

He ate, and drank a little water. He drifted off. A strange sensation woke him seconds later. Maybe more. A feeling he hadn't had since childhood, the knowledge of falling out of bed before fully waking to stop it from happening. He jerked awake, just as the sheet of metal finished sliding off a knee he hadn't meant to raise. It clanged on the hard floor, a noise that rang like a bell, rolling along the tunnel in both directions.

Skyler whipped his gaze to the guards. They were up, moving toward the center of their barrier and crouching behind it at the same time. One of them shouted something. Lights came on, from their weapons as well as two floodlights he'd not noticed before, embedded up on the walls. Another command caused a small device to lower from the ceiling. It resembled a turret. Skyler took aim at it, but held fire when he saw it spewing forth a cloud of white powder.

Virus. Immune or not, he still suspected they served as a kind of meshed sensor network. Trillions of little biological machines. A cloud of eyes and ears. As the bank of billowing dust rolled toward him, Skyler clenched his jaw, took aim, and fired. No time to even notice how still his hand now was. A beam of reddish energy tore through the air, creating a visible tunnel through the virus fog. It hit one of the Scipio guards square in the face, vaporizing the flesh in a sudden, wet burst.

The guard fell away, behind the barrier. His companion smartly ducked as Skyler swept the beam in his direction. He lowered his arm to compensate, tracing a glowing path across the barrier's surface.

Skyler knew he had to end this quick, before they could report what had happened, assuming the virus wouldn't do that on its own accord. He kept the beam fixed on the position he guessed the enemy to be in and willed it to increase in power. A flash of heat bloomed across his wrist and hand, crawling up his arm, and then came a blinding flash. The beam pulsed, bright and hot as the Sun, for an instant. The barrier exploded, flash-heated to incomprehensible temperatures, the moisture in the air exploding right along with it in a column that stretched all the way back to Skyler's wrist. It rocked his arm upward, wheeling backward, sending him sprawling onto his back.

He sat up, shook away the dizziness of the impact. The center of the barrier had been obliterated. Of the Scipio guards there was nothing left, nothing identifiable from here, at least. "Fucking hell," he whispered, glancing at his arm. He wondered how much of his "ammo" that blast had used. No way to tell with that part of his visor smashed.

Instincts honed from years of scavenging in the wastes beyond Darwin propelled him to his feet. More Scipios would come, he had to get through now. Skyler raced ahead to the barrier. He dove over it at one edge rather than rushing through the blood-smeared center. One glance at the gore there was all he needed to know. The poor creature had been liquefied.

He tucked midair, rolled, came up at a full sprint. Weaving amid debris, Skyler ran until he could no longer see the scene of the brief skirmish behind him. Ahead, the tunnel had flattened out and changed.

The source of the light he'd seen. It wasn't sunlight, but some kind of underground junction. The vehicle he'd seen was parked in the center, and several Scipios moved between it and a platform it had pulled up next to. Skyler slowed, pressed himself to the wall once again. He had little shadow left to work with. That they had not spotted him, or heard him, was some incredible luck. He looked around, frantically seeking a door, a vent, anything he could tuck himself into before they glanced this way. But there was nothing.

Skyler stood there, ready to fight, ready to run. Expecting to be seen at any second. And then they were gone. The Scipios all went into a hallway just off the platform, pushing a few long narrow pieces of cargo that floated as the vehicle did. As the aura shards had in Belém, he thought, filing that, unsure what it meant, if it meant anything at all.

He ran ahead, crossing to the same side as the platform, intending to dive to the base of it if anyone came back out despite knowing that would make near as no difference. No one came out. He hopped up onto the platform and waited. Steal the vehicle? It looked too small for him inside. He stood a half-meter taller than any Scipio he'd seen, after all. But even allowing for that, the vehicle looked cramped.

The platform itself, then. He scanned it hopelessly. There was nothing. Nothing! Nowhere to hide. Just a big flat slab that abutted the parked vehicle, and the iris-style door the four Scipios had entered with their cargo. He glanced at the wall around the door. It went up about three meters, ending at the ceiling where a row of wan lights had been embedded along the length, providing all the illumination for the area.

There came a hiss. Footsteps. The Scipios were coming out. Skyler remained utterly still. He stood only centimeters away, his back pressed so hard into the wall he could feel his suit adjusting for the pressure against his supplies at the small of his back. The Scipios were oblivious, though. Chattering, walking in their odd gait, as they returned to the vehicle. Not a single one of them even glanced in his direction.

He rushed inside, ducking into the iris door before it could hiss closed. A second after he passed through it did just that, leaving him utterly alone in a narrow, low corridor.

Outside the group of Scipios was chattering to one another.

His visor rapidly scrolled through the translations, the shattered glass able to display only the first few words of each sentence. Something about how they'd found two this time, and that was very good. The parting words were "Hunt well!"

Parting, he decided, because the engines on that vehicle were starting to roar again. Skyler crept deeper into the hall. He stopped at a junction just a few meters inside, pressed himself to the wall, then made a quick glance around the corner in both directions. Rooms, to either side, behind iris doors. Next to the one on the left were the two items they'd removed from the vehicle and brought in. They hovered like aura shards, one on either side of the door. Curious, he moved to one. There was a small display on the top, and a little clear section. A growing unease filled him as he approached. Part of his mind already deciding what these items were, the rest unwilling to accept it. Yet as he reached the object, he could no longer deny it. The proof was right in front of him, behind the glass.

Coffins.

Behind the glass of each lay the expressionless face of a Creator. One, Skyler realized to his horror, he recognized. That vertical scar. The one he'd sat with in that small dusty chamber while the aircraft searched for him. The one who'd told him how to get here.

Anger grew within him. He heard movement behind and turned, one arm raised and ready to fire, content to vaporize the two dock workers or whatever they were out of a sheer and sudden desire for revenge. His other hand rested on the coffin. He felt something, and held fire. A thud. And something else. Warmth.

Skyler glanced down. The face behind the glass had not moved at all, save for that third central eye, high on the forehead. It was open now. Staring at Skyler. Fear coursed through his veins, a terror like he'd not known since childhood. He started to step back, involuntarily. Another thud from within the coffin. Weak. A hand, Skyler thought, tapping against the inside.

Wait, some part of his brain said. This was no coffin. Skyler looked at the thing with fresh eyes. A medical device, maybe. A stretcher. Or something purely to restrain a prisoner. His fear abated.

He'd forgotten about the two Scipios. Skyler whirled just in time to see them disappear through the iris door in the opposite direction. They hadn't seen him. Hadn't even bothered to look. And that said a lot.

They weren't on alert despite everything. If these two encapsulated Creators were indeed prisoners, then their hosts were utterly unconcerned about the chances of them escaping or being rescued. Moreover, they'd yet to discover the carnage just a few hundred meters back down the access tunnel. That might change, Skyler realized, if the departing vehicle went back the way it had come. They would find the destroyed barricade and the smears that had been their comrades. Of course they might drive the other way, deeper into the city, but he couldn't count on that. No, any second now an alarm would be raised, and they'd be back on his scent. Skyler turned back to the strange life-support capsule. He looked helplessly for some way to open it, but there were no buttons or switches. No obvious latch. He placed a hand on the window and mouthed, *Be strong.* The gesture felt lame, inadequate in the extreme, but he couldn't simply walk away.

Weighed down by guilt, Skyler went to the iris door the two medical pods were waiting in front of. Its segments swept out of the way and he stepped inside.

Another hall, this one sloping upward before reaching a sharp corner. Sterile white walls free of any markings. The floor was dark like graphite, with little grooved channels running its length. Some kind of rail for small robotic transport, maybe. Skyler rushed ahead to the corner and found another section of similar length and incline, another sharp bend. He moved to it and found the pattern repeated, like a spiral staircase. A dozen turns later, winded, Skyler reached the end of the hall and another iris door.

This one looked different, though. He stood before it, keeping his distance, unsure why. Skyler studied the lines where the segments curled together, traced their Fibonacci paths outward. It all looked fine. *So why am I standing here?*

The words registered then. Glowing letters in the corner of his vision, only visible when he focused on a small faded set of symbols just above the circular portal.

TRANSFER STORAGE

The translation seemed so simple, so innocuous, he'd only subconsciously registered its presence. And Eve's language skill had already produced its share of bizarre conversions. Yet here, now, after what he'd seen below and what he'd come through to get here, some deep part of Skyler found grave concern in those two words.

Transfer storage. A place to stage items being transferred to orbit. This was it, the gateway, the first step toward leaving. Toward finding the others, and confronting Tim. They were up there, somewhere. Unless they'd already found a way to leave, or a worse fate. Yet he couldn't make his foot take that step. He glanced down, actually stared at his own goddamn foot. *Move, for fuck's sake!*

The sound of a footstep, but not his own. They were coming up the spiral ramp. A different part of his mind came forward. Skyler took the step without another thought. He was in the open, nowhere to hide here or anywhere behind him. The door was all he had. It hissed open as he reached it, and Skyler ducked under the low bulkhead.

He entered a vast warehouse. Scaffold shelves stretched away before him, marked at regular intervals by massive support pillars that had lines of light running up their entire height, fifty meters or more. Virus-dust swirled in the air, gray and fine, somewhere between ash and snow that just refused to fall.

Skyler ignored the scale. He paid no mind to the handful of Scipios milling about, some just at the edge of his vision, so vast was the room. What held his gaze was what the shelves housed. Those capsule stretchers. Thousands of them. Tens of thousands. "So many," he whispered.

The door hissed behind him, the sections clicking softly together as they met again in the center. The sound snapped him from his entranced state. He was in danger here. An intruder. A killer, in fact.

Skyler glanced right, saw nothing of use. To the left, along this wall, were a series of large cylindrical tanks. Ugly, grimy things, like everything the Scipios seemed to make. They'd been added haphazardly, not part of the building's original design, he guessed. Because of this they stood about a half-meter out from the wall. Skyler ducked that way and squeezed into the shadowed gap. He pushed farther and farther into the darkness. Banged his knee on a pipe that he registered as hot, but he knew he could not back out now.

The door behind him hissed open.

Skyler was about five meters away. He tucked himself between two of the massive tanks and pressed himself against one, waiting. In his mind's eye he saw Scipios all staring at one another, some pointing at his hiding place, others rushing off to call security, or drawing weapons and beginning to encircle him.

Something caught his eye. Strange indentations on the side of the tank, just visible in the weak light. He craned his neck upward, and realized it was sort of a staggered set of ladder rungs, indented into the surface rather than protruding out. The tank must be twenty meters tall, but in this gravity if he climbed it and slipped it wouldn't be too bad. Would it? For the first time, he recalled the propulsion system his suit contained. He hadn't tried it since the battle aboard the *Chameleon*. Had no idea if it still functioned.

It was a gamble, but one he had to take. Staying down here, without a line of sight on the enemies around him, was to put his fate entirely up to luck. *Fuck luck*, Sam had once said. Wise words, though he hadn't told her that. Sam was hard enough to handle on her own. Sam with an inflated ego? No and thank you. The thought filled him with guilt. *If I see you again, I'll tell you just how brilliant I found that phrase, Sam. I never gave you enough credit for my own survival. I'm sorry for that.*

Skyler climbed. He didn't bother to look to his right through the occasional gaps in the pipework, to see if the workers were still going about their business, or standing slack-jawed, watching the alien scaling their storage tank.

He reached the top without incident, and hauled himself over and onto the roof. A maze of tubes snaked in every direction, connecting this tank with those adjacent. In several places, large bundles ran off toward the storage shelves that dominated the room. Skyler decided in the low gravity of this world they could probably take his weight. They were big enough, and metal. He climbed atop the nearest trunk and, on hands and knees, crawled across it. A harrowing five meters to the other side.

Halfway there he paused.

Movement below, glimpsed from the corner of his eye. He flattened himself, waiting for cries of alarm or bullets to ping and spark in the darkness around him. Nothing happened. He leaned out and looked down. Below, the Scipios were gathering around the two white pods brought up from the subterranean tunnel. Their chatter could only be born of excitement, he thought. They each leaned in, remarking on the contents. One reached out and did a strange little slapping motion against the glider-flap of one of the newcomers who'd shepherded the device up. It was, to his admittedly alien sense of body language, a pat on the back. Job well done.

Puzzled, Skyler glanced at the vast room full of similar lozenge-shaped pods. Why, he wondered, were they so excited about two more when they had a million or more here already?

And if this was transfer storage, why were so many just sitting here? A traffic jam? A backlog?

Curious. He crawled the rest of the way across. The bundle bored straight into a channel that perfectly fit its size, disappearing into the complex scaffold of shelves. Too narrow by far for him to continue, so he stood up and climbed onto the shelving. He went sideways, to the corner, and then turned in and continued deeper into the vast space. He was twenty meters up, only darkness below. The pillars that supported all this were spaced at least forty meters apart, the lights embedded in them providing only minimal visibility. It was darkest between these, so he kept going until he reached the halfway mark and then started up. He'd go as high as he could, he decided. Maybe find a way onto the roof. He found he wanted that, to see the sky, to see that graceful line of a space elevator soaring higher than the mind could easily comprehend.

But first, the capsules. Skyler paused. He hooked his arm around one of the thin beams of the shelving stack, and craned his neck into the narrow space between. The capsule here was identical to all the others, placed feetfirst so that the little viewing window was on the outside, closest to him.

Dust coated the whole surface. Or dead virus, if there was even a difference here. He swept one hand across it and cleared the view. Dark inside, not like those below. And no status lights, either. Skyler leaned in farther and waited for his vision to adjust. It was almost pitch-black here. But not quite. There was enough light to see, after a minute or so, that this capsule was empty.

As was the next.

And the next.

Skyler climbed up and up, checking each capsule he passed, growing more and more confused. They were all empty. Every single one. Which explained, he supposed, the excitement of the Scipios far below.

At the top his hopes proved true. A large fan whirled slowly inside an indented section on the ceiling, pulling air upward, probably for filtering. Next to it was a hatch, an iris door embedded right into the surface. Skyler crawled across the tops of capsules and support beams to reach it. Each pod he passed he glanced down at, almost wanting to see a face now. He never did.

"So many, and all empty. What the hell does it mean?" he muttered, aware he was talking to himself and not really caring. Something about this place did not add up, did not match Eve's description. He just couldn't figure out what.

The hatch led to the roof. An inclined surface, marked in random places with the machinery he guessed was cooling, ventilation, and power. The building was, compared with those around it, quite low. Skyscrapers rose all around him. These were Creator built. Elegant, bright, with swirling patterns of windows here and angular, geometric patterns there. All had been marred, though. Protrusions grafted on, ugly and out of place. The work of Scipios, and not just the powdery virus cells, which coated everything like a light snow. Their own gear marred everything: pipes, vents, cabling, and all the rest. In many ways, it reminded him of Darwin, the way people had been forced to retrofit the city to support the population trapped there.

Nothing Eve had said implied the Scipios lived in a similar state, though. This was no prison for them, just a ready-made city that needed to be adjusted to support their culture and physiology. Indeed, the most common out-of-place addition to the structures around him were what he had to assume were perches. Little poles protruding from the corners of buildings at random heights. He let his eyes take it all in, and yes, there, in the middle distance, he saw several Scipios gliding between these perches. Poles and platforms, even little huts in some cases. All grafted right onto the sides of the original buildings.

He forced his gaze away. Cast his eyes skyward in search of some glimpse of the Elevator. But he saw nothing. Worrying, but he shunted that aside. It was here, somewhere, close. Blocked by these massive buildings. He would have to go around.

Skyler worked his way to the edge of the building, wondering when day would come, when he'd lose the natural cover of night and the deep shadows created by the erratic lighting across the city.

"Tim," he said, deciding to risk the transmission. "Tim, you asshole, answer me."

No response came. Not then, not ten minutes later when Skyler finally ambled to the edge of the roof and glanced down on the city below.

He heard them before he saw them. The noise of life. City life. Vehicles, like the one from the tunnel, trundling down the once-picturesque plazas and paths the Creators had favored. The batlike Scipios milling about in small groups, some shuffling to home or work or whatever they did here. Still others, gliding from perch to perch, building to building. Always a slightly downward path. How they got back up again he could only guess from the spiraling ramp he'd ascended himself.

There were many Scipios here, though the city had none of the vibrance or lived-in feel of Darwin. Still, it was night. Plenty more could be asleep in all these massive buildings, assuming they kept to such a day-night schedule. A guess, yet Skyler still decided he needed to be gone before the sun rose, if only to take advantage of the cover of darkness. Skyler racked his mind, trying to recall how long a day lasted on Carthage, but that detail remained steadfastly out of reach, if Eve had ever bothered to share it. His only option was to watch the sky for signs of an approaching sunrise.

He walked along the rooftop to the far end, to get a better look. Below, a wide plaza seemed to be the central place for Scipio nightlife to gather, at least in this part of the city. He found their movements and social patterns mildly fascinating, like watching a colony of ants for the first time, marveling at individual interactions as much as that of the whole population.

A gravity began to tug at that population. Something he couldn't see, drawing their attention. They began to move toward a place directly below his position. Skyler backed away, fearful. They'd seen him, were ambling over, curious.

No, he realized. None of them were looking up. They were looking at the base of the building. Curious onlookers began to cluster, becoming a crowd. He didn't know why, or what they wanted, or how to get them to leave. This must be how Russell Blackfield felt, he realized, when crowds would surround the gates of Nightcliff. Only he knew what they wanted. Food. A better life. They were angry, scared. These Scipios, on the plaza below, were neither. They seemed almost giddy with excitement.

Skyler leaned out to get a better look. Far below, at street level, several Scipios had emerged from the building, pushing the two medical pods. Even from here he knew they were the same ones because of their softly glowing status lights. Their movement became a procession, with Scipios lining up on either side to watch the two capsules float through the long, narrow plaza. At the far end the parade ended. Both pods were guided into the open doors of another building. Skyler studied the façade, but it was too far away to see clearly. Until his gaze focused on the middle. There, above the doors, tacked-on signage covered the original. He could not make out the details, but his visor could. It translated the words into perfect English.

TRANSFER FACILITY.

13

ABOVE CARTHAGE

The small shuttle drifted on a preprogrammed path, first climbing to the midpoint of the space elevator where gravity would be effectively nullified at this speed, then beginning its trek to the selected location. The cramped space quickly became uncomfortable, with each member of the group gravitating to their own place and settling in for the ride. Tania remained in what she considered the pilot's seat, though with everything automated the true purpose of the position seemed more like that of a conductor.

Still, it allowed her to monitor the various displays aligned around her. Something of a chore considering the translation system her helmet provided. Anything she wanted to read she had to hold in the center of her vision long enough for a suitable English version to display. For simple signs inside the space station, that had been trivial, but a status screen for a spacecraft was a whole different thing. Not only was the information dense, but it changed rapidly. Because the numbers no doubt had to also be converted into something a human would appreciate, often her visor's readout could not even finish displaying something before it had to wipe the whole mess and start again.

Trying to follow it only made the headache she already had that much worse. The vitals at least seemed in order. They had fuel, they had air, and they had a destination. Tania decided the only thing she really needed to know was if their course had been altered by an external force, or if another craft was approaching them with an intent to dock, ram, or otherwise impede their course.

So she stared out the window instead. The ship was on autopilot, but she could roll it on its axis without affecting their course, so she manipulated the angle until her window looked down at Carthage. Nobody complained, or even seemed to notice.

Sam and Vaughn had taken positions on either side of the small airlock, ready to exit the craft at a moment's notice if a battle was imminent. Prumble similarly clung to the wall directly opposite the same door, ready to face anyone who might try to board them. That left Tania at the "nose" of the ship, and Tim all the way aft, in a small chamber that appeared to be used for storing the personal belongings of the passengers. He had his eyes closed, and drifted lazily, held in place only by one foot, which he'd looped through one of the luggage webbings. He'd lived most of his life in space, as had she, which made the materials and design of the vessel the only thing about this that felt truly alien.

Tania let out a long sigh. It fogged her visor, temporarily obscuring the view. She let it fade, slowly revealing the details of the planet below as the moisture was removed from her air by the suit. She studied the landmasses, the oceans with their odd milky coloration. A topography she'd all but memorized while aboard the *Chameleon,* but seeing it in person was always so different. *It's so close,* she thought. To come all this way and not make it to the surface. This outcome made her feel profoundly empty inside. All that had happened, here and on Earth and in between, for nothing. To end in retreat, with the knowledge that the Builders would simply continue their galactic sorting algorithm in order to find another possible candidate to achieve this rescue.

And worse, so much worse it made her heart feel as if

gripped in a vise, was the knowledge that they would leave people behind. Skyler, Vanessa, even the crew of the *Wildflower*. Missing, presumed dead, the report would conclude. She could see it now, and it made her want to scream. Tania did not expect the Universe to be fair, never had. She knew it for what it was; a mostly empty container of atoms that sometimes came together in interesting ways. Such a thing had no sense of fairness. It had no sense at all. But it was supposed to *make sense*. That, at least, she always had believed. That if you looked hard enough you could find a reason for something being the way it was.

An overwhelming sense of confinement took hold of her. She wanted, more so even than seeing Skyler alive again, to be outside. To feel the air on her face. To not be in a tiny box with nothing more than someone else's technology to keep her from the cold vacuum of space.

She took some advice Skyler had given her, years ago. To act on instinct, rather than think everything through. Tania reached up and undid the seal on her helmet. She ignored the warnings and lifted the bulk away before anyone could stop her. Tania let it drift into a corner and shook her hair free from the ponytail she'd tied it in.

"What the hell are you doing?" Sam asked.

Tania inhaled deeply. The air tasted of metal and grease and the faint traces of chemical recirculation. Like home, to her, though it was far too cold and very thin. She turned to Sam, exhaled, and said, "I couldn't stand the staleness anymore. Besides, we knew it was breathable."

"Only just," Prumble observed.

Tania gave an apologetic shrug. "I only want a few minutes. Besides, one of us was going to have to test it at some point."

She drifted between the group clustered around the airlock. A tight fit, but she didn't care. She just wanted to move, feel wind on her face. Nothing like what she'd experienced falling toward Hawaii, of course, but it made things a little more bearable.

The burst of conversation had not woken Tim. He'd twisted in his sleep, and settled in a corner as free-floating debris in zero gravity often did. Tania had no interest in waking him. She performed a swimmer's turn, rolling in midair so she could push off with her feet, and launch back toward the nose of the ship.

A display caught her eye. She'd left her visor behind, and so had no translation, but the imagery required no such system to be understood. It was a map. A top-down schematic of all the space stations and space elevators around the planet, as well as some markers for various installations on the surface. Something about it was wrong. It didn't match Eve's depiction.

Curious, Tania pushed back to the cockpit, retrieved her helmet, and put it back on as she crossed aft once again. Prumble, Sam, and Vaughn watched all this silently, heads swiveling in unison like spectators at a tennis match. Once at the screen, with Tim's sleeping form bobbing just centimeters away, Tania scanned the display again, this time with the English translation appearing just below the alien symbols.

There were so many that it took her a moment to realize it was the quantity that had caught her attention. Of course, that made perfect sense. Eve's data had been woefully out of date. It was only natural to expect the Scipios to have expanded in the centuries since Eve had last visited. What wasn't new had probably been moved or removed as well.

"What is it?" Prumble asked.

"A map," Tania replied, almost unaware of her own voice. She'd already become lost in the schematic, studying its details wherever her eyes spotted something interesting. It took a moment, but she found their own craft, indicated by a small red shape that was evidently their iconic representation of a transport or shuttle. Their path, a softly glowing yellow curve, took them halfway around the planet to another space elevator, which ascended to the farthest point and terminated at a space station marked simply DEPART. *Well that's tidy*, Tania thought. Now she knew why Tim had picked it. She just hoped it meant depart as in leave the system, and not the Scipios' version of a morgue, for nowhere did it say who was departing or what it was they were departing from.

Still, she had to agree with Tim's choice. It made sense to have a dockyard at that outermost point, if only for the gravitation assist such a position provided.

Chewing her lower lip in concentration, Tania scanned the

other stations around the planet. Their purposes were often obvious—NUTRIENT PRODUCTION—and alternately, utterly baffling—EXCITING ALLOCATE being one example she could easily envision as the type of T-shirt tourists would buy in a foreign country purely for the novelty of the poor translation. She theorized that section of connected stations to be the Scipio version of a theme park or vacation spot. Probably used a slogan like "A place to get your yearly allocation of excitement!"

On a certain level she knew her giddiness came from the air she'd breathed, but that same air also made her not care. She continued to study the map. Doing so gave her an odd sense of joy, a feeling she'd known since childhood, that very first time she'd seen a physical globe map of Earth and spun it around. "The pleasure of finding things out," a book she'd read many times had described it. A phrase that had defined her life.

Two details caught her eye, one after the other, each so alarming she felt momentarily trapped between them, unsure which to focus on. "Oh my God," she whispered.

That drew Prumble over. He shouldered himself into the cabin, pushing the sleeping Tim against the wall. He still did not wake. The space was now utterly cramped, made worse by the fact that all three occupants had their aura shards strapped to their backs. "Found something?"

"Two things," Tania said, breathless.

"Be calm, be calm," he said. "Show me."

Sam and Vaughn came over as well, though they had to remain just outside the narrow bulkhead, unable to see the screen.

Tania pointed to an odd icon flashing erratically on the planet's surface, near the base of one of the space elevators. The text below it translated to two phrases that it faded between rapidly: UNEXPLAINED FATALITIES, and DEORBITED OBJECT.

"That," Prumble said, "is something indeed."

Tania nodded. She didn't want to voice her theory, as if putting his name out there might somehow dispel the chance. Besides, she could see in Prumble's eyes that he thought the same thing she did. "There's more," she said, tracing her finger up the length of that elevator thread. This was no error or even a warning, but merely a stack of space stations along its path, perhaps a third of the way around the equator from the position of their little shuttle. On their path, in fact, a bit less than half the distance to their destination.

She pointed to one station after another along the line of the Elevator, lingering briefly on each so Prumble could digest their meaning. PRIMARY VIRAL PRODUCTION, VIRAL REALIGN, VIRAL ANALYSIS, and so on.

Sam must have seen a great change in Prumble's expression. "What the hell is it?" she asked, loud.

Tim stirred.

"I'm not exactly sure," Prumble replied, "but I think we might not want to leave just yet."

14

ABOVE CARTHAGE

"This is insane," Tim said. "Suicidal."

Samantha battled back a powerful urge to punch the young man in his stomach. If not for his armor, she might have. Words would have to suffice. "Your cowardice is really starting to piss me off."

It felt good to say it. She'd been thinking it since the first time he suggested they look for a way to leave despite having agreed with that plan. The difference in their motivations being what allowed this little bit of hypocrisy.

From the sudden wrath in his eyes, though, Tim did not care for this assessment. "I fought those creatures as hard as any of you before the *Chameleon* exploded, taking our way home and our *guide* from us. All I want to do now is survive this . . . this mess."

"Tim," Tania said, with just the right amount of soothing and authority, "this place is on our way. We may not be able to accomplish our mission, but we might at least have a chance to do some real damage. To give whoever comes after us better odds."

"She's right," Prumble said. "Our mission here is over, no one is saying it isn't. But if we can knock out their plague factory, who knows how long that would set them back."

"It might not set them back at all," Tim rasped.

"True, true. Or, it may set them back years. Decades. They may be utterly vulnerable during that time, allowing the Builders' next attempt to succeed."

"Exactly," Tania said. She was next to Tim now, her hand on his arm. "Come on, Tim. We've come so far, taken so many risks, surely this is worth the tiny bit more."

He looked at her. *Really* looked, Sam noted. Probably trying to find evidence of what he no doubt assumed: that Tania wanted to stay longer only to give Skyler a chance to join up with them. Sam was a realist, though. She could feel it in her bones that Skyler and Vanessa were gone. Mourning would have to come later. Maybe she'd find that same hangar in Darwin where she and Skyler had drunk a toast—several, actually—to their lost friend, Jake. She'd sit up there again and drink for Skyler, and Vanessa, and the fact that everyone and everything she'd known on Earth was centuries dead and gone. Part of her saw this prospect as a fresh start, a new beginning on a once-again prosperous planet. And part of her saw it as a strange sort of cheating, leaving Earth at its lowest moment only to return centuries later when everything was back on track.

Tim's gaze drifted down, stopping on Tania's arm. He reached up and lifted it away. "It's clear you've all made up your minds. So be it. But I'm staying with this craft. It's too useful to abandon." He glanced at Sam, then at Vaughn and Prumble, too. "Do what you can in there. I will wait as long as possible for you."

This last he said to Tania.

"Good enough," Vaughn proclaimed. He moved to the airlock, forcing an end to the conversation. Sam joined him a moment later. Prumble followed as well, leaving Tania with Tim in the storage area at the back of the craft. They floated side by side for the remainder of the journey, speaking to each other only occasionally. Most of the time they both just watched the display. Tania with an expression of fateful confidence, and Tim with something more like that of a counselor who's just given up on a troubled patient, and is now content to let them make a great mistake so that it can be learned from. She'd seen this before, in her own face reflected in a mirror, working at a summer camp helping troubled teens. A life that felt impossibly far away now.

She'd left those kids there, to die. Fled, in truth, for they'd become something not quite human. The fact remained. She wondered if Tim would do the same, and was surprised to find that she didn't care. Something had changed inside her with this discovery of the Scipios' own plague forge. There was a chance, after all, that Skyler's death would not be in vain. And there was a chance she could meet an end as he had, fighting the good fight, not growing old on a world she no longer recognized.

"We're here," Tania said, gripping the bulkhead and propelling herself to the center of the cabin.

The four of them clustered around the door like a team of special forces soldiers about to raid a bomb lab. The sudden shift in mood and purpose flooded Sam with that most addictive of chemicals: adrenaline. Battle-sense. She coiled herself opposite the door, ready to power through into whatever waited beyond. "I'll take point," she said, though she sensed the others already understood that. They should, by now, but it was even more important here. She was the only immune in the group, and therefore the most nimble.

Prumble positioned himself to one side of the airlock, Vaughn across from him. Tania loomed at Prumble's shoulder. Notably she'd not said goodbye or good luck to Tim, and he'd been silent, too.

The sensation of movement made her stomach flutter. The craft slowed, matching speed with the docking port of the approaching station. Sam grunted as the gravity piled on, all the way to Earth normal and beyond, then abruptly eased. A clang rolled through the ship. The hiss of air, equalizing.

"Docking complete," Tim said. "Keep in contact, please. We don't know the range of the comms."

"Will do," Prumble replied.

"Here we go," Sam said.

The airlock door irised open. Sam rushed in, both arms held in front of her.

She dove left.

Scipios were arrayed in the hallway before her, huddled behind improvised barricades. One of them wore a thing that looked like a backpack vacuum cleaner. A choking plume of white erupted from it as Sam hit the floor. The fine particulate, a much denser version of that which permeated everything here, seemed to freeze in midair, and then the particles formed strands. The crystalline structure she'd seen in Darwin, and again aboard Eve's ship. Sam rolled backward and pushed herself to her knees. She raised her arms and let loose both beams, sweeping them inward until they converged on the place she thought the sprayer stood. The sizzling beams of energy ripped through the crystal growth, leaving two angular swaths of empty air in their wake.

Something strange happened. Around the airlock door, as if pulsating out, a bubble began to form. Or rather, a spherical cavity where the crystallized virus structure shattered into powder. This invisible ball of empty air pushed toward the enemy for a meter or so before she realized what was happening. Two more beams joined hers. Vaughn, coming in, and the aura shard on his back was negating their viral cannon blasts.

Together they unleashed hell on the welcoming party. Four beams that danced, sliced, and cut through a defensive position that seemed, to Sam at least, odd in its apparent hasty arrangement. Why were they still so unorganized in their response to this incursion? Sam swept her beam up the chest of one. A vertical line of gore as its neck, then face, split into gushing halves. It fell, lifeless, behind the barricade. Three more took its place.

"They know we can't resupply," Vaughn shouted over the battle. "We're going to burn through all our ammo doing this. They're cannon fodder, literally."

Then Prumble stepped into the frame of the still-open airlock. "Let me show you how it's done," he said.

Arms raised, he let loose. Only, the protrusions above his wrists were not throwing forward their usual lines of sizzling energies. Or rather, Sam thought, they *were*, but they were turning on and off a hundred times per second.

The result was like two energy-based mini-guns. The very

air vibrated with the constant pulse. Shoot, stop, shoot, stop. The flashes of light were infinitesimal in duration, but no less effective. Any Scipio caught in their path was just as dead. Pulverized as if hit by machine-gun fire rather than the smooth slice of a heat blade, but death was death.

"Now for the fun part," Prumble said. Then he roared, like a rabid bear, shouting *"Everybody die!"* as he plowed forward. Not running, Sam realized, but propelling himself on the thrusters in his boots. Prumble lowered a shoulder and slammed into the barricade at 80 klicks an hour or more. The whole thing exploded. Chunks of shattered wall flew off in all directions, along with the cartwheeling bodies of their enemy. Prumble, at the far end of the hall now, landed in a tucked ball, rolling several times until he came to a stop. At which point he stood, turned, dusted off his suit, and started back. No thrusters this time. Just his heavy steps and enraged posture. To the Scipios, who stood barely more than a meter tall, he must look a giant. Prumble stepped up to the first one and swung one fist up and over in a high arc, then straight down onto the top of the poor alien's head. Sam winced as the thing's skull caved and the creature went down.

But Prumble wasn't done. He kept his swing going, opening his hand. He picked up the Scipio by the scruff of its neck and swung it like a bat—which, considering their batlike appearance, Sam found distantly amusing. This did little physical damage to their ranks, but the psychological effect was, it turned out, not unique to human foot soldiers.

Sam finally snapped out of her initial shock. As the Scipios began to break formation and stumbled over one another to get out of this enraged giant's murderous path, they backed up toward Sam and Vaughn. She had no idea how he'd changed the way their wrist-cannons fired, but that didn't matter. She didn't need to use hers now, their enemy's numbers thinned so and their mindset fully switched over to "Get the fuck out of here." Sam pounced, landing a flying kick into the back of the nearest Scipio. It flew forward, arms flailing, right into a well-timed punch by Prumble.

A bloodbath ensued.

Sam would feel a little guilty about it later, but in that

moment, the chance to unleash pent-up aggression made any such concerns just distant noise. She punched, kicked, clobbered, swung. She twisted necks and heaved limp corpses into the faces of a fresh second wave, breaking their resolve before they'd even had a chance to fire. The Scipios went into full retreat then, as the battle spilled out into the station proper. This station, being at the outermost end of a space elevator, meant the sensation of gravity was all from centrifugal force, the spin of Carthage throwing them ever outward. Being at the level farthest from the planet, effectively the bottom of this station, meant the Scipios could not simply glide away on their wing flaps. Nowhere to go but up.

They stumbled over one another, running to the railing, climbing it, leaping off to grab the nearest handhold. Up they went and with shocking speed, nimble as monkeys.

By the time Sam, Vaughn, and Prumble reached the rail, their prey was vanishing into the hazy darkness far above. Sam felt a sudden wave of exhaustion, like a fist of its own. She slumped against the rail and stared up at the disappearing bodies. They leapt, hands and feet nimbly grabbing the nearly invisible divots in the walls, until darkness had almost swallowed them.

She watched them go, deciding pursuit was not required. They'd gotten the message. "You ain't seen nothing yet," Sam said to the last of the vanishing bodies.

Vaughn and Prumble took it upon themselves to make a circuit of this bottommost level of the station, each moving off in a different direction and passing each other on the opposite side. Sam watched them, feeling numb. Tania joined her at the railing. The scientist gazed up into the darkness and said mildly, "I'm afraid."

Sam looked at her. "You're afraid? Why? They're the ones who just got their asses handed to them. You should be . . . okay, maybe not happy, but emboldened."

"I'm afraid," Tania repeated, "we may have just let them know what they're truly up against."

"If you're saying we should have held back, well, fuck that—"

"No," Tania said, shaking her head. "You all did, well, what you're good at. I can't fault you. I just have a feeling we've been an unknown up until this point. They might not have even truly realized we were here until this confrontation."

"Their welcoming committee were a bunch of hacks. I noticed that," Prumble said, returning from his search of the level. "This place is a ghost town now, by the way."

"A bunch of hacks," Tania repeated. "Yes. That's what I mean. But this time they were waiting, at least. They're beginning to recognize what's happened, I think. They know they have intruders in their midst. And now they know their virus 'spray' is ineffective against us."

"That may be the only weapon they're trained to use," Vaughn mused.

"Exactly," Tania said. "We have to assume that they're now considering other tactics. We know they have them. Compare this response with the efficiency and competence of the swarmers that bored into the *Chameleon* and fought us there."

"Night and day," Sam said. "Are you saying they had all their best soldiers out there, on the front lines, so to speak?" She gestured vaguely at the space beyond this station, where the distant Swarm Blockade had converged on Eve thanks to the unfortunate arrival of the ship from Earth.

"It's a theory," Tania said. "Best I've got. The point is, we know they're more capable than this, and sooner or later they'll come at us with something more"—she nodded toward Sam's wrists—"appropriate to our defenses."

"We'll be ready," Vaughn said.

Tania gave a wan smile. "Let's hope so. Honestly, I'm worried they'll just disconnect this whole station and let it, and us, drift off into space."

That gave the man pause.

"Prumble," Sam asked, "can you show us how you turned your fists into Gatling guns?"

"Is the interface not intuitive?" he asked, only half-serious.

Sam rolled her eyes and then listened closely as he ran the group through the menu options within their visor displays. He and Eve had actually included four firing modes: beam, rapid-fire, single shot, and shotgun. This last made Sam want to simultaneously hug the big man as well as punch him in the face. "Shotgun?! You didn't think to tell me about this?"

"I thought you'd just elected not to use it!"

"Goddammit, Prumble."

"Hey. A little gratitude would be appreciated."

Sam narrowed her eyes at him, then let out the grin she'd been trying to hide. "Thanks, you magnificent bastard."

"*De nada*. But listen, the shotgun firing rate is not so good. It has to cool down for a few seconds between shots."

She picked the option, anyway. Disadvantage or not, it was too tempting. She'd scored thousands of subhuman kills with her old sawed-off back on Earth. Selecting the shotgun mode now made all this somehow feel *right*. "Let's go find something to practice on."

Sam took point. She heeded Tania's sobering advice, forcing herself to take their opponent just as seriously despite what had happened back at the docking tube.

As a group, they agreed not to pursue the enemies into the dark levels farther up the station's central spine. It smelled a little too much like a trap. Instead Sam led them on a winding path around the circular access hall, staying near the railing so that she could see anything coming down at them. Prumble matched her, but at the outer wall, in case any Scipios came out of one of the many doors along its length.

"Tim, do you read?" she asked, when they'd already ascended two levels.

"It's cutting in and out, but I've been listening."

"Status down there?"

A pause. "I'm trying to figure out how to enable a radar or something like that. Their interface is, well, alien, and I suspect this map view is only going to inform me about—"

Sam let him prattle on. The gist was clear. He was bored, he was ready to leave and looking for any reason to do so. She suspected if Tania had remained behind with him, he might have spent all this time talking her into an early departure. He might even go as far as forcefully leaving, given his behavior of late. But with Tania here, she thought he'd wait. In fact, she counted on it.

Sam realized he'd stopped talking. "Sounds good. We're going silent for a bit."

"Understood. Um. Godspeed."

"Yeah, yeah."

She left her link open, setting it to receive only after instructing her companions to do the same. Their transmissions were hopefully indecipherable to the Scipios, but giving away location via their emissions was still very much possible. She wanted the element of surprise.

Four levels up and still no contacts.

That was when the power was cut.

Absolute darkness consumed them. Sam saw nothing save the red lights inside the helmets of her friends. She flipped her lamp on immediately, as did Vaughn. It took Prumble and Tania a few seconds to get over the shock of their new circumstances and do the same.

"Something's happening," Tim said, voice garbled now by distance and other interference.

"What is it?" Sam asked, enabling her transmitter.

"Incoming ships. Lots . . . them. Converg . . . level."

"Say again?"

"Converging on the planetside," he said, and then it was all static.

"They're jamming his signal," Sam said to the others. "I think. Could just be distance. Interference."

"We should get back there," Tania said, enabling her own transmitter. "He might need us."

"Negative," she replied. "He said they were converging on the planetside level. Covering the evacuation of the others, I'll bet."

Tania's face pinched in concentration. "But without a way to contact him, we won't know if he has to leave. We'd lose our way out of here."

"A risk we'll have to take," Vaughn put in. "Besides, I think we all knew coming in here that the likelihood of making it back out again was slim. We've got a chance to do something here, so let's do it. Tim's a big boy, if he needs to leave, fine."

Sam looked to Prumble. He nodded once, agreeing. Tania did, too, though not before some serious weighing of her options. A mental debate Samantha could only imagine. It was, ultimately, a decision to die. She wondered if Tania would have made that decision if here alone, or if it was enabled only by the peer pressure of those around her, but in the end, what difference did it make? She'd nodded, and that was good enough.

"Let's keep going, then," Sam said, "and see what they've got waiting for us up there."

"Direct approach?" Vaughn asked, a hint of pleading in his voice.

"Yeah," Sam said. "That sounds good to me."

Before Tania or Prumble could object, Sam jumped up onto the nearest railing and ignited the thrusters in her boots. She rocketed into the central tube of the station and powered upward at maximum speed. As she flew, she cranked the lamp built into her helmet to maximum brightness. She hoped the red hue, viewed from above, would look intimidating. A demon rising from the depths of hell, if they were bothered by that kind of thing.

Sam saw the ceiling and veered to one side, powering over the railing of the last level and turning in a fluid motion to avoid collision with the wall. She flew a circuit of the ring hallway at speed, shotgun-augmented fists held out before her.

No takers to the invitation, though. Disappointment hit her as she reached her starting position. Vaughn and Tania waited. Prumble crested the rail and joined them as Sam arrived. "Now what?" the big man asked.

"Pick a door, I guess," Sam said. She moved to one. Unsurprisingly, it did not open at her approach. Sam raised an arm, happy for the opportunity to try out her shotgun mode.

"Hold on," Tania said. "Look here."

Sam turned. The scientist had walked several meters down the hall toward another door. "What is it?" Sam asked, moving that way.

Tania gestured at the ground. "Footprints," she said.

Oldest mistake in the book, Sam thought as she studied the floor. Sure enough, the Scipios had all piled into the same chamber, and their constant dust storm of virus gunk had betrayed them mightily this time. Little markings from their oddly shaped feet were everywhere, all converging on this one place.

"Adjustments," Tania whispered.

"Huh?"

She pointed. Signage on the wall. Sam's visor translated it into the same word. ADJUSTMENTS. "Interesting. Let's see what they've—"

A yellow flash lit the level from behind, throwing Sam's shadow across the wide door that led into Adjustments. She dove to one side, rolling, and came up to a knee with one fist raised. Two more blasts joined the first, leaving three gaping holes through the walls at roughly equal positions around the circular level. One to Sam's left, one right, and the last directly ahead.

She saw the first object push through and recognized it instantly. "Swarmers," she growled. Armored deep-space vessels, each encasing a Scipio pilot. So, they'd finally caught up. Or maybe the Scipios had some here, in-system, and had finally decided the situation warranted dispatching them.

The spherical bulk wormed through the hole, clawing its way inside, spreading segmented tentacle limbs like some kind of robotic octopus. Two of its pincerlike hands gripped the railing before it and it heaved itself toward the intruders.

"Spread out!" Sam yelled, darting to her left. She let loose a blast from her reconfigured arm and winced. The energy release whited out her vision. Her arm recoiled backward as if she'd fired a .44 Magnum with a novice's stance. A shower-spray cone of white glow tore through the air and the enemy alike. The swarmer's momentum did not change, but all across its surface a series of little black punctures were left as the blast ripped through it. Eruptions of sparks and debris exited its opposite side, smashing into the floor and walls with a rhythmic pummeling noise.

The swarmer pitched forward, lifeless, skidding to a stop as its bulk slammed into the low wall that ringed the interior of the space.

Another barreled in behind it, undaunted by the carnage that befell its comrade. Sam took aim only to have her arm knocked aside by a tentacle that slapped with blinding speed. Pain lanced up her arm. Before she could recover another tentacle punched inward, striking her full in the chest and sending her flying backward. Her spine erupted in agony as she slammed into the wall behind. Her suit's armor couldn't help her when it was her own body sloshing about inside it that brought the pain. Stars exploded before her eyes. She fell to her knees, gasping. "I guess playtime's over," she muttered at the floor.

Sam glanced up. She fixed her eyes on the one who'd just knocked her backward. She had a vague awareness of Prumble, Vaughn, and Tania all embroiled in combat around her, but Sam's gaze locked on the enemy in front of her. It vaulted the low wall easily and came at her, tentacles whipping about like enraged snakes. She raised one arm and let loose a shotgun blast. Black pockmarks. Slag ejecta. Another fallen foe. Now two more took the place of the dead, one to either side. They both spread out, placing her between them.

Sam tried to fire at one only to have her suit bleat at her about cooldown requirements. Okay, fine. She used her other arm. The spit of energy tore at the very air and eviscerated the encased foe. But that left its friend on the opposite side. Sam whirled. Mortar? No, the damn thing was right on top of her. She powered her boots to lift her away, over the enemy she'd just slain. Behind, it was only smoke and chaos, but she wasn't looking, anyway. She moved backward, keeping her eyes on the nearest foe.

The swarmer climbed atop its fallen comrade and coiled, preparing to pounce. Sam's suit pinged: cooldown complete. She lifted her right arm and let a blinding storm of energy out. But the alien had adapted. It jumped sideways, digging clawed mechanical hands into the wall and heaving itself closer, going higher, leaping away finally to come in at a downward arc toward Sam's head. She grimaced, raising an arm in useless defense.

A beam caught the thing in mid-flight. Melting a hole right through the center of it and continuing to slice until only burning remains landed in little splats and clangs around Sam's feet.

She glanced in the direction of the beam and saw Tania perched on the railing, smoke trailing from the weapon on one wrist. "Down!" the woman said.

Sam needed no more prompting than that. She flattened herself to the floor as Tania unleashed another beam past the space where Sam's head had just been. Sam turned to see the target, and was surprised to find Tania cutting a hole in the center of a door. "In!" the woman shouted as a human-sized

159

opening fell away. "Prumble, Vaughn, here!"

Sam gathered her wits and rushed into the opening. Into darkness. She swept the twin cones of her headlamp across a room of indecipherable machinery. No enemies, that was all that mattered. Sam positioned herself behind the opening Tania had made and provided two blasts of covering fire as her three companions found their way to the temporary stronghold. "Anyone see what the signage read?" Prumble asked, the last to join them.

"'Imprint,'" Tania replied. At Prumble's confused reaction, she shrugged. "Beats me, we just needed to get out of that death trap."

"Not arguing!" Prumble shot back, clapping her on the shoulder as he ducked inside and turned to join in their barrage aimed at the few visible Swarm ships. Smoke and licking flames had dropped visibility to nearly nothing out there.

Sam left them to it and examined the room called Imprint.

It looked to her like a factory upon entering, but on closer inspection a sense of medical purpose wormed its way into her perception.

All the pipes and machinery in the vast chamber seemed to converge at one point, about twenty meters away. There, a semicircular array of six small pillars faced inward on a pristine white platform.

"Tania," Sam said, without looking. "Tania?"

"What is it?"

"What do you make of this?"

"Take my place here," Tania replied, "and I'll check."

Fair enough, Sam thought. She turned back and swapped spots with Tania at the improvised door. The space behind was too hazy to see much of anything now, and both Vaughn and Prumble were holding fire as Sam took up her spot with them. The trio kept their arms raised, aimed into the swirling smoke lit orange with dying fires from smoldering corpses. "What a mess," Sam observed. Her back still rang with jolts of pain, and her whole body felt like one giant bruise. *Still, could be worse,* she thought. That tentacle strike to her chest would have punched right through her under normal circumstances, or crushed her rib cage if she'd had on lesser armor, like a Kevlar vest.

"It's quiet," Prumble said.

Sam winced. "Vaughn, don't—"

"Too quiet," Vaughn said with all the swagger in the universe.

"Dammit, Vaughn. And damn you, too, Prumble." Sam shook her head. Vaughn chuckled, and soon Prumble took up the laughter.

Samantha glanced back at Tania.

The woman was standing before the little array of pedestals or broken pillars, whatever they were. A screen had come to life beside one of them, and Tania seemed to be reading it as if it were the daily gossip. "What is it?" Sam asked her.

Tania said nothing. Instead, incredibly, she began to strip out of her armor.

"What the hell?" Sam rushed toward her. She shot a glance back at the two men. "Guard the door."

They both nodded, as confused as she was.

She crossed the space as quickly as she could without burning more thruster fuel, watching as Tania slowly extracted one arm from her suit.

"What are you doing?" Sam asked her.

But disrobing was not the woman's goal. It was only her hand she'd meant to free. And once done, Tania reached out and placed her palm and fingers on top of one of the little half-pillars. "It's just like in Africa," the woman said, so distant she might as well have been there instead of here.

"What is?" Sam asked.

Red light flickered around Tania's hand as her skin met the dull gray surface. There was a rumble from below their feet as machinery in the room came to life.

Tania winced in sudden agonizing pain. Sam went to grab her and heave her away, but Tania's cry stayed her hands. "Leave me!" the scientist shouted.

"What the fuck are you doing?"

"An imprint."

"Meaning what?"

Tania, eyes nearly shut in her throes of agony, nodded toward the small screen she'd been reading. "This machine determines what species are granted immunities to the virus. Quick, get Prumble and Vaughn over here."

"Why?"

"Sample size," Tania replied. "We're going to level the playing field."

Sam met the two men at the door and needed to say nothing. They'd heard the conversation, and as soon as she was in position they both rushed off to join Tania. Sam had to force herself to keep watch on the smoky room outside as the trio each placed hands on the sampling devices.

Shadows in the murk. Sam squinted, then raised both fists. "Whatever you guys are doing, time's about up, I think."

"Fifteen seconds," Tania replied.

"That's a wild-ass guess," Prumble added.

Sam clenched her teeth and squared herself as six large swarmers emerged through the smoke. They were twice the size of the others, easily. Standing one beside the other they formed a wall of armor plating and coiled tentacles, sensor pods and stubby—*sensor pods*.

She'd forgotten all about the little cluster of lenses and antennae poking out from between two tentacle joints, roughly where a face would be on a living thing. Somewhere inside, no doubt, the little batlike bastards were watching her, calculating, planning their approach.

Mentally Sam fumbled through her suit's interface. She left her beam weapons on shotgun mode. It was the mortar she was interested in. Working as fast as she could, Sam modified the parameters of the launcher weapon and then fired up the targeting interface. She'd used this once, on the planet where they'd found the skin for the yet-to-be-named *Chameleon*.

Sam stepped through the hole in the door.

The six Scipios surged forward at the sight of her out in the open.

She took a knee and gave the instruction to fire.

Her back erupted in fresh pain as the launcher pressed downward in six hard, rapid-succession punches. The projectiles flicked out through the air on jets of superheated exhaust, their flights lasting only a second. The first three struck home. Direct hits, straight into the sensor pods of their victims where they exploded with only minimal force. The fourth projectile was knocked aside by a lucky swing of a tentacle arm. Five and six hit home, their sensors cracking in a cloud of fire and mechanical chunks.

Sam had known the full destructive power of the missiles would have taken out the entire station. This less ruinous option, though, was enough to leave gaping wounds on the hulls of the enemies she'd hit. Blinded, they flailed about recklessly. The one she'd missed was knocked aside by its own companion, struck full across the center of its mass by a tentacle. The limb broke in half at the point of impact and the smaller chunk came cartwheeling away. It flew right at Sam like a boomerang.

She twisted and ducked, too late. The spinning tentacle struck her across her turned shoulder and upper right arm. Her armor tensed a spilt second before impact, suddenly hard as cement and then relaxing just as quickly, but the force of the hit sent her spinning herself, flipping around and slamming into a wall. The air rushed from her lungs. Her shoulder buzzed as her nerves there overloaded, all shouting their concern at once. And then the pain came like a tsunami.

Sam grasped at her arm as she staggered to her feet, unable to tell which way was which. She gulped in air and gagged on it, and wanted nothing more in that moment than to rip the helmet from her head and breathe the real thing. To be away from this wretched place.

"Three seconds!" Tania shouted. "Twooooo . . ." Her voice took on an odd elongated tone, trailing into silence.

"Now would be good!" Sam barked at her companions. She chanced a quick look back. The three of them were still standing exactly where they'd been, only now a semiopaque dome of purple enveloped them. "Oh shit."

Sam hobbled back from the door, firing off a few more shotgun blasts from her wrists just to keep the enemy from getting any ideas. The pain in her shoulder and arm still flared, but thankfully now at a level she could mostly ignore. She turned and raced toward her friends, mind reeling. They'd been trapped, one of those freakish time-desync bubbles or whatever Eve had called them. From here they seemed frozen in place, which meant for those inside the sphere time had been slowed. They probably hadn't even realized anything was wrong yet, and it could be minutes or hours—hell, years—before they turned and managed to move outside the sphere of influence. The perfect trap.

Sam's thoughts caught up with her actions a split second before she barreled right into the pearlescent dome. She skidded to a stop just centimeters from entering it herself. She'd be trapped right along with them.

Instead she pivoted and turned to face the door. Smoke curled in through the ragged frame they'd carved. Beyond, there were hints of movement in the choking haze. Scipios, gathering, scheming. Sam took a quick glance around, looking for anything that might help. *That dome,* she thought. *There must be a way to turn it off.* But she could see nothing. No power cables snaking toward it. No obvious beam projecting it or anything of that sort. It was just there, covering the platform.

The platform.

Sam circled to one side of it. As she moved she switched her wrist-cannon back to beam mode, and let off a scintillating blast through the hole in the door. On a whim she fired another mortar in there, this one set to medium-yield with no target. It zipped through the door, pushing a column of smoke out of its way as it crossed the threshold into the space beyond. There was a crushing *whomp* that almost lifted Sam off her feet. The explosion ripped the rest of the original door away, leaving a massive opening now.

"Oops," she said, but there was nothing to be done about it. Sam circled the platform. There, behind it, a groove in the floor. She blasted it away with her beam weapon, opening a hole to some kind of crawl space below. Bundles of cables and pipes of unknown purpose all converged on the center of the platform where her friends were trapped. Samantha paused, staring at the mess. Slice one? Slice all? What if that caused the whole place to explode?

She had to assume a civilization capable of building a facility as advanced as this would factor into their design the possibility of some cables getting severed, but then the Scipios seemed oddly inept in some areas. "Ah, fuck it." Sam raised her arm and gave the thought command to fire her beam.

". . . Ooooooone!"

Tania's voice. Sam killed the weapon in the same instant it

came on, dealing only minor damage to the edge of the first pipe. She looked to the platform and saw her three friends just as they'd been, evidently no worse for wear. The purple dome had gone.

"Everyone okay?" she asked.

Vaughn just about leapt from his boots.

Prumble answered her question with his own. "How'd you get over there?"

"No time to explain. Tania, did it work?"

"I don't know," she replied, studying the lone screen again. "Their method of graphing results—"

Sam annihilated the screen with a quick snap-fire of her beam weapon. "We're done here," she said. "Time to go. Now."

"Why?" Prumble asked.

"Because of that thing." Sam nodded toward the now wide-open door to the chamber. It was filled, corner to corner, ten meters across, by the hulking form of a single, giant swarmer. The largest Sam had yet seen. Its surfaces were all shiny, as if dipped in chrome.

The behemoth's tentacles curled in around the gaping hole in the wall where the door had once been.

Behind it, three more loomed.

Prumble's shoulders dropped, more out of annoyance than any concern. He casually lifted one arm and unleashed a torrent of rapid energy bursts that flicked and blazed in Sam's vision like the flare of a welding torch.

The energy ricocheted off his target, as if it had struck a mirror. Little parcels of roiling heat spraying outward like a firework from hell. Sam just managed to duck as one streaked past her head, disappearing into the complex machinery behind her.

"Mortars!" Vaughn shouted. He took a knee to incline his back and launched a round at the same enemy, which had advanced several meters into the room. *Too close,* Sam thought.

Vaughn was a smart son of a bitch, though. He'd lowered the yield, just enough. The round hit the thing dead center and its entire bulk rocked backward. For a moment, smoke and shrapnel obscured the result. Sam waited, teeth clenched.

The beast pushed through the haze, undamaged. Undaunted.

"Uh," Prumble said as the four humans backed up, "ideas, anyone?"

For a second no one said anything, and in that brief silence Samantha felt the first pang of fear begin to crack her battle-lust. Then Tania spoke. "The legs," she said. "These things are built for zero-g."

The swarmers had six tentacles, three mounted on the top hemisphere with one in front and the other two behind. The others were on the lower half, arranged in the opposite fashion. Optimized to give it stability no matter what surface it needed to cling to.

These bastards, though, theirs were polished to a mirror finish, just like their bodies. Sam tried a mortar, the idea hitting her at the same instant Vaughn reached it. Without planning, they both fired half-yield rounds at two different legs, each striking their targets a split second apart.

Two explosions shook the room. Debris sprayed against Sam's visor, the smoke now so thick she could see only a few meters. Then came a great crash that shook the floor. Sam was knocked off her feet, but she'd been ready for it, turning the fall into a backward roll that left her pressed against the machinery that made up the bulk of the chamber. The pain in her shoulder flared, and she held it back with clenched teeth and a powerful will not to die here.

Sam rocked back onto her feet and scanned the area before her. Vaughn and Tania had closed ranks with her. Prumble was somewhere near, but she could not see him.

A vibration came up through the floor, like an earthquake. Sam ignored it.

Ventilation finally cleared the view enough for them to see their attack had worked. The massive swarmer lay on the floor, rolling, trying to find a way to get up. That would be only a matter of time, Sam knew. It had a healthy set of tentacles on top to stand on, once it figured out how. But there were more enemies behind the fallen one, and they were as yet undamaged. With a meaty swing, one of them swept their wounded comrade aside as if it were trash.

"Up here!" Prumble shouted.

Sam scanned the area around them, but saw nothing. Of course, he'd said "up," and she'd failed to process that. She looked up and saw him. He'd found some kind of Scipio-style handhold ladder leading up to a raised walkway that snaked off into the tangle of pipes and machinery. A crack ran across his visor, Sam realized, and she wondered when that had happened. She wondered if it would affect his displays. Something to figure out later.

The vibration in the floor had grown, and kept growing. Something coming? The station moving? She felt no change in gravity, though.

Sam motioned for Vaughn and Tania to join Prumble. She turned to follow, ready to defend their backs if the Swarm monstrosities gave chase, when something truly bizarre happened.

It took her some time to process it afterward.

One second she was running, Tania right in front of her, the handholds looming just a meter away. Vaughn was there, reaching for the first.

Then the floor shook like a struck drum before going utterly still. A purple sheen flashed around her vision. Tania and Vaughn looked normal, but everything beyond them became almost completely obscured and blurry, tinted pearlescent purple.

She had time to think only two words: *Oh fuck.*

And then it was gone. The purple bubble. The machinery. The walls.

Sam was falling, her view only that of Tania and Vaughn against a backdrop of stars, their limbs suddenly flailing for purchase as hers were. Sam felt a pressure against her back. Air, smoke, fragments of machinery all flowing past her and outward.

A flash of motion caught her eye. Prumble, in space, using the thrusters in his boots to keep from falling away. Arms held -out, flashing with their mini-gun chatter of blazing energy at targets unknown. Somehow Sam managed to spin around and look behind them.

Her mind caught up with reality.

It was a brilliant tactic, of course. Trap your enemies inside a weird-ass time sphere and figure out how to deal with them at your leisure. A heartbeat for them, hours for you. Sam had no idea what was required to set up one of those purple domes, but they clearly were not easy to make.

Only problem was, they hadn't quite caught everybody.

Prumble, you sneaky bastard.

Behind her she saw the wreckage of the room they'd been in. While Sam and her team had been pinned down at the back of that platform, fighting for their lives, the Scipios had moved the device beneath them, under the floor. Only they'd been too late. Prumble had already moved away, outside the literal sphere of influence.

And from the wreckage, he looked none too pleased at seeing his friends caught like statues in a museum. Even now he continued to fire. Not at the enemies, but at the machinery. A rapid continuous drumbeat of destruction. Flickering explosions roiled through the exposed pipes and conduits. He had, evidently, carved a massive hole through the outer wall. Whether on purpose or not, he'd caused everything not bolted down to be sucked out into space. Then he'd gone to town on the device generating the time bubble, destroying it as he floated out with the rest of the ejecta. It had all happened in the blink of an eye for Sam.

"Sorry it took me so long," Prumble said, voice crackling in her ears.

Sam remembered his damaged visor then. "Prumble, your helmet!"

"I'm okay," he said. "It's holding. You guys all right?"

"Yeah," Sam replied. Vaughn and Tania echoed her response.

"Then maybe you could start shooting?" He was falling with them now. Away from the planet along the length of the long, tall station. Somewhere below, docked at its outer edge, Tim would be waiting. Should be.

As the four of them fell toward that point, they raked their weapons across the length of the Scipio space station. Prumble spraying it with his rhythmic, now-silent thrum. Sam and Tania still in beam mode, tracing molten lines across the metallic surfaces. Vaughn took a different approach. He used his mortars only, aiming them at windows. All above them the station cracked apart like an egg. Secondary explosions began to rock its very core. Sam suddenly feared the whole thing would go up in a giant nuclear inferno before they were clear.

But that's why we came here, isn't it? Go out with a bang?

"Tim," Tania said. "Can you hear us?"

"I read you," he replied instantly, though he sounded like he was whispering, or talking through clenched teeth.

"Undock and move clear if you can. Things are, um, heating up."

"Would if I could," his response came. "But I'm afraid I've been captured."

15

CARTHAGE

He watched from the rooftops for several hours, telling himself he'd move as soon as the horizon showed any hint of an approaching dawn. His goal, at least the one he sold himself on, was to learn the schedule of their climbers, and perhaps catch a glimpse of how they were loaded. Security precautions, inspections, anything like that.

In truth, though, Skyler needed to understand. How these beings went about their business, how the machinery of their society worked. Did they get breaks? Did they go somewhere to sleep? Anything he could learn that might help him feel a bit less out of place, he'd take. But then, of course, one could learn only so much skulking about in the shadows above a city. This was no comic book, and he did not have superhuman senses. If his visor hadn't cracked, maybe, but not now.

Moving from roof to roof, he slowly worked his way toward the building dubbed the Transfer Facility. Little made sense here, but a place to transfer cargo on and off climbers? That he knew. *That* Eve's delivery of space elevators to Earth had prepared them for.

So he climbed, scaled, and walked, avoiding the use of his thruster boots in case their heat or noise would give his position away.

Nagging at his mind was another odd fact. They still did not seem to be looking for him. Granted, there may be a whole team of forensic investigators in the tunnels below even now, picking through the wreckage and studying burn marks to determine what had happened at the guarded barricade. Same went for the ruins across the bay, where more Scipios had surely died. Part of him wanted them to declare a state of emergency. To fill their streets with foot patrols and broadcast announcements about a possible saboteur. Something. And it wasn't because Skyler craved recognition, oh no. He wanted something he could understand. An enemy who reacted was an enemy who could be predicted. But this . . . this total obliviousness, it made no sense.

He thought back to his first encounters with subhumans on Earth. Years of campy zombie sensories and films had prepared humanity for a similar event. But in all those, at least the few Skyler had seen (not really his cup of tea), the monsters had been predictable if nothing else. They'd shamble, they'd want to consume the brain, they were relentless about it. That was simple. Subhumans, though, had not quite meshed with this ingrained cultural expectation. He wondered, back then and again now, how many people had died because they'd expected something else. He'd come close, that much he knew. He hadn't been prepared for the ones that weren't full of murderous intent, but instead wanted to flee and hide, or laugh for all eternity, or *play,* as one had so terribly asked of him in Nightcliff.

So he fought the urge to map the behavior of Scipios onto what his expectations were. The need to anthropomorphize was deeply seated in the human psyche. It took a force of will to overcome. A constant vigilance. Not so hard when sneaking about, alone and in no immediate danger. Much harder when in the heat of combat.

In those hours he learned a few things, the most important being that all of the climbers he'd seen were coming down. Not a single one had returned back to space. Granted, it hadn't been long enough to get a complete picture, but as much as he tried to view things through this lens of no expectations, he couldn't get over the fact that they weren't alternating between directions. A space elevator was in many ways identical to a single-track rail line, with the space stations along the length serving as sidings where the climbers could be moved to let others by. But here, at the terminus, it didn't make any sense to only receive, to never send out. Traffic would back up, surely. And he'd seen a lot of it. At least twenty climbers had lowered themselves into the city since he'd arrived. Busy times, evidently. Or maybe they just ran them no matter what the passenger count was.

Yet nothing went up.

The only explanation he could come up with was that they were worried he'd be aboard. Hard to escape the planet if there was no way off. Yet this did not mesh with the near-total lack of pursuit they'd sent after him so far. That fact, viewed on its own, implied they were waiting for him to make his escape attempt. Indeed, counting on it, with ample forces waiting to grab him when he reached the departure facility. So why not run the climbers up and let him think there was a reason to head there?

He kept watching, hoping to spot some clue that would unravel this. Or, barring that, at least spot a way to get a climber to head off-world. If he was successful in that it would lead to its own problems, most notably that they'd then just be waiting for him above, but one thing at a time. Get off the planet, get far away from the planet. That was the plan.

Another thing bothered him. Transfer Facility was directly adjacent to the structure that received climber cars descending the cord. In his mind, he dubbed the place Centraal Station, after the bustling rail hub in Amsterdam, a place he'd spent way too much time in his youth doing what poor kids do: loitering.

Fitting that he loitered now. Skyler grinned to himself at the irony as he sat, back against a wall, and watched the climbers come down. They were oddly small compared to the ones humans had built, but then the Scipios were diminutive. Their climbers were a mix of very sleek, lozenge-shaped things that looked quite weathered, and others that were utterly functional in design. Ugly, angular, studded with vents and pipes and other machinery, all built atop a wide, flat circular platform. Instinct had him labeling these as passenger versus cargo, respectively, but he forced himself to set aside that assumption and really think about it. In the end he reached a different conclusion. The sleek ones had been built by the original inhabitants of this place, the Creators and their Builder AIs. The ugly ones were Scipio-made. What either carried probably had nothing to do with how they looked.

Probably.

Skyler sighed. The moment was quickly approaching when he'd need to go see for himself. And if they weren't going to send anything up to orbit he'd have to figure out a way to turn them around himself.

He tried to envision himself an alien in Darwin, crash-landed and ignorant of all things human, whose only goal was to leave. What would he have done? He'd seen the control room in Nightcliff where climbers were received and dispatched, where entire teams of very smart people planned and managed the traffic, manipulating computer programs for special cases, letting algorithms handle the day to day. Comprehending that system well enough to change it seemed ludicrous, even as an average human. It would have been impossible for an alien, no matter if they had a translation tool.

No, in that scenario he would not have tried to decipher the climber control systems. He would have pointed a gun at someone who did, and forced them to help.

And that, he thought, *is the only way to do it here, too.*

He certainly couldn't just *ask,* amusing though the idea might be.

Skyler allowed himself a few swallows of water, and some of the bland nutrition paste Eve had provided. He tried not to think about how long it would last, or what stretching that time would do to his health and energy. His body ached in a dozen places, but no worse than a friendly spar against Sam might have left him.

A strange whisper fell over the entire city. Skyler felt it as one feels the air change before a storm hits, and the Scipios sensed it, too. He leaned and looked down, expecting to see a gas leak or some kind of quiet electric vehicle powering through the wide plaza below. But the sound did not come from below, he realized.

173

It came from above.

Skyler glanced up, his gaze immediately drawn to the line the space elevator traced up into the dark sky. Nothing out of the ordinary there. A few climbers working their way down.

Perhaps it was a storm. The sky had gone opaque, an even cloud covering made all the more ominous by the lack of ground lighting to give it texture and shape.

A change did register then. The virus-fall, which had become like dust or powdery snowfall to him after being in it all these hours. It was coming down much faster now. Falling straight, as if weighted. He held his armor-gloved hand out and watched it accumulate there. Little white clumps, not quite dust and not quite snowflakes, but something in between.

Before, they'd swirled and danced in the air almost as if alive. They may well be alive, of course. But lots of things on that scale were alive yet showed no outward movement other than the utterly random. The Scipio virus, though, had so far seemed to him to move like microscopic fish, the air their ocean. If he tried to focus on the falling powder before, he would see swarming patterns, schooling almost. Shifts that were not from a sudden gust of wind, but rather some signal that pulsed through the "crowd," causing the little microscopic machines to alter their position.

This behavior had now changed. They were falling as if they'd decided in their trillions to just *stop*.

In seconds the rooftop around him had gone a dirty white. It was on his arms and legs, and starting to obscure his already broken visor.

What did it mean? Skyler came to his feet and tried to shake the powder off. He felt as if he were a tiny creature under the sudden deluge of powdered sugar from a baker's sifter. It just kept coming and coming. A centimeter deep now, and growing by the second. Maybe they intended to just bury him and sort it all out later.

No, he thought, it couldn't be that, but perhaps the point was to force him indoors. Usually the opposite would be the goal. You didn't flush your prey *into* hiding, after all. Unless . . . Skyler licked his parched lips as he scanned the sky above. An impossible task, the air was positively full of falling virus cells now. He could barely see the end of his arm. Thick as a Rotterdam fog, only falling. The size of the clumps grew larger and larger. That made sense. The stuff higher up had had more time to gather on the way down. He wondered how big the chunks would be when the "storm" peaked.

An eerie thought bored into his mind. The bigger, faster-falling chunks would catch up to those below. This might all end in one big sudden crescendo. Maybe the goal wasn't to bury him but to crush him.

Skyler made up his mind. He turned to the wall behind himself and carved a hole in it with his plasma beam. He stepped inside and flipped on his headlamp. He doubted anyone could see either light show with the air so choked, and any concern he had about the virus itself being some kind of surveillance tool was gone now, too.

It was like it had all just died.

This thought, too, gave him pause. He crept into the room he'd made a door into and swept his beam around. Empty. Some kind of living quarters, it seemed. Spacious, with elegant curved surfaces and simple, clean lines. He pushed as far in as he could go and turned, watching the powdered virus pile itself around the gap he'd carved in the wall. Within a minute it had piled high enough to start spilling into the room.

Like it had all just died, he repeated in his mind, and his thoughts returned to the plague forge. That bizarre pyramid-like factory he and Tania had found in Africa, the source for the virus that had, invisibly in Earth's case, permeated the world and left everywhere but Darwin unsafe for humans. Most humans, anyway.

He and Tania had done something there. Deactivated the machinery that churned out the virus cells day and night, replenishing their numbers. Could this be the same thing? The others were out there, somewhere. Tim had proved that much. Perhaps they'd spotted this world's plague forge. Bombed it from orbit, or just rammed into it. Found the proverbial kill switch.

This train of thought reeked of wishful thinking, though. Skyler wanted to slap some sense into himself for allowing it.

No, his friends were far off. This was something else. A tactic, one he just couldn't yet see the purpose behind.

And no matter. "I'm immune to your shit, or haven't you figured that out yet?" he asked of the growing pile of off-white grit spilling into the room.

With this came a new fear. One that he'd buried deep, refused to believe possible. Skyler swallowed as he watched the powdery stuff begin to push across the floor, a growing mountain like sand poured into a loose and circular pile. Perhaps they'd figured him out. Studied a scrap of DNA he'd left somewhere, or worse, captured Samantha or Alex and analyzed them. Maybe this was a deliberate extinction, making way for version two.

Viruses were life-forms, after all.

They evolved.

16

MAGO

They moved swiftly on the base. Vanessa again took point position at Gloria's behest. She had alien armor, weapons, had spent years fighting subhumans, and—potentially the most important thing of all—she had the immunity. No one argued the choice.

As before, Xavi followed close behind, then Alex Warthen in the middle, in front of Gloria. Alex insisted he would help them, fight if it came to that, but Gloria still had not decided if she could trust him. Besides, he was unarmed, just like Gloria and Beth, who brought up the rear. The three of them were a liability until they could arm themselves, and that seemed unlikely to happen anytime soon.

Unless . . .

Gloria tried to keep the thought from her head, but it was too tempting. If Dawson was here, alive, then her gear might be, too. Hell, the whole ship. The question was, what state were they in? She imagined dissection, both biological and mechanical, and shuddered. They needed to hurry. Every second may matter now.

Vanessa took a serpentine path. Direct, but opportunistic in its use of shadows for cover. The outer wall of the facility came into view, just beyond a rock-strewn rise of blue-gray. Sunlight bleached the landscape at a forty-five-degree angle, blinding where it fell, making the sky a ceiling of total darkness. Gloria felt glad for that. The night sky always drew her gaze. Always. Her very first memory was of trying to capture the moon in her tiny hand, frustrated that she could not, her mother laughing and soothing at the same time. Now was not the time for such distractions.

At the crest of the last rise Vanessa angled toward a small depression and waited there for everyone to catch up. Gloria pulled up next to her and scanned the view.

The wall was no defensive barrier, of course. Nothing to defend against on this rock, at least not until this moment. But the facility was one large complex of interconnected buildings, and so presented a continuous exterior surface that jutted out in various places. From above she thought it probably resembled an overly complicated puzzle piece. Lights dotted the roof, reds and yellows mostly, indicating who knows what. They painted the areas currently lost in deep shadow due to a large mountain on the opposite side of the base.

Gloria spotted several spherical structures in the middle distance, perhaps chemical tanks, perhaps reactors of some kind. She knew from history classes that humanity used to build them aboveground like that, too, something they'd grown out of ages ago. Maybe these Scipios weren't quite so advanced as they seemed. She grinned at that thought, then quickly set the feeling aside. Vanessa was on the move again. She'd stopped only long enough to pick a point of entry and, now evidently having selected one, was off. Xavi followed, then Alex, then Gloria. She felt Beth's presence behind her, pleased that the engineer was keeping pace.

Nearer the wall Gloria eased off her pace, putting a hand on Alex's shoulder to keep him with her. She wanted Vanessa and Xavi to gain some distance, and Alex Warthen, a career security officer, understood and made no complaint. They allowed a gap of twenty meters to open.

Of Dawson's errant radio communication, they'd heard

nothing more. The distant anguished sobs had ended a minute after they'd started, and not returned.

Vanessa reached the wall without incident. No alarms, no sudden appearance of defensive turrets. Now came the tricky part. Well, the *first* tricky part. Breaching the outer wall of a building on an airless moon meant exposing the inside to vacuum. Not something to be done lightly, especially when there may be people inside you wanted to remain breathing. Had there been an obvious airlock to enter through, that might have been better, but Vanessa and Xavi both discarded that option right from the beginning. Those, undoubtedly, would be watched. And they'd be too easy to become trapped inside.

Gloria bounded across the last twenty meters, watching as Vanessa teased a hole in the wall with her wrist-mounted beam weapon. A gout of moist air plumed from the hole. It kept coming for several seconds, then diminished, then vanished altogether. This implied much. Rather than some field or self-repairing wall, the Scipios' base used emergency bulkhead doors to seal a breach. Easier to enter, then, but also her team must now work on the assumption that a repair crew would be dispatched immediately.

Vanessa stepped back and carved a two-meter-high oval in the wall, stepping aside to let it fall away into the gritty "soil" of the moon's surface. Then she was in, going right. Xavi followed, pistol raised, heading left.

Pushing Alex ahead, Gloria and her group followed. They would remain close to the advance team, following Xavi if the lead pair decided to split up. That was what everyone had agreed to, back on the crater rim. That had been the extent of the plan. Anything more wouldn't survive contact with the enemy, as Vanessa had put it.

Gloria escorted Alex into the hallway. Beth came in a second later. They paused to let their eyes adjust.

Dim red lights illuminated the space. The floor was a thick metal grating with pipes and other infrastructure visible below. The walls were simple and dark, adorned only with two stripes that ran the length at chest level. Gloria had to stoop slightly to fit. She'd never seen an actual Scipio, but from the dimensions of this place they probably stood a bit more than a meter tall.

Sure enough, emergency bulkhead doors had closed and sealed the punctured hallway, each perhaps five meters away in both directions. Xavi stood near one, ready if anyone came through. Vanessa had moved toward the other bulkhead, but she stopped short. On the interior wall there was a door leading to a connecting room or hallway, and the immune now crouched before it, attempting to decipher the control mechanism. Gloria moved to her side and eased her away. She pointed at the emergency bulkhead and tried to mimic holding a rifle. The other woman understood and moved into a defensive position.

Gloria studied the door. Beth joined her, and after a few seconds they managed to work out the control. A little lever embedded in a C-shaped groove in the frame, that slid around in the half-circle. Twelve o'clock for closed, six for open. So she guessed, at least. She moved it, had to use her pinky for the groove was small. Nothing happened. Perhaps refusing until atmospheric integrity returned. Perhaps it just didn't recognize her, or she'd misinterpreted the function of the lever.

Then the door opened.

She found herself staring into a square room, housing what looked like tables and chairs. One chair still spun about, another had been knocked over. A hasty evacuation? With a hull breach just meters away, it made sense. There was another exit on the opposite side. Gloria ushered her friends in and shut the door behind them. Within seconds a thin hissing could be heard as air was fed back into the chamber. Other sounds bled back in, too. Something like an alarm—high-pitched E followed by a low *doop*, repeating every few seconds. The sound echoed, giving the impression that it was bleating site-wide.

Gloria moved aside as Vanessa and Xavi rushed to the opposite door, ready for anything. Just in case, she took a knee behind one of the tables and waited. Beth and Alex followed her example. Since air had filled the room, Gloria decided a small gamble was prudent. She switched on her suit's external speaker, then instructed the others to do the same. "Just keep the chatter to a minimum, right?" They all nodded. "Vanessa, Xavi, check the next room and make sure we're not going to get ambushed in here."

A light above the door went green. Vanessa, copying what Gloria had done, opened this inner door. It reacted instantly, and so did Vanessa, pushing into the space beyond as soon as there was room to do so. Xavi followed her, again covering the left to mirror her focus on the right. They moved like they'd worked together for years, Gloria thought with more than a little pride in how her navigator was handling himself.

Beth moved past her, but not to the door. Her focus was firmly on the table nearby. Dismissed as being empty, she realized now that was wrong. Or rather, it was empty because it wasn't a table. It was a display, and on it information and graphics begged to be noticed. Gloria allowed herself to rise from her hiding place and stand across from Beth, looking down.

Terror and dread flooded into her at the sights displayed there. X-rays. A rib cage. A skull. Human.

Close-up imagery of limbs and organs. One showed an entire intestine splayed out, with several Scipios hunched over the gore.

Gloria's stomach heaved. "Xavi," she managed to say.

He must have heard the strain in her voice, the fear, because he came back in almost immediately, pistol raised, ready for anything. He saw the look on her face and came to her directly. "What is it?"

The question needed no answer. He followed her gaze and tensed up. "Oh. God."

"Some of them may still be alive," a voice said. It took Gloria a moment to realize it was Alex Warthen. "If we hurry."

If *we* hurry. Somehow the tone and delivery of that single word told Gloria everything she needed to know about Alex Warthen. Whatever his ultimate motivations or goals, he was with her. He would help. She realized she was nodding at him and stopped, turned to Xavi. "This place is huge. We need to split up."

"We talked about this. Bad idea."

"That was before we saw what they're doing in here, Xavi. I don't care about our safety now, and you know what? Fuck radio silence. If they figure out how to break the encryption on our signals then so be it, because then they'll have to figure out our language."

"It's triangulation I'm worried about, boss."

Vanessa poked her head back in the room. "What's the holdup?" she asked.

Gloria pointed at the display table, ignoring the gasp that came a second later. Her eyes never left Xavi's. "I've made up my mind. Beth? Go with Vanessa. You too, Alex. I'm with Xavi. Remember we have two goals: Get our people out of here, or barring that, make sure there is nothing left of us, them, or their ship big enough to study without an electron microscope. That clear?"

Alex moved without a word. Beth, however, lingered a moment, no doubt trapped between the fear of being separated and the desire to spend more time with the two historical figures they'd become allied with. Soon enough curiosity won, and the young engineer relented. She moved to Vanessa's side.

Gloria looked at each of them in turn. "We meet back here, go out the way we came in unless a better option presents itself. Our comms are different, so Beth, your job is to act as relay between Vanessa and us."

"I can do that," the woman said.

"I know you can. I'm counting on you." She gave Xavi one last, hard look, pushing the doubt from his expression by sheer force of will. After a second he jerked his chin toward the door and was off.

By unspoken agreement he went left in the next hall, leaving the other direction for Vanessa and her team. Gloria ran along behind him, no easy task in the weak gravity and low-ceilinged hall, but soon enough she found the right stride and posture and was managing to keep up. She and her navigator fell into a rhythm. He would stop at a door, put his back to the opposite side of the hall, and wait for her to trigger the lever. As it opened he would push inside and clear the room, as if he'd trained for this kind of thing all his life. Probably learned how to do it from all those police sensories he lost himself in.

Three times they repeated this without finding anything. No humans, no remains, not even a Scipio to fight or interrogate. Just empty rooms of vague purpose, all with signs of hasty abandonment. All the while the warning lights flashed and their odd erratic version of a Klaxon wailed.

She was approaching the fourth door when white powder

began to flood through air vents in the hallway ceiling. It was as if someone had turned on a fan covered with baking powder.

"Virus," Xavi grunted, stepping back. Only there was nowhere to go. The hall behind them was no less inundated. In seconds her visor had a dusting that obscured her view. Gloria wiped at it, but the arm of her suit was no better off, making the problem only marginally better.

"Suit integrity?" she asked.

"Holding. Beth, are you guys okay?"

The reply came a second later. "Powder all over the place here, too, but we're managing."

He didn't bother to ask if they'd found anything. She'd have said if they had.

Visibility fell to a few meters. Gloria decided this wasn't such a bad thing, assuming the Scipios didn't have some way to peer through the fog. For her, unarmed, it meant no one could shoot at her from afar. Given the enemy's diminutive size, she liked her chances in a fistfight.

Then Xavi struck gold. The door he'd just opened entered into a chamber tailor-made for analyzing technology. Bins of spare parts lined the walls. Half-dissected machinery lay on knee-high tables under bright work lamps. Gloria followed him in, looking for anything that resembled human gear. Her heart sank quickly, though. This was no analysis room, she realized. It was a repair center, or assembly plant. Everything on the tables was run-down Scipio tech. Xavi went to the bins and started rifling through them, stooped over to get a close look.

"Don't bother," she said. "Remember the goals. Their crap is not important."

He stood, holding something up to examine. "Not so fast there, boss." He tossed the item to her.

It was a length of pipe, about a meter long. White porcelain in color and sheen, and though solid as rock it felt extremely light, almost like paper. She understood immediately, and gave one of the tables a swift whack to test it out. The pipe did not bend or crack. The table, on the other hand . . . it folded in half, crumpling under the force of the strike.

"This will do for now," Gloria said with honest admiration.

183

They continued the search. Two more doors, same lack of result. The hall took an elbow corner, and then ran off into the haze of the virus spray. Gloria kept closer to Xavi lest she lose him in the murk. Hefting the pipe gave her a surprising surge of confidence she tried to quell. To let her guard down now would be foolish in the extreme. She had to remind herself of where they were, and that they had no way to escape this cursed moon. At best, they'd die on their own terms. At worst, they'd be torn limb from limb, their organs stretched out on metallic tables for Scipio scientists to ponder.

Xavi slowed, held her back with an outstretched hand. "What is it?" she asked.

He pulled her forward to stand beside him in the hall, both of them pressed against the walls. The space widened, Gloria saw, and the ceiling angled upward into blackness and smoky blur. Perhaps some kind of junction, she thought. The place had a modular style to it, not much different from human outposts on moons all over the Sol system and beyond.

Undulating red lights created glowing orbs of the virus powder, giving size and shape to the otherwise hidden space. It was large. One of the towerlike buildings she'd glimpsed, located at intervals throughout the complex. She'd assumed they were multistory structures, but the lights here told a different story. They were simply high-ceilinged, square buildings.

"Xavi," came Beth's voice.

"Go ahead," he replied.

"Vanessa's visor can translate some of their words. We think we've found the . . . security office, or something. Anyway, we're going to try to turn the lights back on, and kill that alarm."

It was a lot to process. Xavi glanced at Gloria, eyebrows raised in a "That sounds good" kind of way. She replied, "We're ready, go ahead. Anything like camera feeds or a blueprint there?"

"No," Beth replied. "Just controls for the alarms and such. We think."

Under any other circumstances Gloria would have told her not to touch anything. Tactically, a bad situation that was known beat out an unknown alternative, any day. Any day except today, rather. "If you can do anything about the powder spraying from every air vent, that would be nice."

"No promises," her engineer replied.

Even through the tinny speaker and interference, Gloria heard the renewed calm in Beth's voice. Perhaps due to the company she was in, or maybe that she'd found some way to contribute, Gloria couldn't be sure. She felt glad for it, though. It had hurt to split up her crew back there, a direct affront to some deeply seated need every captain had to do right by the people who'd placed trust in them. It couldn't have been helped, though. She needed a way to communicate with Vanessa and Alex, and this was the only option.

All at once the red glow of emergency lights vanished, along with the erratic sirenlike noise. There was a second or two of absolute darkness, long enough for terror to grip and squeeze Gloria's heart, and then the lights came on. Bluish white and strangely calming. In the absence of the Klaxon came the sound of the laboring ventilation system. Laboring, to Gloria's ear, at least. It sounded raspy, clanking and grinding inside the ceiling as it struggled to flood the base with the powdery air.

That did not go away. Beth was right not to have promised, Gloria thought wryly. She shifted her focus to the expansive chamber they'd arrived in.

To her surprise it did not just extend upward, but down as well. The hallway they'd arrived in ended at a railing that ran around the interior perimeter of a deep, square shaft. It descended perhaps thirty meters below, to a grated floor. Gloria counted two other levels between here and there, with similar railings and doors leading off into rooms or more hallways.

"Bad news," Xavi said, for both her and Beth. "This place is bigger than we'd thought. Goes at least three levels underground." He glanced up. "Maybe the same above."

"No," Gloria said. "Not above. We know that from what we saw outside."

"Good point," Xavi conceded. "Still, there's potentially a lot more area to cover."

"Do you have somewhere else to be?" she asked him, managing to add just enough sarcasm to her voice to let him know she didn't mean it. Gloria racked her brain, wishing she'd studied the layout from their perch on that dune a bit more closely. Then she smacked herself.

"What is it?" Xavi asked.

Gloria ignored him. She brought her left arm up and began to tap through the menus there, an interface decidedly difficult to manipulate with thickly gloved hands. Her navigator shifted uneasily, waiting, no doubt feeling as if the walls had eyes.

There! She tugged at his arm and pulled him over to look. On the curved screen mounted on her forearm, she'd accessed the video feed constantly recorded by her helmet, pausing the image on her view of the Scipio base from outside, thirty minutes ago.

"So what?" Xavi asked. "We don't know what any of it is."

Gloria shook her head. Something had bothered her about this view earlier, she just hadn't known what. But thinking about the small tower they now stood in had triggered her memory of that vague concern, and now she saw the solution. Plain as day. "Here," she said, pointing.

She enlarged the image. On the far side of the base, one building did not match the others. It was of medium height, its walls of a different material. Easily overlooked when one didn't know the purpose of any of it. All she had to do was apply the one thing she did know: They had Dawson here. And Dawson had been aboard the *Lonesome*.

"That look like a hangar to you?" she asked him. "And a temporary one at that?"

He scrunched his nose.

Gloria pointed to the walls. "Look. No moon dust. These are clean. This thing was just put up."

"How the hell'd we miss that?" he asked.

She zoomed back out, then pointed at one of the few tall buildings. "I think we're here," she said. Xavi nodded agreement. "So, we go this way." She pointed ahead and to the right.

"On it," he grunted.

As he bounded away, Gloria marked up the image with her finger and shot a copy of it over to Beth's suit. "Meet us there," she said when Beth acknowledged.

Given a purpose, a true goal, Xavi moved like a man possessed. The slow progress and careful checks of doors were set aside. But the path was still invisible to him, and twice he led them into a dead end. It was as they backtracked down the second of these hallways that Gloria noticed the doors on either side had small porthole windows, a feature not present anywhere else. She slowed, curious, and had to bend at the waist to look through one.

Her breath caught in her throat. Human feet pointed upward, the skin bloodied, scabbed. A hand swung at the end of a limp arm. The rest obscured by the medical—presumably medical— bed upon which the person lay.

"Xavi," she hissed. He heard her and doubled back, at her side in a second. He knew this tone; he knew not to question it. Her navigator took his standard entry position and waited for Gloria to open the door. Only, she hesitated. Afraid of what they'd find in there. What it might mean, and who it might be. Gloria couldn't help it. She closed her eyes as she yanked on the lever and let Xavi in.

He moved past her in a rush. She felt the wind of it on her suit. And then the pop as his gun fired. Two times. By the time Gloria made it into the room, two Scipios lay dead. Xavi did not spare them a second glance. He was at the table, holstering his pistol. She'd never seen that expression on his face before. She hoped she never would again.

"It's Dawson," he said. "It was Dawson."

Gloria liked to think of herself as tough. She'd been called a cast-iron bitch by her medical officer on more than one occasion, always acting hurt by the remark but secretly proud. Not now, though. She could see Dawson's body out of the corner of her eye and could not bring herself to focus on it.

"What were they doing when you came in?" she asked Xavi, her words so skewed by nausea that she started to repeat herself, but he'd heard. He stopped her.

"Poking at her brain."

Gloria staggered to the other side of the room, her gaze unfocused on the dark wall, the corpse at her back, a thing to mourn but not see. Her hands found a surface and she leaned on it, willing her knees to keep her upright.

It was another table before her, a narrow one, higher. There was a bundle of silvery fabric on it. A helmet, tossed carelessly aside. A backpack.

Dawson's gear. Gloria stared at it for a moment and then, with a shaking hand, she reached into the pack. Her hand curled around the grip of a service pistol. Identical to Xavi's. Standard issue on a fold-ship.

Gloria pulled the weapon free and turned it from side to side in front of her face. She didn't even remember dropping her pipe length.

"Good," Xavi said, seeing what she held. "Come on."

He moved with absolute purpose. From room to room, finding the same situation in each, his pistol barking once or twice, sometimes three times. Some part of Gloria knew these were just scientists or coroners, studying specimens, but she did nothing to stop him. Because she knew what the Scipios were hoping to learn, and knew what would happen if they found it. That, and because she needed the revenge.

"We need to get to that ship," she said when the rooms Xavi crashed into started turning up empty. "Make sure they can't access the data core. Leave nothing but—"

"No argument from me, boss," he said. "Beth, status?"

"We took a wrong turn," the engineer replied. "Backtracking now."

"Hurry it up. We found the *Lonesome*'s crew."

"Alive?"

Such hope in her tone. Gloria fought fresh tears.

"Far from it," Xavi replied.

"Oh . . . oh no."

"And if they're treating that ship the same way they treated her crew . . . ," Xavi said.

"We understand," Beth replied. "We're going as fast as we can."

There was nothing more to be said. Xavi stormed through the halls, pistol held in front of him, cradled by his other palm, swinging about with each hallway entered or junction crossed. Gloria did her best to mimic his posture, covering the hall behind them and double-checking the halls and doorways he passed.

A minute later the state of alarm returned. Gloria found she didn't care now. She didn't much care what they threw at her at this point. Maybe that was the pistol talking, but so be it.

Another turn, another junction. Xavi pushed through, moving by some internal map she could do nothing but trust. He was a navigator, after all.

In the junction now herself, Gloria heard a sound to her left. She turned in time to see three Scipios burst through a bulkhead door about ten meters distant. They were dressed differently from the torturers. Blues and grays, their gliding flaps covered. And they wore helmets, full-face. She noted the moon dust on their shoes and lower legs. They'd been outside, maybe just come in. Out searching the wreckage of the *Wildflower,* perhaps.

They froze at the sight of her. Gloria had her weapon up already, aimed right at them, but for that instant she'd forgotten it. She wanted to march forward and swing that pipe she'd left behind. Feel the connection against skull ring up through her arm.

"This will have to do," she said, and fired.

But they were scattering already. She winged the middle one, literally punching a hole in the gliding flap that stretched from forearm to shin. The creature yelped, but was not slowed. The other two scrambled for doors on either side of the wide hall. The third, the one she'd wounded, turned and ran back for the airlock.

Indecision gripped her. Who to shoot at? She settled on the one she'd already hit, not caring that it had its back to her. Not caring that they were unarmed. She fired three times, all misses.

"Focus, dammit," she rasped at herself.

Then Xavi was beside her, matching her pose. His presence gave her the mental push she needed. Together they felled all three, the last one dying with its foot protruding from the door it was trying to escape through.

"Don't think about it," Xavi said to her. "Just keep moving. Remember Dawson."

"Remember Dawson," she repeated, for her own benefit. But she hadn't been able to look at Dawson. She hadn't given her that little bit of respect. Didn't want to remember her old friend like that.

No, that wasn't true. It had been the gore. She'd never had the stomach for that sort of thing. Could never have been a surgeon or a killer, not of humans, anyway. Not on purpose.

These three aliens, though, with their pinkish creamy blood splattered about the hall, she found that didn't bother her. They were bastards, all of them. A parasite species whose designer viruses were merely extensions of the way they behaved themselves.

Gloria turned and followed Xavi, her own blood as cold as ice water in her veins. She rounded the next corner and almost slammed into his back.

"We're here," he whispered.

Gloria moved to his side and took in the sight before her. A vast room, ceilinged in a white hard-shell structure supported by metal trusses and girders. A glorified tent, really, hardened against the airless environment outside. Since receiving that first distress call she'd envisioned a room like a forensics team's setup after a bombing. Clean, with bits of unrecognizable shrapnel and remains laid out in a careful grid, tagged and numbered, photographers and sensory drones moving methodically from piece to piece. She expected to see an imploder core surrounded by a scaffold, teams of scientists swarming over it, probing at the atomic level to unravel its secrets.

Her knees buckled at what she did see. She dropped to her knees, mouth agape.

It was the *Lonesome*. Fully intact. Barely a scratch on it. One of its imploders still loaded in the launcher. The implications crashed down on her one after another, threatening to pummel her all the way to the floor.

We have a way off this rock.

We have a way home.

We can still stop them from learning our secrets.

Through all of this she failed to notice the Scipios in the room. They were tiny compared to the ship, which was nearly twice the size of Gloria's diminutive *Wildflower*. It had been custom-built to test the new imploder technology, while the *Wildflower* had been only hastily retrofitted.

"Beth," Xavi said. "If you're going to get here, do it quick."

"Did you find the remains of the ship?"

"Yes," Gloria found the voice to say. "Better still, it's all in one piece. We need you guys here. It's surrounded."

Surrounded wasn't quite true. There were a lot of Scipios, but they seemed to be working on their analysis of the ship, just not in the invasive manner Gloria had pictured. Surrounded implied an organized defense, but once again they appeared to have caught the Scipios off guard. She saw no reason to explain any of this to Beth, though. Surrounded was wrong, but it would get the others here sooner.

"Vanessa says to hold on to something," Beth replied.

Gloria glanced at Xavi, who looked at her in turn, with the same clueless expression she felt.

The Scipios finally seemed to notice their presence. They erupted into chaos, chattering as they scrambled for exits or cover in equal number.

Several came toward Xavi and Gloria's position, and only belatedly did she realize they were armed. They held small devices in their hands that looked more like black exercise weights than weapons, but when the Scipios lifted them and Gloria saw the ports open and extend, their purpose was not in doubt.

Xavi fired before they could, dancing back at the same time to take cover behind the corner. Gloria found her knees a second later and managed to stand. Something seared through the air beside her helmet. *One breath of this air,* she had time to think as she dove for cover.

Then the ceiling of the great room exploded inward, punctured and carved by a white-hot beam of roiling energy.

Air rushed from the giant chamber, sucked out into the vacuum beyond. Debris flew up into the air, as well as one unlucky Scipio who went flailing out into space.

And then Vanessa dropped in. She crashed through the hole she'd carved and landed neatly in the center of the floor, taking a knee as she did so.

The Scipios held on for dear life as their air rapidly vanished through the new entrance. The security team no longer aimed weapons at Xavi and Gloria. Instead they clawed at crates and floor tiles for purchase as the air around them rushed inward and up.

Vanessa stood and flicked her beam weapon on again. She drew the beam across the room like an artist with a brush, leaving not paint in her wake but a blackened scorch line and neatly severed bodies.

Another form entered through the roof. Alex Warthen, landing beside Vanessa. His suit, though similar to hers, lacked the weaponry. But he was a capable fighter, and as soon as his feet hit the ground he leapt again, powering into the midsection of a hapless Scipio who crumpled under the weight of the much bigger human.

Beth Lee entered last, through a door at the back of the room, unseen in the chaos except by Gloria.

"Beth. Let them deal with the Scipios," Gloria said. "Meet me inside the ship."

Far across the room, through the literal fog of the virus-filled air and the figurative fog of battle, Gloria met Beth's gaze. She saw the same wonder there she'd felt upon seeing the ship, saw the same realizations slide home in Beth's eyes. "I . . . understand."

Gloria shifted all her attention on the prize. "Cover me, Xavi."

"You got it, boss."

And they were running. Hopping, more like, but used to the gravity now and moving fast. Xavi loosed calculated shots from his pistol, more to scare and pin than to kill. Gloria poured all her focus on the ship, and the open airlock halfway down its side.

Xavi stopped at the end of the hallway, taking a knee and opening fire on another of the armed Scipios who was off to their left. Gloria didn't bother to look. She raced forward. From the corner of her eye she saw Vanessa whirling, beam weapon dissecting the room.

"Down!" Vanessa said.

Gloria dropped, sliding like a baseball star as Vanessa's beam tore through the space above her. She watched the line of white fire sweep overhead, and above that, the hole in the ceiling revealing the black of space beyond. Two more Scipios were carried up toward it, only to fall and collide with each other as the air in the room finally, fully evacuated.

And something else, too. Gloria glimpsed it, if only for a second, but it was enough. Against that blackness beyond the ceiling, a pair of silvery orbs hurtled toward them from the darkness above.

She didn't have time to shout the warning. The two swarmers exploded through the fractured ceiling with far more violence than even Vanessa's grand entrance achieved. They hit the floor in two corners like meteor strikes, the twin explosions showering the room with debris. Vanessa was thrown to the floor. The upright-standing *Lonesome* rocked on its landing legs. All around, the erected structure of the hangar began to falter and collapse.

And in those two corners, the huge swarmers drew themselves up to full height, each standing on three tentacle legs, the remaining three already stretching out, aiming weapons. They looked different from the ones she'd seen before. Like orbs of liquid metal, polished to a shine.

"Get to the ship," someone said. Gloria realized she'd said it, and repeated herself over and over.

One of the swarmers focused on Vanessa, galloping toward her, closing the distance in a half-second.

Gloria had only just managed to find her feet when Vanessa let loose with both arms. Two white rails of energy that filled the space between the immune and her attacker. Only the beams did not punch through. They reflected off harmlessly.

Gloria swallowed. "Oh shit. Oh shit oh shit oh shit." She took her own advice and bounded toward the *Lonesome*, eyeing the ladder that led up to the airlock. *Fuck the ladder,* she thought. In this gravity, she might be able to—

A tentacle slammed into the ground in front of her. The whole floor erupted around its length, and Gloria, somehow, managed to use this failed attack to her advantage. Just the boost she needed. As the floor heaved, she leapt. Some instinct she did not know she had guided her muscles, propelling her more forward than up as the buckling floor gave her the lift she needed. Gloria soared through the air and slammed into the hull of the *Lonesome* just meters above the airlock door. She let herself slide down until her feet could swing into the chamber. She swung, landed on her back, not hard, and was up in an instant.

She ignored the sounds of fighting outside. Her weapon would be useless against swarmers that could deflect those terrible beam weapons. No, she had only one task now, and Gloria meant to accomplish it. She let herself into the ship and began to climb.

17

ABOVE CARTHAGE

"Captured?" Sam asked. Tania would have, but she'd been struck speechless by Tim's news.

His reply took a moment, mumbled, like someone talking when they didn't want anyone to see their lips moving. "They came through the airlock in force, a compact swarmer and a dozen of their regular . . . security, I guess."

"Use your weapons."

"Waiting for the right moment," he replied. "Swarmer is mirrored, the beam failed, sliced off a whole row of harnesses in here."

Sam didn't ask about the mortar. No point, Tania realized. In that cramped little transport craft the mortar would be a suicide weapon.

"Just hang on," Tania said. "We're coming." She decided not to mention the reason she'd contacted him in the first place. That they needed *him* to come to the rescue. Tim, it seemed, had problems of his own.

Sam barked, "The ship, now!" The woman did not wait for

reply, debate, or even acknowledgment. It was the only option left. She turned and jetted down the length of the station. Tania fell in behind Vaughn, with Prumble somewhere just behind. They followed Sam's path, which she took pains to keep close to the hull despite the explosions tearing the place to pieces behind them. Sam twisted and turned, dodging protruding antennae and other equipment, uncaring if those behind her were keeping up. They had to.

Tania did fall behind, though. Her boots were intuitive in atmosphere but here, essentially falling through vacuum, she had to pulse them just so in order to dodge to one side or another. It required a different way of thinking, one that she had only limited experience with. Prumble fared no better, and soon the two of them were a hundred meters behind their more adept friends.

"They're bringing something into the cabin," Tim said. He'd abandoned his mumbling.

"What is it?" Tania asked.

"I'm not sure. It looks like—"

The connection ended.

"Tim? Tim?!"

No reply came. Ahead, Sam slowed to wait for her to catch up. Tania waved her on. "Get to him!"

Sam flashed a thumbs-up and really took off now, Vaughn at her side. A few seconds later, Sam's voice filled her ears. "I see the transport."

Tania held her breath, expecting some ominous addition, like "Or what's left of it." Instead Sam said, "It's moving away."

"Where?"

"How the hell do I know? Away. They're pretty far already, still accelerating."

Tania asked, "Can we catch them?"

"We're not going to have a choice." It was Prumble. His tone caused a chill to spike up Tania's back. She glanced in his direction, then followed his gaze to the planetside portion of the space station, where they'd exited less than a minute ago.

Roiling explosions began to cascade through the hull, tearing chunks of it away with fire and debris spilling out through the cracks.

"Move away now!" the big man shouted.

Tania followed him, pushing the thrusters in her boots to the maximum. She could see Sam and Vaughn darting away, too, and thankfully in the same direction. She adjusted her angle to bring her on a trajectory that would hopefully intersect theirs.

Prumble's words made sense then. "Head toward the transport," Tania said, angling herself once more.

"No way we'll catch it," Sam shot back.

"No choice. The station itself isn't going to exist in a moment. If we don't chase Tim, we'll be adrift out here. We have to hope at least that wherever they're headed is someplace we can reach." *Before we run out of food, or water, or power.*

Tania could see the transport now and it was still under thrust. It was trying for another Elevator. She had an idea then. "Everyone, forget the transport. Pulse toward Carthage."

Toward the explosions.

"Why?" Sam asked. "That's not where they're going."

"Orbital mechanics," Tania said. "It's counterintuitive, I know, but listen. We need to make our way down this Elevator, to the middle, then we cross. We might not beat them there, but we'll have most of our fuel left."

She'd organized and even piloted, remotely, enough cargo missions between Darwin and Belém to know the drill. Moving between two space elevators was counterintuitive, at least at first. Every station was at geosynchronous orbit by definition, and due to the forces involved you never wanted to let go of an elevator cord unless you were near its center, where everything basically canceled out.

They were near the outer end of this Elevator, and thus already being flung, albeit slowly, out into space. The transport had probably come out this far on some preprogrammed course that would see it heading off to visit the moons, or something, only to drop back toward home later. But now it was burning hard, trying to overcome that outward momentum. It was heading for the next space elevator over, if Tania's guess was correct. The only other option was for them to keep burning and head for the planet, but that little transport did not look to be atmosphere rated.

"We need to grab on to a climber and ride it in to the Elevator's middle."

"If you say so," Sam said. "Feels like we're leaving Tim behind."

"We're not," she said. "Trust me."

"I was going to say I wasn't too bothered by it," Sam admitted.

Tania found she couldn't really blame her. In fact she could not explain her own sudden sense of loyalty to the young man. She may not desire his company in a romantic sense, and worried constantly about his apparent jealousy toward Skyler, but she was far from the point where she'd leave him to be a prisoner of this evil species.

"There," Prumble shouted. "Our ride!"

Tania looked. They'd cleared the station, which burned behind them, but had not fully exploded. Not yet, anyway. Tania's slim hope worked out. The space elevator's thread heading toward the planet was crowded with climbers. Evacuees, most likely, all racing along toward Carthage. Prumble flew on ahead, pulsing his boots to find the right velocity. Tania more or less kept pace, and seconds later she saw Sam and Vaughn approaching from her left. They flew like they'd been born to it, and reached the nearest climber a full ten seconds before Prumble did. Tania herself landed last, grabbing on to a little groove in the hull of the vehicle. She could feel the vibration of its motors as it pulled itself toward the planet, still accelerating. Glancing back, she saw the inferno of the station they'd departed, like a nascent star trying to ignite. Huge sections now pushed away from the elevator cord, no doubt a safety mechanism to keep it from being shredded in the carnage. They'd done some damage, all right. The question was, would Tim be punished for the crime?

"Vaughn," Sam said, "eyes forward. If this climber traverses the next station through a hole made to fit, we're all going to be smeared on the outer hull."

"Absolutely right. I'm watching."

Sam crawled back toward Prumble and Tania. "Are you two okay?"

"Never better," Prumble replied.

Tania offered a thumbs-up, which Sam acknowledged with a quick nod.

"I wonder where they're taking him," Sam said to no one in particular. She gazed out into space, trying in vain to see the small transport Tim had been inside.

Tania looked in that direction as well, but the tiny craft was already too far away to spot. "No way to know, of course, but I'm very worried. It's bad enough they have him, but . . . God, I hope he can't hear me right now . . . but I fear what he might tell them. About why we're here, and where we're from."

"And what that giant thing is strapped to his back," Prumble added. "Not his goiter, of course. I mean the aura shard thing. I'm guessing these chunks of virus repellent are a bit of a shock to them."

"I hadn't thought of that," Tania said. "If they take it from him . . . and open his suit."

"What if he's bait?" Vaughn said from the other side of the climber.

"How do you mean?" Sam asked.

"Just what I said. What if they're using him to get the rest of us to come to them."

"I don't think so," Sam replied. "I mean, so far their encounters with us haven't gone so well for them."

"True," Tania said, "but they're adapting. Those mirrored giants . . ."

Prumble grunted. "Tough bastards, no question. Still, we managed."

"And with the next thing they throw at us?"

"We'll figure that one out, too. C'mon, Tania, we were brought here for this reason. We improvise. It's obviously why they picked us."

Tania frowned. "I highly doubt creativity is a trait unique to humanity."

The constant tug of acceleration faded as the climber reached its cruising speed. Sam led the team around to the other end of the climber, reorienting them for the presumed shift to deceleration.

Tania had only just looped her arm around an antenna when it came, that sudden force of what the body thought was gravity. The press was hard, three or four g's, she guessed. So hard, in fact, that she feared this was an unscheduled stop.

Sam and Vaughn evidently had the same concern. In unison, they scrambled to either side of the climber's endcap and peered over the side.

"Station approaching," Sam reported.

"How close?" Tania asked.

"About a klick," the woman said. "I think we should go."

"Agreed," Vaughn said.

"All hands abandon ship!" Prumble said, voice raised but not so loud that anyone might mistake it for an actual alarm.

Sam got on her hands and knees. "Follow me, everyone. Let's go get Tim."

And she leapt.

Tania went after her, powering up the thrusters in her boots and matching Sam's speed and trajectory. Their path took them clear of the approaching complex of space stations, which the Scipios had arranged in a snowflake-like pattern connected by glowing beams. Sam let their momentum carry them past the complex, diving through a gap between two segments of the bleak and complicated structures.

"Is it bad that I just want to shoot everything?" Sam asked the group.

Tania couldn't help but smile. She'd thought the same thing, but never would have voiced it.

"Save your ammo," Vaughn replied.

"I am. I know. Just . . . thinking aloud." Sam started to curve her path as they flew under the cluster of stations. Carthage loomed below, a patchwork of grays, greens, and milky whites.

The globe's presence, and the coming sunrise, made it easier to spot the adjacent space elevators. Not the cords, they were much too thin to see from here, but the clustered space stations that marked their path. Somewhere over there, Tim was being held by the Scipios. Tania stared at those stations, wondering if she'd been too hard on the young man.

His actions since their crash landing had seemed so selfish, driven by jealousy. Yet she knew his heart was in the right place. She had no doubt that all he really wanted was to see her safely home, no matter the outcome of this endeavor. Viewed so, Tania could see herself as the irrational one now. Clinging to a baseless hope that Skyler and Vanessa were still out there, somewhere. She had been the one who had resisted the efforts to flee this place, and in doing so she might have doomed them all. She was the reason they were still here, which had led to Tim's capture. Some friend she was.

No wonder he'd become so sullen and bitter. She'd built a wall, steadfastly refused to see things from his perspective and analyze the situation objectively. She'd forgotten herself. Her scientist's mindset, the very thing Tim had known and no doubt loved about her for years now. A terrible thing to see someone you thought you knew become someone else.

"There," Sam said, pointing.

Tania steeled herself for what was to come, silently vowing to give Tim not only the benefit of the doubt, but also the respect he'd earned as her peer and friend these last few years.

Ahead and below, another cluster of space stations grew nearer by the second. They were attached at the midpoint of the elevator cord, and not spinning. Null gravity inside, then. Tania took a hard look at the stations themselves, attempting to apply what she'd learned on the few she'd visited already in hopes of discerning their purpose. That effort was hopeless, though. The Scipios' architectural style was functional in the extreme, but without their cultural context it all just looked haphazard and messy to her. Occasionally she glimpsed one of the stations the Creators must have built. Sleek, elegant things, though their windows were mostly dark now, and their surfaces largely hidden under the additions of their oppressors.

Minutes passed. She felt utterly exposed, adrift in the vacuum, nothing connecting her to any solid object. And yet at the same time, Tania found a sense of power in it. The feeling that she could go anywhere, do anything. Literally an entire world lay beneath her.

The stations grew slowly larger, the distances involved making it hard to judge speed. Arrival came almost out of nowhere, confusing Sam as much as everyone else. The woman overshot their target and had to make a wide loop around. This proved useful, even if it hadn't been the plan, for it afforded the whole team a three-hundred-sixty-degree view of the stations clustered here at the center of this cord.

"Bingo," Prumble said. Everyone looked to what had caught his attention.

It took Tania a moment to spot it, but when she did she knew instantly they'd found the right place. There, tucked up against a protruding hallway, was the transport craft. It had the same designation emblazoned on the side that she recalled seeing on the displays glimpsed within. Tania activated her comm. "Tim," she said, "make a sound if you can hear me. We're close. We found the transport."

A silence stretched. No reply came, not even static. She wondered if they'd already extricated him from his suit, or found a way to power it off. What would they do to him? Her mind conjured terrible images. Horrible punishments, dissection, and all because he'd wanted to leave instead of quenching some petty thirst to leave a scar on the Scipios' apparatus.

"I'll keep this channel open," Tania added, aware of the bleak tone in her voice, unable to mask it. "We're coming for you. Stay strong, we're coming."

"Behind us," Vaughn said.

They all whirled.

From the direction they'd come, a dozen flares had lit up against the background of dimly twinkling stars. Engines, firing to slow the approach of what could only be a pursuit. "What do we do?" Tania asked.

"I'd rather fight them inside," Prumble said before anyone else could talk. "They have to worry about collateral damage. We don't."

"Unless Tim's in there."

"Fair enough, but their risk is still greater."

"Agreed," Vaughn said.

Sam was nodding as well. Without prompting she took the lead again. Her boots flared and she took a direct path toward the docked shuttle. At the last second she pulsed to one side and flew past it, on a path parallel to the airlock tube extending out from the main station to the little craft. "Remarkably like how they approached the *Chameleon*," she said, and then let off a mortar round. The projectile traced a line toward the tube, slamming into it right at the middle. There was a bright flash instantly followed by debris radiating out in all directions. Sam did not slow, did not waver. She flew right into the hole she'd made. Prumble followed her in, and Tania, without even really realizing she'd started moving, found herself flying in only seconds behind him.

"I'll check the transport," Vaughn said. "In case they haven't moved him out yet."

The tiny shuttle craft was still connected to a length of the severed hallway, drifting away from the station proper at a slow speed and tumbling slightly. Tania glanced back in time to see Vaughn fly into the ragged end of the tube and disappear inside.

Sam and Prumble moved directly to the airlock door at the end of this part of the now-bisected hall. By the time Tania caught up to them, Sam had started cutting through. "Latch doesn't work," she said by way of explanation. "Bastards locked us outside."

"Can you blame them?" Prumble asked.

Tania wasn't so sure, but decided to keep the theory to herself. Sam had just destroyed what served as the airlock, so it made sense that the inner door would automatically lock if vacuum was detected outside.

Sam was almost through.

"Move aside," Tania said. "That door is going to shoot outward from the pressure difference." She flattened herself against one wall. Prumble moved to a spot opposite her and Sam took up her own place above. A few seconds later the cut was almost finished. The door began to bow, held on by only a slim bit of metal now.

"Transport's empty," Vaughn said. "Coming to you."

"Watch out for the door," Sam said. "It's coming loose any sec—"

The circular slab tore free and shot outward, straight down the hall, missing Tania and Prumble by mere centimeters. Vaughn needn't have worried, the tumble imparted on the transport had taken it away at a slight angle, well out of the door's path. Tania watched him emerge from the still-attached section of tube and push free. He powered up his boots and started toward them. "Our pursuers are close," he reported, "and coming in hot."

Foam the color of mucus started to push out from small

nozzles around the airlock doorframe. Emergency sealant.

"Inside," Sam said. "Now." She led by example.

Tania pushed in behind Prumble, the view of the interior obscured by his hulking form. As humans went, you couldn't get much more intimidating than Samantha and Prumble, Tania mused. As soon as she passed the bulkhead she drifted to one side, one arm raised as if she were truly adept at such an incursion. She aimed where she looked, and only after a second, hearing both Sam and Prumble exclaim "Clear!" did she do the same.

This station was much different from the others. The layout registered first. This room was really just a large hollow sphere, broken only by a single thick column that rose up from the floor and exited at the ceiling, those directions fresh in Tania's mind because she'd seen the planet below them upon entering, and considered that "down." The shaft cutting through the center of the spherical room no doubt housed the space elevator cord.

The second thing she noticed was the style. This place clearly was not of Scipio design. There was an elegance to the curves, a thoughtfulness to how it flowed. Even the fact that connecting tunnels entered the sphere at seemingly random locations from all around, somehow their presence worked. It had an artful quality.

"Now what?" Prumble asked.

"Well don't just sit there," Vaughn said, coming in behind them. "The swarmers are right behind us."

"Yeah, but where do we go? This place is gigantic."

"They would have taken Tim somewhere they could study him," Tania suggested.

"That does not help at all," Prumble noted dryly.

"Just pick something!" Vaughn yelled, coming in through the hole carved in the airlock door.

Behind him, only seconds later, the temporary seal around the ragged hole they'd made in the airlock became a solid mass, hard as concrete. Tania heard the hiss of air being recirculated into this part of the station.

"Down," Sam said, and was off again. She pulsed toward the spot where the column that housed the space elevator connected to the bottom of the sphere. All around it were circular openings—passages leading downward, parallel to the sheath that protected the cord.

Sam aimed toward one of them, then once adrift she spun herself around to face the airlock they'd entered through. Tania pulsed her own thrusters to move slightly to one side, giving Sam a clearer view behind them, more than happy to let her handle whatever might follow them in. She moved into the lead, nodding to Sam as she passed her, seeing agreement in those eyes. This was Tania's mission now.

All right, Tim, she thought, *where did they take you?*

She glided into the tube, just meters from the shaft where the space elevator's cord drew a path all the way to the planet's surface. The temptation to carve a hole in the wall and dip in there, to ride that insanely long zip line all the way to the ground, nearly consumed her. Instead she focused on the chambers opposite her. Door after door, marked with symbols that her visor refused to translate. What could that mean? Words new to the Scipio lexicon? Or maybe just proper names?

Tania realized each door had a small panel beside it, with softly glowing symbols in rhythmically changing patterns flashing across the screen.

She slowed and moved toward one, aware that Sam and the others were right behind her. Most of the words here, too, were unknown to the translator Eve had provided. But some were recognized. Tania scanned symbols and found words like *mixture,* and *pressure,* and *nominal.*

And another thing. What she presumed was a date, though with no concept of their timekeeping methods the numbers meant little. The word beside the date, though, that she understood well. " 'Departure,' " she read aloud.

The last thing, which the screen flashed every few seconds, was TRANSFER STATUS: PENDING.

"Pardon?" Vaughn asked.

Tania wasn't listening. She moved to the next. And the next, and then one more. All of them had different configurations of mixture and pressure, all of them had nominal status, and all of them had different departure dates. TRANSFER STATUS: PENDING.

TRANSFER STATUS: PENDING. TRANSFER STATUS . . .

COMPLETE.

She opened this last.

"Is he in there?" Sam asked.

For a second she thought she meant Skyler, not Tim. In truth Tania had not expected to find either one. What she did find, for the first time since coming here, matched her prediction.

"What the hell is it?" Sam asked. Her three companions had stopped in the hall, forming a line ready to fight enemies from either direction.

"An alien," Tania said. She moved a half-meter inside. The door led into a small viewing chamber, the inside of which was entirely transparent. Thick borosilicate glass, or something like it, from floor to ceiling. And beyond, in a thick haze of violet-tinged air, a lanky alien being lay on a long bed, straps keeping it from floating about. The three-meter-long creature resembled a stick insect, yet with a bulbous head. Its skin looked almost like polished stone.

For a second Tania thought the creature was asleep, but then it moved one hand up to its face and scratched. The hand went back to its side. A very human gesture. Tania reached out and tapped on the glass. The creature's head turned and strange eyes, great pools of black, looked into hers. Or perhaps not, hard to tell with no discernible pupils. It continued to swivel its head around, confused, she thought.

A one-way mirror, perhaps. She turned and studied the wall just inside the door. There was another control screen there, and this had more words. One said OBSERVATION MODE, so she tapped at it. The words changed to CONVERSATION MODE. When she turned back the creature had sat up, looking directly at her now. It made a sound, guttural and raspy, something like "ghvast t'yolk."

To Tania's surprise, her visor translated the words. WHO ARE YOU?

"What is this place?" Tania asked. "Why are you in here?"

She could see glowing symbols appear on the outside of her visor, a written translation for the alien to read. It stared at her, unblinking, eyestalks twitching.

"Uh," Prumble said from the door. "What the fuck?"

Tania shooed him off without looking.

"Do we have time for this?" Prumble said. "I don't think we have time for this."

"If it's not Tim let's get the hell away from here," Sam urged, farther out in the hall but no less loud for it.

The alien undid its straps and rose from its bed. It came to the glass, tilted its head slightly, and pressed one stalky finger, or maybe that was its hand, against the surface. [ERROR] CARRYING TO GESTATION WORLD. HERE UNTIL IS TO RECOVER.

"Recover from what?" Tania asked.

REJUVENATION.

"I knew it," Tania whispered. She pushed back out into the hall and closed the door. "We need to split up," she said to the others.

"Out of the question," Sam replied.

"Listen," Tania urged. "This is the Elevator they use to bring mind-transfer patients back up from the surface. This is where they recuperate before departing back to their own system."

"You learned all that in thirty seconds?" Prumble asked.

"I learned enough," Tania said. "There will be ships here. At the far end. Big ones. Interstellar capable, like the *Chameleon*."

"What about Tim?" Vaughn asked.

Tania looked at him. "We still need to find him, but if he manages to escape, he would head there. And if they're trying to use him to find Earth, that's where they'll take him."

"You're making a lot of guesses, mate," Sam said.

Tania had no reply that would satisfy that. Sometimes you just knew. Like the first time she would sit before a computer interface she'd never used. Like in the station they'd destroyed, with its imprint chamber. Baffling at first, then all the little glimpsed and confusing pieces suddenly made sense.

"I still don't see why we have to split up," Prumble said.

Tania looked at all three of them. "This is the Elevator where transfer patients are brought up from the surface. Which means down there"—she pointed toward Carthage—"is where they perform the procedure."

Prumble and Vaughn both glanced at Sam. Her face was pinched in concentration, a deep furrow across her forehead. "We should stick together," she said after a moment.

"But—" Tania began.

Sam's glance stopped her. "Remember when you dropped that farm platform on Russell? In Africa?"

A chill went through her. "Of course."

"Maybe that's the answer. Maybe Eve was testing us on that, too."

"No," Tania said vehemently. "They could not have known anything about that situation, or our ability to move farm platforms. And anyway, we can't do that; it's possible they took Tim down there."

"We need to cover both possibilities," Prumble said.

Tania nodded toward him. "Exactly."

"We should go," Vaughn said. "I mean if there's ships above we should just go. We've done our part here. We pick up Tim on our way up and get the hell out of here."

"Did you hear what I just said? We don't know which way they took him."

Vaughn only shrugged. "If we find him, we find him. Look, we're not going to get many more chances. I say we leave. Get up there and find a ship."

He was looking at Sam, not Tania. Sam moved to Vaughn, as if to side with him. Tania resolved then to stay. She was going to the surface, no matter what they decided.

But Sam surprised her, as she often had. She put a hand on Vaughn's neck, just below the collar where the helmet attached, and drew him toward her until their visors touched. "Yes," she said. "Get up there and find a ship. And then wait for me, you sorry son of a bitch. Leave without me and I'll kill you myself."

"You're going—"

"I'm seeing this through," she said. "But I also know if we don't secure a vessel now they'll block that avenue off really fucking soon."

Vaughn searched her eyes. "I kinda wish you'd make up your mind on this. Thought we were trying to find a way out. Now you want to stay. It's confusing."

"This whole situation—"

"Guys," Prumble said. "We've got company."

Everyone turned. Only, the wrong way. Prumble was facing down, toward Carthage. Tania reoriented herself.

207

The enemies had not come from the main spherical room of the station, but from points lower. Four of them that Tania could see. Not swarmers, but regular Scipios in pale blue garb and full-face helmets. She saw what had to be weapons in their hands. The four of them were clustered around the lower end of the tunnel. Watching. Waiting.

"Feeling squeezed all of a sudden," Prumble said through clenched teeth.

"This station houses aliens who've undergone the transfer procedure," she said, puzzling it out for everyone's benefit. "Makes sense they'd have security, in addition to ships ready to take their allies back home."

"Why aren't they attacking?" Vaughn asked.

"Because," Sam said, "they've got us trapped and they know it."

"We should spread out," Tania said. "If they hit us with one of those time-compression things again . . ."

"Don't stand on any plinths and you'll be fine," Prumble said. "I don't think they can conjure those just anywhere."

"You can't know that for sure."

"True. I just wanted to use the word *plinth*."

Sam was still glancing back the way they'd come. "Back to the sphere," she said. "It's not blocked off yet. At least there we have options."

"Agreed," Vaughn said.

The pair began to move, as if their votes were the only ones that mattered. Tania bobbed against the wall, frozen with indecision. Any movement away from the world took them only farther from the goal.

No, Tania reminded herself. *We have different ideas of what the goal is.*

An odd crackle of static, barely heard above the pulse in her ears and her own breaths.

"Tim?" she asked, activating her comm. She scanned the nearby signals. Vaughn, Sam, Prumble . . . and a fourth. Faint, but close. Its source was automatically triangulated by Eve's sophisticated tech. Tania activated positional iconography and swiveled about. Above, and to her left. She moved as if on autopilot, floating past Sam and the others as they took up positions around the elevator sheath. None of the swarmers had followed them into the station. The hole they'd carved in the airlock door, however, had been sealed.

"Um, Tania?" Sam asked. "Where are you going?"

She motioned for them to follow her, not wanting to speak in case it caused her to miss Tim's voice. If his helmet was off, or damaged, he may not be able to transmit properly, but he'd sent something. Who else could it be?

Tania almost stopped then. Her breath caught in her chest. She'd been so focused on rescuing Tim, it hadn't even occurred to her that the signal might have been from Skyler, or perhaps Vanessa. The idea made her dizzy, and were it not for the null gravity she thought she might have fallen.

"Tania?" Sam called after her. "Seriously, we've left enough people behind already. I'm not letting you wander off. I will throw you over my shoulder and carry you out of here if I have to."

She picked the tunnel closest to the virtual marker hanging in front of her, projected on the inside of her visor. Another long, tubelike corridor that curved gracefully upward to bring it parallel to the elevator cord. More doors, just like the other tunnel.

But here, there floated a glowing marker just inside one of them. Tania kicked off from the wall and flew toward it. "In here," she said. Then, with the comm active, "Tim, can you hear me?"

No response.

The status display beside the door did not read TRANSFER PENDING or TRANSFER COMPLETE, but HOLD AND OBSERVE. She opened the door, surprised that the Scipios had not yet locked the whole place down, until she remembered their distinct lack of security. Complacency had that effect, she mused, and in a way she felt glad that Eve and her kind had failed for so many years to penetrate this far into the system.

Again the small alcove of glass, and the small chamber with a single bed. Tim did not lie on it, but rather sat, helmet in his hands, held close to his face like a bowl. *Helmet in hands,* she thought. *Exposed to the air.* She couldn't see his back to tell if his aura shard was still strapped there, but it didn't appear so.

Oh God.

Tania turned to change the glass from observation to

conversation mode, only to stop with her finger just millimeters from the display. Tim was speaking, and for a second she thought he could see her, that his words were meant for her. That he was talking to her through the comm. But no, her comm was silent. He was talking to his helmet.

". . . chose me, Skyler. She chose me! And I decided it was time to go."

Skyler?

A garbled response, familiar, too quiet to understand.

Tim squeezed the helmet so hard his knuckles turned white. "No, we don't. We owe them nothing, less than nothing. The only reason I agreed to come was for her. That's how we're different, you and I. You put this ridiculous mission first, allowed her to tag along. Endangered her. I came to protect her. To find the chance to get her away from this wretched violence."

He's talking about me. Tania shifted, uneasy. Inside her warred the emotional fallout of knowing Skyler lived, and that Tim was able to speak with him.

Unless the virus had infected him. The way he held that helmet, it looked as if he were speaking to it, not to whomever might be listening through its comm. Tania moved from side to side, looking at his neck for the telltale signs of rash that appeared on those with the SUBS virus back home. She saw nothing, but of course SUBS had been an invention of Eve's, meant to simulate how the Scipio technology worked. As of yet she had no data-point for what, if any, symptoms or effects the real thing conjured.

"I'm telling you this . . ." He paused, swallowed. For a brief instant his eyes went to the glass. A mirror to him, Tania reminded herself. Tim studied his own reflection for a time. "I'm telling you this because we failed. The others . . . the others did not make it." Tim stared into his own reflection as he spoke, his eyes like two stones. "I don't know why Eve gave me the ability to communicate with you. I'm not sure why she'd trust me with that, but I did what I thought was best.

"You should focus on the mission now, Skyler. Forget about us. Do what you need to do, but forget about us. It's all over now."

His head slumped to his chin then, and he let the helmet go. It drifted, slowly, about the small chamber.

Tania fought back tears. She fought the primal urge to rip this man limb from limb. She wanted to fire her beam weapon straight at his face, let it bore through the glass and then him, melting the mind of the person who could betray her like this. Betray all of them.

She whirled and tapped the conversation mode button on the wall, ignoring the blank stares of Prumble, Sam, and Vaughn, who she hadn't realized were clustered behind her. "I'll handle this," she said to them, and closed the door.

Tania turned around. Tim still had his head lowered. The helmet bobbed gently off the glass in front of her, started to float off to one side.

"Why?" she asked. Her voice sounded like someone else's. Like a person capable of the worst imaginable things. Was she capable?

Tim didn't seem to hear her at first. He didn't move at all. But then his face slowly came up and he met her eyes. Just for an instant. He could not hold her gaze. He may have been able to stare into his own reflection, but he couldn't face what he saw in her eyes.

"Why?" she asked again.

"I don't know."

"When did you know he was alive?"

"Does it matter? The mission is a failure. I only wanted to get—"

"When, goddammit."

Tim scowled. "Soon as I woke up."

Tania bit back the flood of pure rage welling inside her. He'd kept this from them, and advocated they leave. She rasped, "And Vanessa?"

He said nothing.

"*Tim.*"

"I haven't heard from her. I swear it. Tania, look, I only wanted—all I ever wanted—was to—"

"Enough."

His mouth clapped shut.

Who was this man? How had this side of him come to the

fore? Had it always been there, lurking beneath that innocent youthful veneer? She felt sick. And so tired of this. "Where is he?" she asked finally, when she could make the words come.

Tim took his time replying. Perhaps concocting a lie. Perhaps even now, exposed as he was, trying to salvage something. She wanted to leave him there, to his fate, or kill him herself, but not until he told her what she needed to know.

"Last chance to redeem yourself, Tim," she said, her voice flat. Controlled. "Tell me right now what you know, or never speak to me again."

He kept his jaw firmly shut. A silence of stubborn misery filled the space between them.

"I don't get it," she said. "Did you really think this was the right thing to do? That no one would find out?"

"Forget it," he said. The defeat in his voice so thick she could barely understand him. He straightened up a little. "I made a mistake." He pushed off from the bed, then floated up to the glass and placed a hand on it. "I'm sor—"

"No. Don't you dare say that."

Tim bit back the rest of the word.

"What did you tell them?" she asked. "About Earth. About us."

"The Scipios?" he asked. "Nothing. They haven't asked. Put me in one of those time bubbles and the next thing I knew I was in here. He's on the planet, by the way. Skyler. That's where he crashed. Said he found the city where they do the mind transfers."

Right below us. Tania swallowed hard, fighting to still her trembling body. They were so close, and had almost gone the wrong way. "And Vanessa? Is she there, too?"

"I swear I don't know. I've had no contact with her."

"Tim," she said very patiently. "Can you put me in touch with them? Can you transfer that ability to me?"

He thought about it without looking at his helmet. That meant he already knew if it was possible. He was simply deciding *if he should* . . . "Tell me what you want to say, and I'll relay it to—"

"Not good enough," she said, sensing his gambit. "Not nearly."

"If I give you that, you'll have no more need of me," he reasoned, voicing what she'd already sensed. "It's the last thing I have. Without this I am useless, expend . . ." The word trailed off. He stared at her now, with none of the affection present before. He was sizing her up as an enemy.

"That's not true," she tried lamely.

Tim's gaze went distant. He twisted, slowly, and grabbed the helmet. Pulled it on. Glowing icons began to shuffle around on the inside of his visor.

"There," he said. He popped the helmet back off, scowled at her. Tania saw a message pop up. A transfer of access.

"Another gift for you," he said in a ragged, defeated voice. "I'm always doing things for you. Story of my fucking life."

"Tim," she tried. "I never asked."

" 'Course you didn't. Your mind was always elsewhere."

"That's not fair."

He slammed a balled fist into the glass. "Don't talk to me about fair."

"What do you want from me, then? An apology? As if I'm the one at fault after what you—"

"Goodbye, Tania," the young man said.

There was a flash from the mortar tube on his back. The blur of the projectile, and then ferocious light blotted out the entire chamber. A *whump* of the blast, and then the awful splatter of Tim's body. Not vaporized, but torn asunder. Tania recoiled. The possibility of her own death from this lunatic action, and the others behind her, had no time to even register because the barrier held, containing the explosion without so much as a crack.

In the blink of an eye Tim became no more than a smear of red and gray on the inside of the glass.

Tania remained twisted away, arm thrown across her eyes, unable to turn back and see.

Two awful thoughts warred in her head. That Tim had done this at all, and also the possibility that he'd meant it to kill them all. That he'd still intended, in that final morbid action, to *take her with him*.

Hands at her back. Prumble or Sam, pulling her. Voices in her ears. Prumble's. "We've got to go. They're coming. They're . . . Oh shit, Tim."

"Fuck him, he's gone." Vaughn talking.

"Get behind me!" Sam.

She felt Prumble's arm slide under her arm and around her chest, pulling her to him like deadweight. The movement of flight. The sounds of battle.

Go down.

Go down.

Go DOWN.

Skyler. "Go down," Tania said.

"What?" Prumble asked.

Tania ignored him. She accessed the comm, direct link. Skyler's name there, and Vanessa's, where they hadn't been before. *Screw it,* she thought, and selected everyone. "Skyler," she said. "Skyler? Can you hear us?"

A second passed. And then, incredibly, his voice. "Tania?"

She burst into tears. "It's really you."

"Tania, what . . . Where are you?"

"We're coming, Skyler. We're coming."

18

CARTHAGE

"We're coming!"

Tania's voice spilled into his ears, sweet as anything he'd ever known. Skyler slumped against the wall and closed his eyes, fighting tears of his own. "Are you okay?" he asked. "The others? Tim wouldn't let me—"

"I know, I know. He kept it from us. That's over now. We're all alive. Is Vanessa with you?"

Just like that, the despair wormed in again. "I haven't seen her. I hoped she was with you, but Tim said she wasn't."

"That much at least he told the truth about." She paused, catching her breath. "He won't be lying about anything else, though. He took his own life."

Skyler shut his eyes in grief. Not for Tim, not after what he'd done here, but for Tania and the awful position all this had put her in. "God. I'm so sorry, Tania."

Her voice quavered as she spoke. "I'd like to say it was a heroic deed, to hide his knowledge from the Scipios, but the truth is I caught him talking to you. He couldn't look at me."

"The bastard had no right to." He tamped down his anger. "It's not important now. What is important is the rest of us making it out of this."

Some commotion came through the earpiece. Argument, tension.

"What's wrong?" he asked.

"We need to move," Tania said. "Situation still a mess."

"Understood. Keep the channel open, I'll talk as you move."

He sank to the floor then, watching the pile of dead virus grow and spill farther into the room. As Tania and the others sneaked and battled their way out of danger, he talked. Skyler spoke of his rough landing, and what he'd seen since. How Eve had landed him in a city near a space elevator, and the building here marked for transfer.

"I think we're directly above you," she replied then, the first acknowledgment she'd made since he started talking. "We've seen similar markings up here."

"That's the best news I've heard since . . . well, since I heard your voice."

"We'll work our way down there," Tania said. "Sam thinks—"

"Bad idea," he said, cutting her off. "Something's happening down here. I think they're preparing to evacuate. At the very least they'll have the climber port guarded like a fortress."

"Evacuate? What makes you think that?"

"Something happened to the virus. The little flakes in the air, it all just fell. It's piling up on the ground everywhere. Two meters deep and counting."

"When did that start?" she asked.

"I don't know. A few hours ago?"

"Hmm," Tania said. "I think maybe we did that." She quickly explained. A station with a control room not too dissimilar to the plague forge in Africa. How they'd let it sample them.

"Why'd you do that?" he demanded. Then he softened his voice a little. "Tania, you may have just made it easier for them to attack us. What made you think it would help?"

"A hunch," she replied. "This whole place is just a big medical station, if you think about it, Skyler. Aliens are brought here to receive the mind-transfer process, right? And the Scipios must facilitate that, but also guard the tech with total ferocity. I think they use the virus not just to keep the local population mollified, but any unwanted entries to the system, too. When a customer is accepted for the treatment, they reconfigure the virus to let them in, and probably undo that the moment they leave."

"Why's it all dying, then?"

"Oh," Tania replied, "well. We sort of destroyed the station."

"Hmm," he said. "Doesn't make sense to me. They rely on this tech utterly, and it all just dies if one station is knocked out?"

"It's a good point," Tania admitted. "To your left! Sam, left!" Skyler's ears were assaulted by the sounds of swearing and weapons discharge. Tania swore, grunted, and finally howled in either pain or victory, he couldn't tell. "What was I saying?" she asked him, oddly calm.

"The dying virus."

"Right. Okay, good point, we can't be sure our actions are what has caused it to die off. Whatever the case, it has, and I think this is our opportunity to act."

"My turn to act, you mean," he said.

"What?"

"Tania, listen. I'm already down here. Eve sent me here, specifically. She had a plan, poorly explained as it might have been. I don't know what I'm supposed to do down here, for Eve, but I do know what I need to do for me. And that's survive. Get home. Be with you and everyone else. I realize this now, about me. Achieving our goal is not enough. We have to make it out of this."

"What are you saying, Skyler?"

"Find us a way home. Secure one of their craft, and wait for me."

More sounds of battle. This time the cacophony went on for several minutes.

"They're getting tougher," Tania said finally. "That was close."

"Anyone hurt?"

"No. Well, not seriously."

Skyler stood up abruptly. The mound of powder blocking the hole he'd made in the wall had started to vibrate. As he watched it seemed to coalesce. The powdery nature of it shifted to something more solid, like watching a pile of fresh snow suddenly harden into solid ice.

Then, all at once, the solid mass burst and sluiced apart, a liquid ooze now that spread across the floor of the room, slapping against the walls like a wave against a rocky shore. Skyler hopped up onto a low counter and watched the gelatinous fluid settle. Bits of carpet, or something like it, sizzled under the fluid and began to come apart. Acid?

The whole room seemed to boil and hiss around him. Then, as quickly as it had started, the fluid began to drain away.

"Something's happening here," he said. "I think I need to move."

"Move where?" she asked with palpable worry in her voice.

"I'm heading to you, Tania. Even if I don't find a way to break the siege, this has gone too far. I'm heading to you."

"What about Vanessa?"

Skyler battled back a sharp pang of regret. *If we haven't heard from her by now* . . . But then he had only just heard from Tania. That was reason to hope. "Keep trying to reach her. Find us a way home and be waiting for me. Something tells me when I get there I'll have an angry bunch of Scipios on my tail."

"We'll be ready." After a moment's hesitation she added, "Keep the comm open, okay?"

"You too," he replied.

The floor around him had become coated with the slimy residue of the collapsed viral powder. Tentatively he dipped a toe into it. The mucuslike fluid frothed around the edge, but was otherwise totally inert. Skyler stepped onto it and crossed the room, careful not to slip and fall. His feet were armored still, but the rest of his suit had too many holes to count, never mind his wide-open face mask.

At the outer wall he placed a hand on the edge of the ragged hole and leaned outside.

The sky had cleared. Without the virus, night had become day even though the star was dim, a crimson orb hanging low above the horizon. He saw wisps of purple clouds high above, and the thread of the space elevator darting upward to vanish into the clear morning sky. No climbers at the moment. He wondered about that, and then put it out of his mind. Could mean anything. He had to ignore the part of his mind that guessed "all traffic shut down until further notice."

Skyler studied the rooftops around him. He'd descended quite far from his original perch, and now most of the buildings rose high above, blocking much of the view to his left and right. Street level was only twenty meters below him. Given the change in visibility, he decided to go down. Move in the shadows and through the ground levels of the buildings, or drop another level and navigate the subterranean layers again. As long as he was moving toward the goal, he'd do whatever it took. But the rooftops seemed so exposed now. He could see for many kilometers, and had to assume the Scipios were now watching.

He leapt from the balcony outside his hole and dropped in the low gravity, blipping his thrusters a second before impact to slow his fall. Not the most graceful of landings, but no one was around to see.

Quickly Skyler dashed across the walkway he'd come to and pressed himself into the shadow of the adjacent structure. With the star so low in the sky the shadows were long and very dark, but he'd found himself on a lane angled east-west, straight toward the rising orb. He jogged along the façade until he reached something like an alley, though it was wide and had a shallow trench running down the middle, serving what purpose he couldn't imagine. The ground everywhere was slick with the post-viral residue. Great clumps of it fell from above and splatted against the streets and walkways. It was as if the planet itself had just gotten over a centuries-long illness. The goo oozed out of cracked windows and open doorways, and when he stopped he could actually hear it as it sloshed and wormed its way through the interiors of the buildings around him. Perhaps subterranean travel was a bad idea, after all. Everything below street level must be totally inundated with this gunk.

He kept moving, avoiding the shallow trench, if only because it had completely filled with the viscous fluid and threatened to overflow, surface tension the only thing holding back the slick goo. At least here he had shadow. Skyler glanced back every few steps, but saw nothing in the way of pursuit. Or any other activity for that matter. Perhaps the Scipios had abandoned the city. He could only hope.

The alley did not run straight. Several times it bent at a ninety-degree angle, which he guessed was by design. A way to make the lane seem more cozy, as you could never see too far ahead or behind. He wondered if there were street markets here, despite seeing no evidence for it.

At the next intersection he came upon a very wide plaza, a favored feature of the Creator-built city. The pathways here were long, swooping things that were at once chaotic and also harmonious. A work of art, really. They wound around what surely were once elaborate fountains and planters full of vegetation. It had all fallen into abject disrepair, though, but the layout so strongly suggested former greatness that he couldn't help but feel impressed. And profoundly sad, for what had been lost here. This had been a truly great civilization once. The fact that the minds who had devised this place, engineered and constructed it, were still here, only made the loss that much worse. They were trapped inside the bodies of their diseased hosts, forced to watch their once mighty culture decay into total ruin.

He paused there for several minutes, getting the lay of the land. He sipped at his water tube and took a healthy long gulp from the nutrient dispenser, choking the bland goop down. It resembled the slime all around him, and smelled just as bad. If not for the knowledge of its digestibility, he would have left it behind days ago, content to starve. The water, though, tasted wonderful. Cool and clean, quenching his thirst while also removing some of the foul taste in his mouth from the air he'd breathed.

The space elevator loomed, not far now. Perhaps half a kilometer, where it disappeared behind a cluster of squat, ugly buildings. Scipio buildings. Funny how much they resembled the wall of junk that had been erected around Nightcliff in order to defend the Elevator there.

He glanced up again. The cord remained empty. Just a line against the sky, no climbers at all to mark its nearly invisible path. "Getting close to the Elevator," he said to Tania. "No traffic, though. Not sure how I'll get up there."

"How much thrust left in your boots?" she asked.

Not that he'd be able to reach orbit with the tiny thrusters, but he figured Tania knew that already. She probably hoped he could reach an already ascending climber, should one start up soon. "No idea," he replied. "My visor broke. Shattered. I can see a little of the translation display, but that's about it."

"You've been breathing the air?"

"Yeah."

"Side effects?"

"It's made me twice as handsome." She laughed, bright and true. His heart swelled. He had to get back to her. To all of them. "Seriously, though," Skyler added, "it was strange at first, like altitude sickness, but it passed."

Tania considered that. "Good to know. We're running low on supplies."

He caught the undercurrent of fear, but could think of nothing to say that might help. "Going silent for a bit, I need to concentrate. You okay?"

"For now," she said, though he could hear the tension in her voice. He hadn't heard that tone since they'd left the Key Ship together after their first visit, just before she gave him her air, saving his life and almost costing her her own. "Don't worry about us. Sam and Vaughn are in the zone." An annoyed outburst in the background followed that. "No, you're not in the zone, Prumble. You *are* the zone."

"That's better!" the big man replied, loud yet barely audible.

Skyler grinned despite himself. Hearing that voice, and their banter, eased his fears massively. *We can do this.*

He left the link open and continued his journey. He crossed the wide plaza in a dead sprint, sliding into a shadow on the other side and immediately turning, arms raised, in case anything had seen him and decided to pursue. Nothing had. He wasted no more time, jogging off along a high wall that lined this side of the plaza. Intricate patterns were embossed into its sandstonelike surface. Art, perhaps, or even something as mundane as signage. Impossible to tell now, so weathered the surface was, and covered in moss and creeping roots. About a hundred meters along the wall, near the center of the plaza, a gap opened to a terraced maze of irregularly shaped plots that may have once been gardens. The section was unruly, with no obvious purpose or plan, but it stood between him and the ugly, squat buildings the Scipios had erected around the elevator base, so Skyler began to work his way up the twisting path.

He took a route that favored shadows and cover, until that proved insufficient. He'd come to a small alcove with a cathedral-like dome of vines above it, all dry and bony, skeletal fingers interlaced above him.

Being here, in the daylight, reminded him of his first explorations of Belém, and the day he'd spotted Ana dancing in a long-abandoned courtyard. A chill ran up his spine at the memory. Not because of the place or who he'd seen there, but because of the strange way this place made him think of it. Once again he found himself wondering if this had been the Builders' plan all along. If Eve had somehow known his path would take him to this particular place in this particular city, and that what she'd ultimately caused him to go through in Belém that day would somehow be relevant here.

On higher ground now the slickness caused by the viral residue abated. As he walked on he tried to recall the events of that day. How Ana had run from him, startled by the sudden presence of another person in her city, and for good reason. How he'd eventually found her and her brother, and helped them free several other immunes from the clutches of a madman named Gabriel. After a time he shook his head. The only thing that could come of searching for similarities between these events would be insanity. A mountain of false correlations and, worse, the second-guessing of his own actions when the time came to act. He did his best to banish the train of thought. He focused on his footing, and stole the occasional glance at the space elevator.

He'd moved at a slight angle as he traversed the maze, and this had given a thickness to the cord's appearance. The Scipio style of space elevator was shaped like a ribbon rather than a cord as those on Earth had been. Tania would probably have theories as to why, but he found no energy to spend thinking about it.

Ahead the first Scipio-style building loomed, and this close he could see that the original architecture had been obliterated to make room for the structures. Foundations left to rot, poking through the caked muddy ground. Portions of elegant wall now just islands, the rest of the structure they'd once supported now just dust. This had happened on Earth, too. Plenty of times. A slum rising up around a once-beautiful and magnificent creation of a long-dead civilization. Only here, the original architects were not long dead, merely held prisoner. A worse fate, in truth. Much worse. All those intelligent minds, trapped inside infected hosts, occasionally called upon to die just to facilitate some alien's longevity treatment.

At the Scipio-built wall Skyler glanced left and right, but saw no obvious door or even break. He sighed and looked up, and decided he'd had enough of hiking. So he jumped, fired his boots in midair, and powered up to the top of the wall where he landed shakily. The wall was in truth more of a fence, barely half a meter thick, supported on the other side by trusses placed diagonally and welded to one another with crossbeams. A hastily erected thing, designed to keep something out. More similar to Darwin's than he'd guessed. Perhaps there'd been some resistance at first. Perhaps there'd been immunes who'd tried to fight their way here. Eve had never implied such a thing, but then why build this wall?

It did look ancient, he had to admit. Rust and dust in even application. Whatever they'd been worried about it had been a long time ago. Perhaps with the installation of the Swarm Blockade at the edge of the solar system, and their mastery of the virus tech, the bastards had gotten lazy. The thought, and not for the first time, warmed him.

Skyler sat on the wall and forced himself to be motionless as he took in the view. The area around the space elevator was perhaps a half-klick in diameter. Buildings ranged in size from one-story huts all the way to thirty-story skyscrapers. Much like Nightcliff, the one at the center of it all was tallest. From here the building looked more like the cooling tower at an old nuclear reactor, only instead of a white plume of steam pouring out there was only the cord, a thin band that punched up from the middle of the wide, tubular tower that surrounded it. The tower was wide enough to accommodate whatever sort of climber the Scipios might use. There were no windows along its two-hundred-meter height. Just an unbroken, dark gray, hollow pillar that looked a bit like a gun barrel pointed straight up. Halfway down its length the buildings began to attach to it. Clusters of angular slabs, studded with antennae, pipework, and ventilation grates. They rose up next to the tower and were connected to it by squared gantry halls, tubes, and bundles of sagging wires.

He must have been staring at the place for five minutes before he realized that, every now and then, words would blip into the corner of his vision. Something out in that industrial nightmare had lettering on it, and his visor was occasionally able to latch on to the words and translate them.

INTELLECT RECOMBINATION, the display flashed.

Skyler swiveled his head until the words appeared and stayed on the visor display. He kept his head still and studied the buildings in the center of his vision. There! A wide, flat, two-story structure adjacent to the main elevator complex. Only a tiny portion of one corner was visible, but that's where the signage was, and it didn't take much imagination to guess what went on inside.

He hopped down off the wall and began to weave his way through the structures. No weeds or roots poked through the hard surfaces beneath his feet here. This had all been patched or resurfaced recently. He kept low and constantly looked left, right, and behind, but saw no one. Maybe evacuation had happened, after all.

Skyler slowed up. Something wasn't right. It seemed with each step the environment around him changed in some subtle way, but he couldn't put his finger on what it was. It felt . . . He paused to think about it. The sensation felt very familiar. Something he'd felt in Darwin many times. He'd be moving through the city and then . . . then what? He glanced up and understood. The sky had changed. The subtle darkening before a storm. He'd been so focused on the uneven ground that he'd stopped looking up, save to check the Elevator for climbers. He'd barely noticed the sky at all. But the clarity that had come when the virus died off was vanishing now. Something new had begun to creep in, like beige, barely coherent clouds at high altitude. Only, these clouds were not starting as small puffs and accumulating from there. This was as if someone was taking an image of a clear sky and slowly cross-fading it to one completely overcast.

He ran, no longer caring if anyone saw him. Every instinct said to get indoors, and quick. He moved as fast as his legs, and the awkwardness of partial gravity, would let him. With each step the sky seemed to dim a shade. It transformed, too. From an even blanket of color to the hazy contours of a cloud layer that spanned horizon to horizon. This seemed to refine itself even as the coloration continued to deepen, and soon Skyler could make out tendrils, like reaching hands, stretching downward from the mass.

The sky, it seemed, was falling.

Skyler switched his thrusters on, skating over the ground now and churning up a huge cloud of dust in his wake. The sound was terrific, booming off the structures all around him and echoing out into the city all around. God, if they weren't aware of him before they would be now. Yet he still saw no one, not even a curious onlooker behind one of the many grimy windows around him.

He weaved and darted, leapt and slid his way through the crowded complex. Finally the building marked Intellect Recombination came into full view. Behind it, the lowest reaching tendrils of the plunging sky neared the ground, like smoke bombs. He'd once seen footage of a volcanic ash cloud as it descended all at once on a nearby village, and this looked exactly the same, save for the coloration.

Skyler aimed for the door, pushed the tiny thrusters to their maximum and slid on his armored feet like he was riding some invisible snowboard. Twenty meters out he lifted his arm, ready to blast the door to pieces, but some instinct made him hold fire. The sky was crashing down all around him. He'd seen no one outside. Not a single one of them, whereas before they'd been milling about, outside the elevator complex, gathering to watch as two coffins were floated in.

They'd gone to ground. They knew this danger was coming. Not him, but the *sky*. And they feared it.

"Tania," he said. "Might have a serious problem here."

The cloud fell, like the powdery wave of an alpine avalanche, only everywhere, all at once. It swallowed the top of the elevator tower and kept falling. A hundred meters above him now. In places the faster-falling tendrils, spearheaded by heavier clumps, began to crash into the city. Skyler watched one as he ran. It hit the roof of a building about half a klick away. The powder exploded outward, flowing over the roof and down the sides of the ten-story structure. The building itself seemed undamaged, as if the impact had been nothing more than a wad of loosely packed confetti.

Five meters to the door.

Skyler looked away from that rooftop and focused. He could hear the early impacts now, all around him, as a strange erratic drumbeat. A shape in the corner of his vision drew his attention back to that first impact. Where the powder ball had struck and disintegrated, something now stood. A large mirrored sphere, studded with blistered sections. In a flash those blisters punched outward and tentacle legs took shape. They slammed down into the roof and the sphere stood up.

A swarmer. A large one, and newly coated in some reflective skin.

"Tania?" he repeated, suddenly realizing she'd not replied the first time.

She made no response now, either.

"Tania?!"

A garbled, incoherent burst of noise assaulted his ears.

"Shit," Skyler grunted, and reached for the door.

All around him, the sky crashed down.

19

MAGO

Other than a thick coat of powdery dust, the *Lonesome* seemed untouched. Gloria Tsandi counted this as the best luck since arriving in this godforsaken system, and hauled herself up toward the cockpit.

Though still a compact ship by fold-spec standards, the *Lonesome* was more than twice the size of the *Wildflower,* and military in purpose. It had been custom retrofitted to use the new imploder, she recalled from her briefing. A process that had taken more than six months, replacing nearly every part with a more expensive prototype version made with the latest lightweight graphene-ceramic composites.

Even the weapons systems. Gloria tapped her comm. "Xavi, get in here. They left everything in place. There will be weapons, somewhere."

"A bit busy," he grunted.

She ignored him. "Beth, you too. I need the ultracaps, reactor, engines. The works."

No reply came.

"Beth?"

"That's what I'm busy with," Xavi said. "She's down."

"Dead?"

"Unknown."

His tone told her two things. He didn't know, and she should shut up or she'd get him killed. Gloria heaved on a rung and powered herself upward five meters, grabbing the next and heaving again. The bulkheads were all open, and the storage containers along the walls unlocked. On purpose? Gloria would have secured everything, changed the codes and thrown away the details. Why Dawson had left everything accessible to the enemy was a mystery, as was why Dawson hadn't gone through with the self-destruct.

Gloria, having had that chance several times since arriving in-system and deciding not to do it, could not blame her counterpart. Dawson probably thought they still had a chance, right to the very end, and merely waited a moment too long. Perhaps she'd opened everything to give her crew a chance when she no longer had one herself.

Gloria powered through the sleeping cabin, into the mess. She made an opportunistic grab at a water pouch left lying out, attaching it to the receptacle on her belt where her suit greedily replenished its supply. She was through navigation a second later, and then at the captain's chair.

Outside a deep boom rattled the ship. Then something hit it, and the whole thing swayed on its landing legs. "Xavi?"

"Not now, boss," he shot back.

She trusted him. She left him to do what needed to be done, and turned her focus to the command console. Dawson had also left this totally unsecured, allowing anyone who might reach it to access the entirety of the ship's controls. *Thank you*, Gloria whispered silently, as her fingers flew across the interface.

Another rattle below her. Gloria turned and saw Xavi clawing his way into the ship through the airlock, one arm around the limp form of Beth Lee.

Gloria said nothing. She turned to the display and found the command she wanted—rapid emergency power-up, and triggered it. Then she yanked her harness off and dropped the twenty meters to where Xavi worked to get Beth into an infirmary bed. "A tentacle arm slapped her across the room. She hit the wall pretty hard, lots of g's. Concussion, minimum."

"Let me," she said.

"No," Xavi said, almost angry but not quite. "Get this bird started."

She nodded, gave his upper arm a reassuring squeeze, and powered back up toward the captain's chair.

At the airlock she flinched. Something punched into her gut and sent her across the narrow space to smack into the far bulkhead, pinning her there. A silvery tentacle arm, barely able to fit in the outer door, held her to the wall, tip squirming around, probing. Lenses and little grated openings covered its surface. The flailing seemed random until, all at once, the whole length of it turned with new purpose and licked out toward Gloria's helmet. She winced, turned away. A useless, automatic reaction.

Nothing happened. She opened one eye and saw the tentacle looming before her. It stared at her with lifeless mechanical eyes and then drifted to one side. A glowing ring came into view, six meters down its length, just outside the airlock.

The whole thing suddenly lurched outward and went tumbling off into the hangar. Vanessa hovered just beyond where the creature had been, the beam weapon on her arm still alive with bristling intensity that stung the eye just to look at. She swept it at unseen foes.

Gloria shook her head, continued her climb. Her stomach hurt like hell, but her suit still had atmospheric integrity so she knew the tentacle had not pierced the material, or her skin. So she bit back the pain and heaved toward the captain's chair.

Alex Warthen waited for her there. She hadn't even seen him come in. For a terrible instant she thought he might kick her away and take the helm, or that he was only there to tell her where he wanted *his* ship to go. But the man merely moved aside, gestured for her to take her place, and moved behind her. He faced not toward the console but aft, and settled into a defensive posture as best he could in this gravity and orientation.

"Whatever I can do to help," he said, "just name it."

"Well don't defend me," Gloria replied. "Make sure Vanessa gets in here safely, and seal the damn airlock the moment she's aboard."

"Copy that," the man replied, and was off.

Whatever he'd been through, or his intentions the very first time he came aboard a ship Gloria captained, those two words settled any lingering concerns she had about him and his loyalties. Warthen was a soldier, a *military man* as the saying went, and when it came down to business he was the type who would set everything else aside. She whispered another silent *Thanks* and refocused on her displays.

"Talk to me, Xavi," she said, tapping through icons and scrolling past the obvious warnings.

The ship rocked to one side, and another echoing boom billowed through the narrow spaces of her hull. Gloria gripped the chair controls and fired the attitude thrusters, forcing the ship upright again. She quickly enabled a launch stability program that would handle that task automatically now. One less thing to worry about, and—*Hey, good news!* she thought—the thrusters worked.

"Reactor is not complying, boss," her navigator said. "Without Beth to—"

"What about the caps? Do we at least have those?"

"Checking." Seconds ticked away. The sounds of incredible violence continued to spill in through the airlock, occasionally singing a chorus with the deep hissing sounds of the attitude thrusters. "Caps are at sixty-five percent."

"Good enough to get us off the ground; we can worry about the reactor when we're out of this hellhole."

"Agreed."

"Beth?"

"She's still out, boss. Might be a coma."

Gloria drummed her fingers on her leg. The ship's state-of-the-art medical pod could tell them more, but it drained power like a minor black hole and she didn't know if they could afford it. "Get her in the auto-med," she said a second later.

"The draw—"

"We can't afford not to have her, Xavi. We need to know if we can fold."

He hesitated, if only for an instant. "I'll take care of it."

Gloria twisted in her chair and shouted down to Alex, who stood gripping the edges of the airlock, watching the battle outside. "Get her in here! We're leaving!"

He glanced up and gave her a nod.

Good enough. Gloria turned back to her console and powered on the engines.

20

CARTHAGE

A white hell enveloped him just a step away from the door. It was as if a thousand tornadoes of bleached sand had converged all at once, then suddenly released and hurled their swirling contents back to the ground in abject fury.

Skyler curled into a ball and let the storm take him. There was nothing else to do. The grit whipped at him, sent him spinning and tumbling across the slimy landscape. It tore through the shreds of his armor and scraped his skin raw. A million tiny cuts.

He screamed and choked, gritted his teeth, tasted acid and the dryness of the freshly delivered viral powder as it swept down his throat and into his stomach, his lungs. He felt it blast his eyes and power up through his nostrils like cold ash.

The force of the wind sent him rolling across the ground until his body flopped against a wall and came to a sudden, teeth-rattling stop. He kept his arms around his face, though it was no use. The powder had found its way through the pathetic defense already.

All the while Tania cried out for him. "What's happening, what's wrong? Skyler, answer!"

He could only cough and gag. The skin on his face bled from countless needle-prick holes where the particulate had struck home. Any more of this and it would scrape his flesh away, leaving only a skeleton in tattered armor.

The rush of sandpaper wind began to abate, and not because the ferocity of the virus-fall had dwindled, no. That would have been welcome, ideal. No, Skyler realized as he tried to open his eyes and felt only the sudden pressure of powder on his corneas. No, the storm had not passed. He'd been buried.

And the pileup only went on. It became a weight on him, a dismal pressure growing to something oppressive. Nasty. Unbearable. Insurmountable, if he didn't move.

Skyler coughed through his pressed elbows, felt a searing burn all along his throat. He strained and strained, willed his legs to move under the growing weight. Somehow he got a foot up under himself and that would have to do. He willed the thruster to power on. Full strength, and then roared in pain as his back became the tip of a very poorly calibrated missile.

The viral sand all around him shifted, rushed in to fill new gaps, but he was moving. He thought he was. Was he? Skyler groaned, strained, tried not to breathe as he pulled, pulled, *pulled* his other leg forward and up, second thruster activated. The press against his back, that goddamn equal and opposite reaction, felt like a two-ton lead weight. He smashed his eyelids together, ground grit between his teeth, held his breath, and willed more from the tiny motors. They howled, slamming his own knees up into his torso, forcing the wind from him.

And then he broke through.

All at once his body erupted from the viral avalanche and arced outward on an erratic curve. He let the boots power off and knew he was falling, but could do nothing about it. He had to hope, could only hope, that he'd land—

A *whoomp* as his body flopped into the loosely piled powder, the softest cushion imaginable. He rolled on it, fought to keep from sinking in again as he heaved in a breath and felt new pain along this throat.

Water! Water! his body screamed.

He searched with his dry, scoured lips for the tube and inhaled all the goddamn powder that had wormed its way into it. He gagged, spit the crud out in a small eruption around his mouth and nose, then sipped again. This time the water flowed. He flushed his mouth, spit, then drank. The first gulp made him retch a pale muddy pile of gunk onto the powder beneath him. He drank again, and this time the water stayed where it belonged. Skyler gulped again, spit the water onto his gloved hands to clean them. The liquid stung the hundreds of tiny cuts, invisible through the pockmarked armor but no less real. He cleared the powder from his palms, spit water on them again, and rubbed his eyes clear.

The liquid burned, but that only made tears, which helped even more. Seconds later he came to a shaky stand, blinking water from his eyes.

The city had gone virtually silent around him as the dust literally settled. Except for the sounds of the chrome-surfaced swarmers. They'd landed all around. He saw one clutching the side of a building, twisting as it scanned its surroundings for its prey. Others lurched as they clawed their way through the freshly accumulated virus-fall.

Then, all at once, the entire area seemed to vibrate.

An earthquake, Skyler thought, but he quickly saw, or rather felt, that this was not the case. The ground, the buildings, they did not shake. Only the powder shifted and danced.

And then it began to rise.

Skyler watched the grit begin to float upward, as if borne on some weak yet pervasive wind from below. Only there was no breeze. The particulate was moving on its own.

Little robotic cells, he reminded himself. Cells had methods of locomotion, and now they were switching on.

This had been a strategy, he realized, starting to run without really deciding to. The Scipios had killed off their old virus and replaced it with a new one, to what purpose he could only guess. Only, they could not afford to wait for it to billow through the atmosphere at its own leisurely pace. So they'd dumped it, like napalm, and activated it once on the ground.

The particles flocked and schooled, took on shapes and flows as they took to the air and began to coordinate.

Some seemed to circle around him, and did not leave. Movement in the distance made Skyler change focus, and he saw the swarmer on the side of the building suddenly twist its main eye toward him.

"Oh fuck," he whispered.

He stood dead center in a cloud of molecular sensors. The cells. A trillion trillion tiny eyes and ears. The evolution of Earth's suddenly primitive-seeming HocNets. And now they had his scent.

He ran, full sprint, toward the building again. His flight had taken him away from the door, but it wasn't far. This time he threw caution to the wind and carved himself a door in the middle of the one that already existed. At the last second he raised an arm and smashed his way through.

Skyler found himself in a small foyer of sorts, with three halls leading off. Left, right, forward. He chose forward, if for no reason other than it was longer than the other two. He needed distance. The viral cloud could not be escaped, of course. It flowed in through the door like an unwelcome ghost, swirling around him.

Scipios scurried like rats from the rooms along the hall, alerted perhaps by the virus that the building was no longer a safe haven. They wore uniforms that were yellow and black, or yellow and white, based on what criteria Skyler had no idea. He let them go. As he strode forward into the hall he saw the ethereal form of the virus cloud move with him, like an unpleasant odor made visible. Skyler swiped at the living smoke to no avail, it just moved out of the way on the air his arm displaced, nimble as tiny gnats.

"Fuck," he muttered, and soldiered on. He needed to get to the Elevator, and doing so unseen, no matter indoors or out in the open, seemed impossible now. The Scipios had recalibrated their tech. He wondered if his immunity no longer made any difference, and if not, how soon the symptoms would start to show.

Something thudded into the ground outside. He turned and saw the mirror-finish spherical body of one of these new swarmers filling the hole he'd made. He fired his beam at it uselessly. The white line of pure energized *whatever* only reflected off, drawing a trail of fire across the little foyer room.

Skyler took a knee and leaned, letting a mortar round loose.

Only, none came.

"Out of ammo," he said to himself. "Perfect."

He shook his head in frustration and felt the powdered virus that had accumulated down in the depths of his collar grate against his neck. Angry and on the verge of collapse from exhaustion and pain and frustration, Skyler hefted a random chunk of debris from the ground and threw it at the enemy.

It bounced off harmlessly.

Ground forces began to swarm in around the swarmer's limbs, dressed in what he could only assume was their military garb, a sort of shifting pattern of camouflage that automatically adjusted based on the surroundings.

Skyler ran.

Why not? he asked himself, feet pounding in that Carthage gait. He rounded a corner and surged ahead, while behind him came the sound of the chrome swarmer as it tore the rest of the doorway aside and moved into the building.

The gunk in the air followed him, always swirling, moving, just out of reach and yet never far. On a whim Skyler shouldered through a door, and then another.

He found himself in a blue room, low ceilinged and nearly totally dark save for the bit of light spilling in from where he'd come. He turned and waited, ready to fight with fists and feet, when he noticed something new.

The virus hadn't followed him in here.

The air in this space was utterly clear, in fact. Unnaturally so.

Curious. He wondered if the swarmer would be blind to his presence. Perhaps he could hide and surprise it. Fire his beam point-blank at one of its vents or eyeholes, there must be some.

He levered the door closed and stepped back. His leg smacked against a low table or something and, delirious and exhausted, he fell backward.

Skyler landed across it and squirmed to get up, only to fall again, a bit farther. Cushioning enveloped his head. Automatically deployed restraints grabbed hold of his torso, arms, legs, feet. The lid of the coffin closed over him at the same instant he recognized it for what it was.

One of those hovering stretchers, like he'd seen in the tunnel. He heard it seal, and then the nightmare began.

21

ABOVE CARTHAGE

"I'm going."

"No."

"He needs us."

"Fuck that. We've got to go—"

"I don't want to *go* without him. Can't you fucking understand that?"

Vaughn stared at Sam. She stared back.

Tania Sharma floated a few meters away, ready to leave no matter what the standoff resulted in.

"We're going to find a ship," Vaughn said slowly, "and make it fly. If you two aren't back by the time that's done . . ."

Sam leaned in and slipped her arm around his neck, pulling his helmet until the glass touched her own. "Then you'll keep waiting for me, because we're going to make it back."

"God damn your stubborn ass," the man swore.

The woman put her hand on the man's visor as gently as if it were his cheek. A rare tender moment from Samantha Rinn, broken a second later when she slapped the same spot and forced a grin onto her face. "You and Prumble better be ready when we get there."

Vaughn could only shake his head, and let go.

Sam moved back, and turned to Tania. "Let's move."

Tania needed no more prompting than that. She turned, too, pulsed out a few meters from the outer hull of the space station, and fired her thrusters, not really caring now that they were so low on fuel.

They'd tucked themselves into the shadowed area between two massive external tanks of unknown content.

Everything inside the station had become filled with a new variant of the virus, one that did not react to the presence of the aura shards, meaning their suits were now their only line of defense. So Tania, Prumble, and Vaughn had ditched their burdens and, if the two men were anything like her, were much better for it. The freedom was exhilarating. She'd gotten used to the awkward bulk, and free of it now she felt as lithe and strong as a tigress on the hunt. Once again she found a tiny corner of her brain musing as to the nature of this moment. Whether or not Eve had foreseen it, indeed planned for it.

Perhaps that was the point, Tania thought. Test us for vague things related to even vaguer distant unknown obstacles, and let the confidence we gain knowing we passed said tests propel us through adversity at the other end. Incredibly brilliant if so, and also utterly ruthless. Somehow that sounded very much like Eve.

She and Sam became like two missiles, arcing and curling along the length of the elevator cord, bowing outward as space stations grew in their visors and then, in a flash, began to recede behind them. The tug of Carthage soon provided all the acceleration they needed, and their flight became a true fall.

Near the top of the atmosphere Tania saw what had prompted their change of plan. Well, aside from Skyler's gut-wrenching cry and subsequent departure from the comm.

An armada of mirror-surfaced swarmers was descending the Elevator, gliding down the ribbon with one or two of their tentacle arms curled around the thin device, using it as a guide. With them were at least ten climbers, virtually in free fall, their contents unknown.

Below, a massive beige cloud spread outward from the elevator base, as if the whole area had been suddenly enveloped in a cataclysmic hurricane. Though Tania knew that was not what it was. No storm moved like this. Straight out, in a nearly perfect circle.

It was the virus, the new one, dropped like an atomic bomb on the city where Skyler lurked. She hoped he'd been underground—deep underground—when that onslaught arrived. From his last transmission, though, she knew that was unlikely.

"We've got to ride one of those climbers," Sam said. She had to shout now, to be heard over the strange thin-yet-loud hiss their bodies generated by friction with the very topmost portion of the atmosphere. "Otherwise the heat from reentry will cook us."

"We don't know that," Tania shouted back.

"Is this the time to find out?"

Tania couldn't argue with that.

Samantha streamlined herself and fired her boots one last time, darting off toward the massed enemy force below. Her mortar tube burped—two, three, four times—the projectiles streaking out on erratic, curling paths as they found the right trajectory to connect with their targets. Her shots avoided the climber cars. Tania didn't need to warn her off that tactic; they both knew that a way back up was somewhat important to the plan.

Four flashes saw four swarmers erupt in nasty tumbling fireballs, tentacle limbs flopping free and cartwheeling as they fell. Sam had smartly targeted the four leaders, the farthest below them. The explosions tore outward, spraying flaming chunks of machinery and Scipio flesh into the paths of those trailing just behind. A sudden frenzy of movement followed. Some angled outward. Others twisted in, then via some survival instinct or a programmed avoidance of the elevator ribbon, they made urgent course corrections back into the maelstrom, or slowed drastically as a last hope of avoiding the mess.

Tania fired. She felt the satisfying punch on her shoulders as the mortars took flight. Four shots, just as Sam had done. They'd both had eight left, now cut in half. Her shots ripped outward, then curled back in as they gained speed. Quadruple pulses of blinding light plumed from the edges of the armada, as those that had fled upward from Sam's attack now ran headlong into Tania's. The massive firestorm would, with any luck, mask Sam and Tania's approach.

She streamlined herself, too, and followed her companion as the other woman punched through that fresh obscuring murk.

Air pounded at her now. A rippling series of kicks and punches all along her body, absorbed by the suit but communicated to her for the sake of her knowing about it. Tania fought to maintain her aim, the ribbon-shaped space elevator making a handy path to follow down. She passed a climber that resembled the transport craft they'd stolen. At the nose she saw a Scipio looking out at her through the window, deep-socketed eyes inscrutable but following her, as if to say "You won't get away with this."

"Remains to be seen," Tania whispered.

She focused ahead, aiming her fall at the climbers closer to the ground. Sam darted in and out of sight several hundred meters below, her beam weapons carving the air. Tania could not see her target, but knew the plan well enough to guess. Time to do her own part.

A climber loomed just below. Tania twisted her body to glide inward, scraping dangerously close to the Elevator now. The sleek narrow vehicle was fifty meters beneath her and approaching fast. Tania held both arms forward and switched her beams on. The twin lines of roiling energy punched into the top of the transport and bored inside. The whole thing cracked apart like an egg, molten fire spewing out through the gaps before the hull came apart and shards flew outward. There was no time to turn. Tania flew right through the center of the chaos, following the path her weapon had carved. She saw the ragged edges of torn-away hull panels and the horrible flailing bodies of Scipios thrust from the wreckage, cartwheeling out into their own awful descent. Wing flaps would not help them at this altitude, surrounded by frigid air too thin to breathe. Some tried, anyway, only to succumb seconds later and begin their final plummet to Carthage.

Tania Sharma forced back a sudden wave of compassion and repeated her attack on the next climber, and the next. She and Sam had agreed to work the plan from both ends, leaving only the topmost climber intact.

A battle instinct she still only felt passing awareness of triggered a sudden departure from her path. She flung herself sideways as the one of the remaining mirrored swarmers tracked her down and hurtled itself in to stop her attack. Tania rolled and swooped a path around its grasping limbs, ignored the sudden blast of viral powder that pelted the back of her armored suit. The display showed no punctures. She wondered if they still hadn't figured the defense out, or if she'd just been lucky in her positioning. As Sam had said, *Is this the time to find out?*

Tania stuck to the plan; destroy the climbers—which seemed to contain some kind of elite ground force from their camolike uniforms and the weapons they held—while avoiding the seemingly impervious swarmers. Mortars were required to destroy the swarmers, and mortars were in preciously limited supply.

In the center of the climber group she held fire as the last of the vehicles came apart, its contents spilled into the now-howling wind. Sam flew past her at incredible speed, heading up. Three chrome swarmers were right behind her, closing fast. Tania saw, too late, that she would collide with one. No time to change course, she acted on instinct and fired her beams. A bad instinct, as the weapons were now ineffectual on these enemies. Tania watched in horror as the twin lasers bent away at strange shifting angles.

The monster rushed toward her, its six arms flung wide as it did its best to avoid her. She tucked her legs and arms in tight and twisted, closing her eyes at the crucial moment, waiting for the impact that would kill her at worst, break her back at best. Instead she felt the wallop of a nearby explosion and her body convulsed as the shock wave ripped through. She opened her eyes, dazed for a moment, seeing only the planet below, clear as Darwin viewed from Gateway.

"What happened?" she asked the world.

It did not reply. Prumble, however, did. "Thought you two could use some company."

Tania twisted about and saw him, and Vaughn, rocketing in from complementary angles.

"Do you two assholes ever follow orders?" Sam asked.

Prumble laughed, full and hearty, as he slammed into one

of the remaining swarmers and grappled with it. Tania did not understand this tactic until suddenly, one of the big man's beam weapons ripped through the other side of the enemy's casing and it began to fall away, limp as a doll.

"How did you—" she started, bewildered.

"Put your fist right up to their eye-thing," he said, "and let 'em have it."

"What happened to the plan, Vaughn?" Sam was asking.

"Too hot up there," he said. "It looks like they brought the entire Swarm in to prevent us from leaving."

"What, all one million of them?"

"Seems that way."

"He's exaggerating," Prumble put in. "There's probably only five hundred thousand."

Tania swallowed hard. "Well," she said, "at least we know we've got their attention now."

The four of them met on the top endcap of the one remaining climber, which still glided merrily along as if its entire escort had not just been annihilated in an orgy of violence all around it.

"Surprised they haven't just stopped," Tania said. "Or turned around."

"Maybe they can't," Sam replied. "Anyway it doesn't matter. We ride this as far as we can and then jump if we have to."

The climber continued its free-fall descent.

22

LOCATION UNFATHOMABLE

He stood on a riverbank, churned water flowing swiftly past. A torrent, and growing, perhaps from a flood upstream. The banks crumbled away at his feet, soil and rock vanishing into the swollen river. He turned to run, only the river was behind him, too.

No riverbank, then, but a sliver of an island being washed away on all sides. In seconds it would vanish under the waters, gone forever, and him with it.

Skyler heard a voice, but did not understand the words. Icy cold swept over his feet as the flood swallowed the last of the land. He would drown. The voice again, above. He glanced up and saw a hand outstretched from a nondescript being floating above him in midair. Skyler grasped the hand and scrambled for purchase on the last little bits of island now beneath the frothy rapids. The hand clasped his forearm and he its, and it pulled.

The person, not human but somehow not anything else, either, heaved Skyler up onto its shoulders and carried him like a child. It walked carefully through the air, one foot stepping right in front of the other as if it negotiated a balance beam.

Another island came into view, this one artificial. Two stairway bridges arching up to meet at a stone gazebo straddling the roaring waters just below. The being jumped the last meter, over and down, spilling Skyler onto the damp stone surface in the process.

He rolled, badly, surprised by the sudden awkward crash. When his body came to a stop, he found himself lying faceup, the spray of storm-driven rain like a perpetual slap across the cheek. Slick cobblestones bit into his back and legs.

The figure stood over him. No, floated over him, as if gravity did not affect it.

"Who are you?" Skyler asked. "Is this . . . What is this place?"

He'd almost asked if this was the afterlife, a concept he'd never bought into if only because it seemed to empower, quite ironically, humanity's worst people. Grillo, being the most recent example in a long and frightening line.

But the being only looked at him quizzically.

He recognized it then. And all at once everything came back to him. The Creator he'd sat with in that ruin of a building as the enemy scouts flew overhead. The same face he'd seen in that strange floating capsule, underneath the city, being brought into the Transfer Facility.

THEY COME FOR ME SOON, the fractured translation on his visor had said. And so they had. And Skyler hadn't figured out, or perhaps didn't want to admit to himself, what this place was, this transfer center.

The being had its hand out, and Skyler only stared at it now. He'd thought it was offering to help him up, as it had pulled him from the vanishing island in the river, but now he saw that was not the case. The Creator was floating away, unbound by the gravity Skyler felt.

This allowed another rush of understanding. The test Eve had performed on Alex and Jared. Alex had mentioned a shared dreamscape, where despite being together they saw different things and different rules applied. It had been another test, so Eve had said, regarding the human mind's ability to align with that of another.

All of it came together in Skyler's head. The coming together of two minds, a bridging, literally and figuratively. A conduit open between them whereby a consciousness could be transferred.

He'd stumbled into it. Fallen into one of the connective pods and inserted himself into the process. As the host? As the mind to be transferred? Was he about to find himself in a new body, or find his own mind discarded so that some alien could plop itself into his head?

If he let this being float away, is the whole business called off? The Creators served as the medium for this transfer, didn't they? That was the whole reason the Scipios had imprisoned them.

Skyler reached for the being's hand. He hesitated. The Creator studied him for a moment with its unsettling third eye and then, bizarrely, nodded. A very human gesture, perhaps glimpsed when he'd sat with it in hiding.

Lightning roiled across the stormy sky. A brisk slap of frigid water across his face.

"Talk to it, Skyler," a voice said, bright and clear.

Eve's voice.

23

THE *LONESOME*

The *Lonesome* spiraled in toward Carthage, engines growling as her velocity bled away and her altitude slowly declined.

The improbable crew stood crowded around Gloria Tsandi, staring at the display in front of her.

"Welp," Xavi said, "no doubt where the bastards are."

The ship's sensors had painted every object of unnatural composition within a few million klicks by now, at least those larger than a football.

The ring of Elevator-anchored space stations around the planet were like a glowing belt. Structured, sensible.

And then farther out, well beyond even where the *Lonesome* now sat, several blips with fine trajectory markers traced long arcs that followed the familiar paths every space captain knew all too well. Injection burns, as they came in to make orbit, or the ferocious push to get out of a planet's gravity well, to achieve escape velocity.

Not unlike what a representation of Earth's space assets looked like these days, in truth. Elevators, stations, and the signs of commerce and exploration.

Except for one glaring, gigantic difference, of course.

The thing they all now stared at in stupefied silence.

One Elevator in particular, around which there buzzed a hornet's nest of icons and calculated vector cones. So many ships the *Lonesome*'s computer had trouble drawing them all, and had marked them with a light gray coloration that Gloria had to look up in the manual to learn the meaning of: The computer used this color when insufficient processing power was available to calculate paths for the number of objects the sensors detected. She had not known this was possible.

"That is a lot of fucking ships," Xavi said dryly.

"It's like they brought the entire Swarm in," Beth Lee said shakily, but at least she was no longer unconscious. Not a coma, after all. Gloria patted the chair's armrest, grateful to the universe for that small bit of good news.

"Perhaps that's exactly what they did," Vanessa replied, thoughtful and somehow still defiant. A warrior, that one. "The question is, why? Last stand, or are they all here to celebrate their victory?"

Xavi made a little grunt of resignation. "Maybe they're massing for an invasion of Earth. Got what they needed, so why wait?"

"We don't know if they got anything," Gloria said. "For now we assume—"

"I know what you're going to say, boss, but it's wishful thinking. We need to warn the OEA about this."

Gloria studied him. "If you think a warning, even now, would help defend against that"—she pointed at the ball of enemy ships on the screen, all clustered around one space station—"you're mad."

"They're all bunched up," Alex Warthen said, more to himself than to anyone. A simple, quiet observation. A rather obvious one, too.

"Alex?" Gloria prompted.

"They're all bunched up. Tactically that's a gigantic mistake. One nuke in there and you'd take out a lot of them. Maybe all of them. Unless . . ."

"Unless?"

He glanced at her. "Maybe they're not preparing to move

outward at all. Maybe," he said, "their focus is on whatever is at the center."

"One nuke, huh?" Xavi said, thoughtful now.

Gloria glanced at him, then sent a private message to his visor. I WANT TO KNOW WHAT KIND OF WEAPONS THIS SHIP HAS, AND I WANT TO KNOW NOW.

He cast her a sidelong glance, gave a small nod.

The *Lonesome*'s current orbit had it circling the world at forty degrees of inclination. She wouldn't pass close to the cluster of Swarm ships for another two orbits. Gloria plotted a small course correction, dragging their path so that, when that moment came, the *Lonesome* would pass right through the center of that mass.

"Is that wise?" Beth asked, watching the adjustments.

"Dear," Gloria said, "I don't think anything can be considered wise at this point. There're only degrees of insane now."

Xavi's reply came. NOT MUCH, I'M AFRAID. LOOKS LIKE DAW BLEW THE ENTIRE WAD BEFORE THEY WERE CAPTURED.

Gloria drew in a long breath. This ship, military, state of the art, designed to survive encounters with the Swarm, had still been captured after unleashing untold devastation on the enemy.

"Are we going to nuke them?" Beth asked. "A suicide run?"

Gloria turned to face her.

Beth Lee held up her hands. "I'm not saying it's a bad idea. I mean, we could eliminate the Swarm, in one fell swoop. Even if this mission is a failure, the next . . . But, please, Captain, we have a right to know. We deserve that. I want the chance to make my peace."

Captain Gloria Tsandi studied her borrowed engineer, the last-minute addition to this voyage, the first crew member she'd not handpicked herself after lengthy consideration and a sizable gut feeling. And she found she wanted to pull her into a mother's embrace and thank her, thank all of them, for being here. For staying by her side through everything. "The truth is I haven't decided yet, but if it comes to that, I will give you your time."

"I don't know about you guys," Xavi said, "but in the last few days I've made my peace more times than I've had a shit." He tilted his head toward Beth. "No offense, mate."

The woman ignored this. She'd grown somber, and stared at her captain.

"Suppose," Vanessa said, "we hit them with an EMP."

Everyone turned to her.

Vanessa shrugged. "Eve tested us for that, back in . . . a place called Colorado."

"The cave, yes!" Beth replied. "Behind the Flatirons!" Before her zeal for the history of that era could get the better of her, Beth visibly shifted to an expression of dubious concern. "That was testing us, though, not the Scipios."

"Exactly my point," Vanessa said. "We survived it. Maybe they won't."

"Hmm. You might be onto something there."

"Doesn't matter," Xavi said. "We don't have an EMP. A couple of rail guns and several low-yield missiles, but no EMP."

No one spoke.

"We could generate one," Beth Lee said, after a moment.

Gloria looked at her. "How?"

The engineer's eyes were darting back and forth, surveying some invisible catalog of the ship's components and how they might be reconfigured to achieve the desired result. "Take the sinks and regulators off the ultracaps, dump them against the reactor's thermal catalyst."

"All that would do is start the reactor," Xavi said. "We could make better use of it than as a bomb, surely."

Beth shook her head. "No. I mean yes, it would start, but we couldn't use it. Dawson shut it off for a reason. The Scipios hit the bleed lines and distribution cluster. If the reactor turned on right now . . . well, it would unleash all the electricity at once, and at maximum output."

"That would fry everything," Gloria said, "including us, no matter what happened in Colorado. How is that better than a nuclear explosion?"

"Because," Beth replied, "the reactor can be ejected. So can the caps."

Xavi made a *tsk* sound. "You realize this would leave us without power, right? The caps are all we've got right now."

"Not true," Beth said, warming to her idea with every word. "We've got the engines. As long as we keep them warm, we can last as long as the fuel reserves last."

Beth glanced at the supply level instinctively and frowned. It was low, very low, and they were going to need a lot of it if they wanted to make an escape velocity of their own.

"You actually considering this, boss?" Xavi asked.

Gloria turned to him. "Degrees of insanity, remember?" She looked at all of them then. "We've got about one and a half orbits before we plow right through the center of that crowd, which means we've got half an orbit before we pass close enough to fling our reactor onto their doorstep. I think," she said, "instead of making our peace, let's make a nice little package for our Scipio friends."

The clock became the enemy.

Beth and Xavi hunched over their terminals, she running calculations of minimum safe distance and when to trigger the various components in order to achieve the result, while he pored through documentation to figure out what fail-safe would have to be disabled or bypassed for any of this to work.

There must be a lot of those, Gloria thought, judging by the amount of swearing coming from his corner of the engineering hub.

She could only leave them to the work. Hovering at their shoulders, questioning or second-guessing, would only distract them. She'd learned, over the years, that being a good captain meant knowing when to let people get about it. Well, that and being an unconscionable hard-ass. She'd lost that last part, somewhere along the path from the Key Ship's destruction to that moon.

Or maybe she'd just learned to trust her new crew. Even Alex Warthen, who now stood quietly by the airlock, watching their target station come into view over Carthage's star-dazzled horizon.

"You okay?" she asked him.

For the first time since she'd known him, the man laughed. A dry, sardonic thing, but still a laugh. It faded, and he glanced at her, then laughed again when he saw she was serious. Gloria couldn't help but smile. He was right. It was a ridiculous question, one of those automatic things one learned to say because it's what they always said in the sensories. A question that always brought about a moment of reflection or deep philosophical understanding.

Alex Warthen sighed, and said, "When I made it out of that AI's nightmare, all I wanted to do was get back to Earth."

"And now?"

"Now I'm starting to think maybe I've lived enough for one man."

Gloria gave him a hard stare. "Don't you get all suicidal on me. I was just starting to like you."

"It's not that," he said. "What I mean is . . . I'm saying thanks. I tried to take your ship, with violence, and here I am part of your crew, and I realize this is where I should be. Fighting the good fight, for once."

She studied him, smiling both outwardly at his words and inwardly that her leading question had actually worked.

A chime sounded. One minute to the point of decision.

"Xavi, Beth, status?"

There was a pause, as if the two of them were waiting for the other to deliver bad news. Xavi spoke first. "I think it'll work."

Gloria digested that. Xavi wasn't the sort for "I think" and "maybe." Still, it wasn't an outright no.

"Beth?"

This reply took longer. As she waited, Gloria tapped in a preprogrammed attempt to fold space, should the crew not be around to try it themselves, in order to get them and their ship out of this predicament forever. Inspired by a very old song, one all ship captains were forced to listen to by their brethren as a rite of passage, Gloria Tsandi set the controls for the heart of the Sun, a program she would have to cancel, not enact.

"Beth?" she asked again, her task done.

"We're a go," the woman said.

Finally, some confidence. Gloria acknowledged it gladly, and reviewed the specifics as they appeared on her screen. The burn would alter their path by just a few degrees, but by the time they reached the "collapsed swarm," as Vanessa had coined it, the *Lonesome* would be a thousand kilometers from the current center of the massed ships. Not the distance Gloria would have wanted, but it would have to do. She added the thrust sequence to the command queue. "Everyone strap in for high lateral burn, and remain so." She followed her own advice, checked her displays, and settled on one in particular. The countdown ticked away the last eight seconds.

"Mark," Gloria said.

A hum as the maneuvering thrusters started their burn. These were not subtle things. On or off was all they knew. The force pressed Gloria into the side of her chair.

"Chaff," Gloria ordered.

Xavi fired the two crude devices, using the last of their supply of inflatable decoys. Captain Dawson had used the technique at least ten times during her own flight from the Scipios, to obvious lack of complete success, but in this case Gloria needed the objects to work only once.

A small flotilla of tightly folded ceramic-alloy objects began to spread in a cloud. Once clear of the ship their panels rotated and stretched, forming buckyball lattice supports that soon contained thick inflated balloons made of a carefully designed fabric meant to return just the right signatures to match the spectral lines an Earth ship's hull would reflect back to any probing sensor out there.

Oldest trick in the book, really, and one the Scipios were very familiar with after so many encounters with humans. Gloria didn't mind. They only needed to present the enemy with multiple targets and, with any luck, not enough time to shoot them all out of the sky before the real payload came within range.

"Launch," she ordered.

Gloria activated the ship's engines at the same instant, the lowest thrust possible, just enough to provide power.

A series of deep clangs and thuds rippled through the hull as single-use explosive bolts sheared the connective supports that held the reactor housing to the hull. Two smaller sequences came a split-second later. The ultracapacitors now. Several emergency alarms began to wail, but Gloria acknowledged and disabled them before her ears received any real damage.

Outside, the three discarded items began to separate from the mother ship, floating away with growing speed. A hundred meters out the two ultracap chunks shifted position slightly, and electromagnets did the rest. The doomed portions of the *Lonesome* drifted together and then, abruptly, snapped into a single entity. They were a kilometer away now, a distance that would double and double ten times over before it was all said and done.

"Settle in, everyone," she said. "Nothing to do now but wait."

The time went by surprisingly fast. Gloria, and she presumed everyone else, passed the seconds by watching the sensor display, where their little gift for the Scipios continued to gain distance from the *Lonesome.* Her eyes darted from their position to the confusing ball of indicators that represented the Scipio Swarm. Like a massive school of fish, it was impossible to focus on any one of them, only to let their coordinated movements fool the eye into seeing patterns and infer a hive intelligence as a result. In truth they were probably all just acting on some individual avoidance programming, but the result was breathtaking. The entire cluster seemed to bulge and dent, bands of it swirling left while others turned back the other way, like a ballet performed by a half-million dancers in zero-g.

"Here we go," Xavi said.

The modified reactor careened toward this mess, and amazingly the Scipios seemed to notice it only in the final portion of its trip. So inward was their focus, the bubble of enemy ships did not begin to realign until the incoming device—and each decoy—was at the edge of its effective range.

Gloria watched as beam weapons licked out across the narrowing gap. The decoys were flimsy, just giant hollow things, really, and so exploded easily and quite undramatically. Little puffs of unsubstantial debris that seemed to scream "Only joking!" as they flew apart.

The ruse had worked, though. Gloria could see it already. She braced herself. She almost didn't notice the plume of Scipio ships that had begun to pull away from the main body, like a detachment of bees peeling off from the hive to confront a new threat. Or, more apt, the curving trail of a solar eruption. The tendril of spacecraft began to stretch outward, an arm reaching right toward the *Lonesome*'s future position.

"Boss!"

"I see it." *And I can't do anything about it. If this doesn't work—*

A thousand klicks away, two ultracaps, all of their safeguards carefully removed, shunted a terrific quantity of raw electric power into the gutted, similarly flawed reactor core. Deep inside that bundle of technical marvel, a minuscule gap at the center of a hundred million tiny amplifiers became filled with argon heated to a temperature of incomprehensible measure. *Hotter than the moment of creation,* a professor had once told Gloria, in explaining the kinds of physics going on around a starship captain, in the hope some care and respect would be afforded the vessels. *If you could see me now,* she thought.

Those tiny amplifiers were supposed to be connected to a whole array of channeling baffles and containment shells that would control and sustain the reaction. None of these things were present, though. Only the converter pods that loved nothing more than to convert heat into electricity and send it onward for use.

Onward, in this case, meaning everywhere, all at once.

In a sphere that grew at the speed of light, an eyeblink really, the swirling ball of Scipio Swarm ships went dark. They went blind, deaf, and dumb all in one fell swoop. No motors to keep them on course, no eyes to keep them from avoiding their multitudes in that gigantic maelstrom. Their paths became fixed things, dictated by their vector at the moment the pulse hit them.

The Swarm mushroomed, and then the collisions began. A hundred thousand high-velocity bodies that bumped, smacked, and head-on collided into one another. Some ricocheted off. Some bounced. Others exploded, and these each added another million objects to the growing orb of deadweight slugs.

All this in the span of a heartbeat.

A cry of triumph had just begun to form on Gloria's lips when the electromagnetic shock wave hit the *Lonesome,* and absolutely everything went dark.

24

THE SHARED NIGHTMARE

Eve.

EVE!

A furious anger boiled in him at her voice. "You've been there the whole time!?"

"I have not. I . . . am very far—" and her voice became garbled digital noise. A transmission from a great distance, then, rather than some voice in his head?

Skyler had the sick thought that this static sound and sudden disconnection was fake, a childish avoidance of guilt. He set this feeling aside. She was back, that was what mattered.

Talk to it, she'd said. Well, okay. "Who are you?" he asked the being.

A delay followed. Perhaps some initiation of translation, for after several seconds came comprehension and, unless Skyler was mistaken, sheer joy appeared on the being's face. "I am many things. All things. An elevated mind, one of the last of our people, and I carry with me the memories of all my species. I need to give them to you."

Well, Skyler thought, *fuck.* Had so much ever been said in so few words? He found himself at a loss.

"I require your permission, Traveler," the being said, hand still outstretched.

Skyler reached up, and took the hand.

The climber began a hard-braking action, prep for arrival. Sam glanced over the edge and watched the vast city rush ever closer, filling the visible landscape. "Get ready," she said.

They'd debated what to do upon landfall, settling on: Stay with the climber, secure the port, then venture out. But one look at the city changed their minds. Swarmers marched through the streets and plazas, like spheres of liquid mercury with spider legs, buoyed by the smaller antlike figures of Scipio ground forces. Or maybe just an angry mob of curious civvies, but whatever. Sam knew the trouble was not in the climber port, and that meant Skyler wasn't, either. They all seemed to be converging on a building a few hundred meters from the Elevator's anchor point. Smoke billowed from the entrance already. Skyler? Defending his position? Or had they already tried to bomb him out?

"Contact," Tania said. "I've got his transponder."

Everyone looked at her.

"Spread out," she said. "We need to triangulate."

They did as she asked, though there was only limited room on the roof of the rapidly slowing climber transport. Sam wondered if it would be enough, if they should fan out now. But Tania's face lit up a moment later, and then, through some technical prowess Sam wished she possessed, Tania made a blip appear on everyone's visor. Sam glanced over the edge and saw what she had already guessed, but the confirmation made all the difference. Alive or dead, Skyler was in that building.

"Vitals look good!" Tania shouted.

Alive and *not* dead, Skyler was in that building.

Vaughn came to her side. "Time to—"

"Don't you dare—"

"—rock and roll," he finished.

Sam punched him in the arm, hard. Then she laughed, a laugh that might be her last. "Yeah," she said, "yeah. Let's fucking dance."

She leapt from the platform toward the army of Scipios, and toward her friend.

He expected something dramatic. To throw his head back and howl as the link between minds occurred and memories began to flow into him. He expected his brain, indeed his whole nervous system, to buckle and thrash under the onslaught and sheer alienness of it all.

Reality didn't care what he expected, of course. What he felt was a curious, calming warmth that spread out from a pinpoint spot between his eyes, up and over his scalp to the base of his neck, and then inward. It tickled. It delighted him. He felt like he had the first time he'd sipped a truly good whiskey, only this sensation went right to the core of his skull, not to his belly. It was even more pleasant, more comforting, than the drink. Exponentially better.

He was conscious of the influx of . . . something . . . into his head. Memories, thoughts, an intellect. Yet it was all out of his grasp. Like knowing someone had entered the room but, just now, he couldn't turn around to say hello. He knew it was there, and that was the limit of his senses.

"Traveler," the being said, "your brain . . . is different."

"Okay?" He felt dizzy. Giddy. At peace.

"We understand you think of this as an immunity," it said. "It is more than that."

"What is it, then?"

A pause. Perhaps it did not understand yet, itself. Perhaps it wanted to keep the knowledge from him for some reason. But then it spoke. "My species has two separate brains. You are aware of this?"

"Yes."

"Humans have one, a trait shared with all others save us. But you, Traveler, you have something in between."

"In between?"

"Not one brain, not two, but a single physical organ capable of holding two states in each tiny quanta of the mind. In effect, the best of both, though from what I gather you've yet to adopt a true use for this beyond a simple hardening of your mental facilities."

Skyler considered this. He'd never really felt particularly hardened, mentally, but he had taken rather a lot of blows to the head in his recent life. "I think I understand," he said carefully. "Will I be able to, I don't know, recall your memories? When this is done?"

"You won't," it said. "But I will. If it works."

"You lost me."

"I will be in there with you, Skyler. A companion, living in this secondary state of your brain's structure."

He hesitated. This didn't sound good, all of a sudden. He felt like a monkey in a lab, if only for a moment. Too late now, he supposed. He'd taken its hand, given permission.

"We must hurry, Traveler," the voice said.

"Why?" Stupid question. He knew why. Still, it answered.

"They are coming."

Samantha didn't need a computer to know the truth of it.

They were going to be late.

After everything, all the vast distances covered, the alien world visited, the failed ruse at the edge of the solar system, the destruction of the *Chameleon,* and their strange calculated expulsion in-system to make one last effort at salvaging this fiasco. After all that, she was going to be thirty seconds late.

"Vaughn, Prumble," she said.

The two were nearby, behind her, in free fall toward the ground. Both acknowledged simultaneously.

"Give these bastards something to think about."

"Understood," Vaughn said.

"A pleasure," Prumble added.

Sam glanced to her right. "Tania? With me."

And Sam streamlined herself, roaring like a meteor toward the blip on her visor that was Skyler Luiken.

All at once the grounds around the complex in which he was located began to bubble with dazzling flashes of white and yellow. A few mortars each, the final supply now held in desperate reserve. The men started in with their beam weapons next, firing for effect. There was little point in attacking the big chrome monsters, but the rest of the alien rabble was fair game. Maybe it would trigger some protective instinct, make them back the fuck off. Maybe they'd get a lucky shot and rupture some fuel tank or another sensitive storage vessel. That would get the party started.

Sam was eight hundred meters off the ground now. Soon she'd be below the roofline of the larger city that surrounded this place. It all rushed toward her. The elegant outer structures and the ugly inner ones. The lumbering shiny bruisers and the flood of tiny scrambling foot soldiers that had heeded the battle call. All of it obscured by the dueling particles of ash and the freshly delivered and updated virus. Explosions tossed their flimsy bodies in all directions, reflected eerily off their larger counterparts. The big ones were of single-minded purpose now. One picked up ridiculous speed and practically galloped.

"Skyler, are you there? Answer! Skyler!" Tania had been repeating the request since finding his signal, so much so that her voice sounded raw and, Sam realized, she'd tuned the woman out.

"We go in through the roof," Sam said to her. "I'll take the side facing away from the Elevator, you go opposite."

"And then what?"

"I have no fucking idea," Sam answered as she blasted a hole in the roof from two hundred meters above. "I'm making this up as I go along."

"We must hurry," the alien had said.

The problem was Skyler didn't really know how to hurry. He was not, as far as he could tell, an active participant in this process. He just had to hold the alien's hand, and not fall off the bridge, which, though slick with rain and the spray of the frothy, icy river below, did have a low wall along each side, and, anyway, he lay in the middle of it, on his back, looking up at his new . . . friend. Companion. Whatever.

So he did his best to relax and let it happen. Vaguely he wondered what it would mean if the process were interrupted.

Was there a fail-safe? Or would he find himself the proud new owner of a half-mind with incomplete memories, insane from the lack of mental completeness and prone to late-night murderous rampages as a result?

Lightning began to flicker across the sky, and with it the sound of thunder. At first far away, but growing nearer quite rapidly. Part of the dreamscape, he wondered, or the real world bleeding through?

Skyler sat up a bit and looked over the wall. The river had swelled, its churned, whitecapped surface now licking the underside of the bridge. It grew higher as he watched, its surface drawn in dark grays save for the occasional—actually damn frequent now—flashes of lightning that inverted the dream-world's colorscape to blinding whites and pastel yellows that lingered inside his retinas.

A pain began to grow from the center of his skull. The opposite of that warm, easy beginning. The warmth became a fire, pushing outward. He wanted to let go of the hand and plunge his head into that water, which now licked at the top of the barrier wall. He felt as if he were cooking from the inside.

"Augh!" he shouted, lying back on the hard stones. He moved to let go, to pull his hand away. But the three-eyed alien clamped down with its long, slender hand. An iron grip that squeezed, squeezed, squeezed, not just his flesh but his mind from the pressure of the transfer. It flooded Skyler's cells, those unused bits he'd evidently had since birth, with all it had. A lifetime. A full consciousness that had lived many lifetimes, and all that entailed.

It all flowed in and he could comprehend none of it. Only the heat registered. The agony as his brain cooked, overloaded like a computer plugged into a HocNet a million units strong, all bursting with information and not a concern in the world for whether or not the deluge could be handled.

That water came over the wall.

It rushed to Skyler and smashed into his face, flooding into his nostrils and mouth, at once cool, which he welcomed, yet choking him. Instinctively he jumped to his feet, his perpetual handshake transformed into a stabilizing grasp. The bridge began to collapse from both ends. In mere seconds they were on an island again, an island of cobblestones already submerged. It was up to his ankles. His shins.

Skyler felt the stone beneath his feet begin to give way. He cried out in alarm, started to fall. The alien held him. It looked at him now, its three eyes suddenly wide open.

Then the middle one, the window to that higher mind, snapped closed.

"Finished," it said, and let go.

Skyler fell back and the torrent took him. And in the dark depths, glimpsed in the now-dim and terrible flash of lightning from above, he saw the silver tentacle come to take him down, down, down . . .

The snakelike chrome limb coiled around his midsection and ripped him from the medical pod. Skyler flopped out, arms and legs flailing, as the Scipio swarmer heaved him out of the machine and threw him against the wall.

He just had time to get his elbow up as the impact came. Coherent thought only returned with the sharp spike of pain that shot from his elbow straight into his thick, overworked brain.

Skyler felt like he'd just recovered from a great illness, the medication far from wearing off. His head, now full of who knows what, had a physical weight he'd never felt before, like someone had stuffed ten kilos of cotton between his ears. An illusion, surely. Memories had no mass. Did they?

The swarmer barely fit in the tiny chamber where the mind transfers occurred. It had only two of its six limbs in front of itself, and it used them now to tear the trio of medical pods from their connective apparatus, crumpling them like tin cans. On the other side of the room Skyler saw the being that had shared itself with him. It had been pulled free first, and now lay against the opposite wall, utterly still, no life in its three dark eyes.

Skyler tried to push himself to his feet, but his brain seemed slow to figure out how to work his limbs. He toppled against a stack of gear that crashed out from under him and found himself on the floor once again. He rolled in time to see the Scipio had shifted its focus back to him. It stared at him with its little array of sensors and lens-studded mechanical eyes, as if in disbelief that he could have survived what had gone on in here. The mind transfer, and the subsequent way in which he was thrown at the wall like a spaghetti noodle being tested for doneness.

Skyler lifted one heavy arm and aimed right at that bundle of lenses. He fired.

Well, he tried to. Nothing happened. He opened his mouth, the foulest of swears on his lips. . . .

And then a miracle.

The ceiling exploded above the thing. Debris rained down, and then something larger. A figure. A human.

A Samantha.

She landed hard right on top of the swarmer's curved hull and planted her wrist against the joint where one of its tentacles was connected to the body. One of the few places the mirror-shine was interrupted. Sam gave it the full force of her weapon. The tentacle sheared and fell away. The body began to writhe, but she did not let go. She moved her arm slightly and aimed into the hole left by the severed limb and fired again.

The beam came out the other side, scorching the floor.

The Scipio fell and rolled backward into the hall, lifeless, as Sam hopped neatly off and landed in front of Skyler. She extended a hand.

The gesture was so like what the alien had done in that shared hallucination that for a second he could only stare at it and shake his head in wonder.

Sam's mouth twisted up at one corner, her annoyed look. "Well," she said, "aren't you a sorry sight."

"Sam, I . . ."

Another figure came in through the door, climbing over the swarmer's carcass. Skyler leaned and saw Tania there. His heart clenched. She looked so tired, yet there was a wild ferocity in her eyes. The face of a soldier who hadn't slept in days because of the bombs falling all around. He reached out for her and she took his hand. She pulled him to his feet and folded her arms around him.

"There you are," she whispered.

Skyler tried to return the hug, he wanted nothing more in the world than to do so, but his arms weren't ready to listen. Tania sensed this, and shifted from hug to supportive hold, lifting one arm over her shoulder.

Sam took the other and together they helped him up.

"Hold on. What the hell, mate," Sam said, "were you taking a fucking nap down here?"

Skyler lifted his head. He grinned at her and let himself be lifted back to his feet. "Not exactly. I'll explain later."

"Are you okay?" Tania asked. She was staring into his eyes, really staring, as if she could not find the person she knew in them.

This worried him, because he wasn't that person anymore. Not exclusively. He could feel it, inside his head. Another. "I'll explain later," he repeated. It was all he could do.

A sharp punch of static in his ears. Skyler winced. Sam and Tania did the same at exactly the same moment. The signal coalesced and then Vanessa's voice filled his ears. "—anyone reading me? Please reply."

They all spoke at once, gushing, overjoyed. Prumble's voice there, too. Skyler wondered where he was, but Sam and Tania didn't seem worried so he filed it for later. Sam's voice won out. "Where are you, Vanessa? Are you safe?"

"I'm better than that," she replied. "We have a way home. A ship. But, uh, the Scipios aren't too happy about it. If we're going to get to you we have to do it now. Please tell me you're aboard that station, the one the Swarm is crowded around?"

"Uh." Sam looked at Skyler and Tania. "We're planetside just now."

"When you say planetside . . . you mean?"

"The base of that Elevator."

"Oh no," she said. "Get out now. Get away."

"Why? What's happened?"

"We're swinging around behind the planet again. Losing connec—et to orbit, all of you!"

"What's going on up there? Vanessa? Vanessa?!"

Prumble's voice interrupted Sam. "She's not kidding. You'd better come and see this."

Reuniting with Sam and Tania, then hearing Vanessa's voice

again, and now the sonorous tone of the dear Mr. Prumble, it was all too much. Skyler faltered, he wanted to lie down and give his brain a few years to cope with it all.

If only he had the time.

Sam and Tania carried Skyler to the hole Sam had made during her magnificent entrance. The three of them flew up and onto the roof in unison.

Skyler, shell-shocked, could not take his eyes away from the sky. It rained fire.

"Vanessa," he muttered to himself, "what did you do?"

The fireballs dripped through the choking haze of the new virus, causing the whole sky to flicker with brilliant oranges and yellows. They fell everywhere, the ones close to the horizon almost totally obscured by the powder-filled atmosphere, just tiny shimmering red orbs that vanished as they reached the ground. Closer, though, the flaming bits of debris made landfall with staggering velocity. Impacts rocked the entire city. Buildings exploded and began to collapse. The streets and plazas were being pulverized.

"To the Elevator!" Sam shouted over the cataclysmic noise. She ran, Tania on her heels, helping Skyler until he shrugged her off.

"I'm okay," he said to her, a half-truth. "Go, go!"

A falling chunk of something slammed into the adjacent building. The ground buckled, the shock wave like a hammer blow across Skyler's entire body. He flew sideways and almost fell from the roof, managing to get his feet under himself at the last possible second.

They ran. They soared. Skyler could not help but look to the sky at first, as if he might spot an incoming strike and avoid it. He knew this would be impossible. There were too many, coming far too fast, to avoid. All they could do was run.

"Prumble and Vaughn are there, waiting," Sam said. "They've got a climber."

The news focused Skyler's mind. Or, the half that was still his. As he ran he felt that second awareness wriggle and squirm. A purely mental sensation, but nonetheless real. It was in there. The Creator. Settling, no doubt struck numb and confused by the alien architecture of Skyler's brain. It could, of course, not be settling at all, but dying, forced into an incompatible structure. He could do nothing about that.

He could only run.

25

THE *LONESOME*

The darkness did not last. Beth Lee had anticipated the power outage aboard the ship and taken measures to shield critical components against the electromagnetic blast by safely shutting them off a split second before the wave hit. Still, it had been a terrifying stretch of pitch-black before the lights flickered and the computers restarted.

The *Lonesome* woke like a spooked animal, but there was no time to let her nerves settle.

Gloria stared at her displays and wondered how the hell she was going to make this work.

Her companions were on the floor. She glanced at the elevator site on her scope and frowned. The whole area around the base, and stretching now hundreds of kilometers to the east and west, was nothing but a constant shimmering eruption of tiny explosions. Landing there would be suicide, but even if the conditions were calm the *Lonesome* was not an atmosphere-rated craft. She could not land.

They'd have to come to her. But even if they could get a Scipio climber moving and left immediately, at best they would only reach a few thousand meters of altitude before the *Lonesome* passed uselessly overhead. Odds were they wouldn't be able to get the vehicle moving at all.

She touched the screen, drowning in a sudden all-consuming grief. If only she'd known they were down there. If only she'd realized what would happen to the ships in that swarm if they were expelled and could not change course. And this was only the beginning. They would be falling to the surface for weeks. There were living beings down there. Diseased and wandering but no less precious. Wildlife, probably, too.

She'd come here to save this place and instead initiated its destruction.

"Snap out of it, boss," Xavi said. He was at her shoulder. She hadn't heard him come up from his station.

"What do we do?"

"About the planet? Sorry, but that ship has sailed. Damage is done."

"And our friends? How could they survive . . . *that*?"

"They've made it through a lot. We have to assume they'll get through this. Anyway, we'll find out soon enough when we swing back around. The more important question is, how the bloody fucking hell are we going to get them aboard?"

Gloria stared at the images, her mind utterly blank. "It's impossible," she whispered. "Xavi, it can't be done."

"Suppose they get a climber working, reach the lowest station."

That would take far too long, but she couldn't bring herself to voice it. "And what, we somehow dock and welcome them aboard? The Scipios just stand aside and let us match velocities and pick them up?"

"They're suited. We don't have to dock."

"But we're going too fast, Xavi. Even if we could slow down in time, which I doubt, we don't have the fuel to get back up to fold speeds again. We'd be too deep in the gravity well. Stuck here, don't you see?"

"I have an idea."

It was Beth, at the ladder, her head just peeking above the hole in the floor that led down to the lower levels of the ship.

She remained there, as if fearful of coming closer, of how Gloria might react. It had been her idea, after all, that had caused the Scipio fleet to shatter and fall to the surface. As much as she tried, though, Gloria couldn't find it in herself to cast blame on the engineer. And besides, it had worked, just too well.

"I'm listening," she said to her.

Beth came up a bit farther, her hands white-knuckled on the ladder rungs. "Suppose," she said, and then voiced the craziest goddamn idea Gloria Tsandi had ever heard.

Insane.

Brilliantly insane.

"You've got to be fucking kidding me," Skyler shouted.

Vanessa indicated she was most certainly not fucking kidding him.

He stood on the roof of a climber, next to Vaughn. Below, on the ground inside the port structure at the base of the Elevator, Tania and the others argued as they tried to figure out how to get the damn thing to move.

Only Vanessa, by way of Gloria, by way of Beth, had just told him how to get the damn climber to move. How to get it to move rather damn fast, in fact.

"Insanity," Skyler whispered.

The walls of the building around them shook. Chunks of loose equipment fell from the high conical ceiling, crashing to the floor soundlessly because the riot of impacts outside drowned all else.

"They're working out the math right now, but it looks like it will work. Skyler, please, it's the only option."

"Okay. Okay. It beats sitting here while the whole planet is blown to shit around us, I guess. We'll do it, we'll do it now."

"No," Vanessa said.

"What do you mean, 'no'? This place is an epic inferno!"

"The timing is critical. You have to do it in . . . Hold on, Beth's running the . . . Yes, okay, I'll tell him. Skyler."

"I'm listening."

"Start a timer on your visor. Set it for one minute and twenty-two seconds, point five."

269

He dialed it in, wanting to laugh and cry at the fractional value, as if he'd be able to accomplish that kind of precision, because his shattered display had room only for the first part.

Vanessa went on. "Start it on my mark. In three . . . two . . . one . . . mark."

Skyler started the timer. Then he told the others what needed to be done. They all stared at him as if he'd suggested they stand around a campfire and sing songs. Except for Tania. Her expression was dangerously thoughtful.

"Huh," was all she said. Then she added, for good measure, "That might actually work."

He'd just opened his mouth to reply when the building shook again. A close one, this time. Skyler staggered and blinked as a rain of dust fell all around him. "Much more of this and the whole place will come down on us."

"Then what are we waiting for?" Prumble asked. "If Tania's on board with this, then . . . well, who am I to argue."

Another blast, even closer than the last one.

"That was no crash," Sam said, moving behind some fresh debris for cover. "That was a landing."

Vaughn matched her positioning, the two of them ready before Skyler, Tania, and Prumble had even realized the truth of their observation.

A horde came through the wall as it exploded inward. Chunks of stone and metal skittered across the wide loading bay at the heart of the climber port. Skyler dove, felt something smash into his leg. Even Eve's armor could not deaden the pain this time. He took a nasty blow that sent him wheeling into a support pillar. He cried out as white-hot pain pulsated in his left calf. Tania was there with him, one hand on his chest to keep him down, the other aimed outward at the Scipios piling into the room. Her wrist-weapon chattered, so fast it almost ran together in a high-pitched yowl.

Across from her, behind the debris pile, Sam and Vaughn moved in unison, firing as Tania was and then, abruptly, unleashing a synchronized barrage from their mortars. The whole room thrummed with violent energies too numerous to do anything but blur. Skyler ground his teeth. The pain in his leg was as bad as any he'd ever known, but it was fading.

Tania shouted something to him.

He glanced at her. "What?"

"The timer!"

"Shit!" he had to blink tears away to see the numbers, and coughed bile when his vision cleared enough to reveal the truth. "Fifteen seconds!"

Tania heaved him to his feet in one remarkably smooth motion, and then thrust him toward the parked climber, wounded leg or not. He limped across the narrow gap, hopping like an idiot. Tania was shouting to the others, giving cover fire as Sam and Vaughn exhausted the last of their mortar rounds.

Prumble had taken refuge behind the climber, and as the group approached he stepped out and let loose with both beam weapons, sweeping them across the throng of enemies and then across the pillars that held the roof up.

"Eight seconds!" Skyler shouted. Could they hear him in this mess? No time to confirm.

The base of the climber was a flat disk, the main body of the vehicle perched atop it giving it the general shape of a drinking glass perched on a saucer, the flat space around the bottom perhaps a meter thick. A ramp extended out to the loading bay at one side, but the rest of the climber was merely suspended over a deep pit stretching down into darkness. Somewhere, far below, the elevator cord plunged into the rock of Carthage and anchored this end to the world.

Skyler landed and took a position on one side of the climber's platform base. He lay facedown and leaned out until he was looking at the underside of the climber, where the mechanism that physically clamped on to the cord and crawled its length ended and the silvery-gray ribbon of the space elevator emerged and ran down into the abyss.

Tania Sharma took up a spot next to him on the left. Sam was on the right. Above, Prumble and Vaughn did their absolute best to keep the enemies at bay. Skyler could feel the presence of that writhing horde. Hundreds of Scipios and several of the large, reflective swarmer vehicles. He did not know if they were here to stop them, or if they'd simply come in desperate search of a way off-world.

Well, he thought, *prepare to be disappointed.*

He watched the timer. Three, two, one, point-fucking-five.

"Fire!"

Here came the question mark. The bit that, in his mind, seemed a dangerously gigantic assumption. The three of them unleashed their beam weapons at maximum strength, full burn, and they *focused.*

Six beams, erratic at first, gradually converged on the ribbon cable that extended perhaps a kilometer below this point and nearly fifty thousand klicks above.

He wondered, when Vanessa explained this, if it would be like sawing through a heavy rope with a butter knife, or trying to sever a tendon by chewing on it with weak teeth.

It was neither. The ribbon, miraculously, snapped like a wire cut with shears.

The planet anchored this end of the cable. At the other end, way up in space, a counterweight anchored the other. As Carthage spun it threw that counterweight ever outward, and the elevator cable held them together, pulled taut by the two opposing forces.

A phenomenal *thwong* marked the end of this relationship. Skyler, Sam, and Tania all heaved themselves backward onto the platform as the entire climber vehicle, clamped as it was on to that now-severed cord, shot upward like a missile.

Vanessa had warned of this. It didn't matter. All five of them immediately lost consciousness as the climber was yanked like a yo-yo away from the grip of Carthage.

Gloria pitched the *Lonesome* into a steep dive, aiming for the Elevator. She could not kill the engines—they were providing all the power now—so she pushed them into a reverse thrust. A light touch. This had to be perfect, and this was her ship to pilot. Xavi had laid the course, but Gloria insisted she take it from there.

She'd never been one to shy away from letting the computers handle flight duties. They could make a trillion decisions in a few microseconds, after all, based on thousands of data-points and readings.

But this was different. She had no idea what to expect here, nor did anyone else, so Gloria knew the moment they'd put this rescue in motion that it would be her gut making the calls this time.

"Boss," Xavi said. "The Elevator."

"I see it," she said. "I'm going to . . . Oh. *Oh!*"

The sight before her defied belief, even though deep down she could not imagine what else would have happened when they severed the cord.

The whole thing, the whole Scipio space station apparatus, relied on that cord. And now it was all coming apart. The orbital structures were bending and twisting along a path becoming more erratic by the second. It had all come undone, quite literally. And somewhere, down toward the bottom, a climber would be dangling from that insane unpredictable mess, and with any luck there would be five likely quite terrified human beings clinging to it for dear life.

"Boss," Xavi said.

"Yeah, yeah, I got it."

"No, not that. Above."

Gloria looked, and her heart fell into her stomach.

"So many," she whispered.

The electromagnetic bomb had done incredible damage. More than she could ever have hoped for. But that compacted ball of Swarm ships had been almost innumerably large. Beth's weapon had disabled half a million, a reasonable guess, Gloria felt, and those had been flung out in all directions. Most out into space. A sizable group had fallen to the world below and many more would follow over time. Some had even slammed into the space stations along the cord, or into other Scipio ships in the area. But that left almost as many unaffected, and like hounds after the hare they had the scent of the *Lonesome* and were coming all at once.

A cloud of death drawn against the moon Gloria had all too recently fled, they poured like a single sentient thing toward the *Lonesome*'s path.

In her heart she wanted to shout at them. To stand and scream, *"Bring it on!"* In her head she knew the truth of it, though. They were far too many, and far too fast. She would not reach the cord. Not even close.

"Oh hell," she said.

Something truly strange happened then. Gloria had to blink because her mind refused to acknowledge what was going on.

It was her radar display. It made a strange sort of chittering sound she'd never heard before, and only after a long second did she recognize it for what it was. It was the sound of a new contact, but so many had been spotted it made about ten thousand of these sounds all at once.

And the screen had erupted in a riot of icons. The uncountable red for the Scipio ships, gray for the space stations that writhed and danced along the recoiling space elevator, and also something new. An armada of "unknowns."

"What is that?!" she breathed.

Xavi did not reply, and she knew him well enough to know he would even now be training their mil-spec sensors onto one of the newcomers. Gloria swallowed hard, wondering what new threat the Scipios had brewed up and dreading the answer. There was a part of her that, just for a second, hoped these were ships from Earth, flying to the rescue. What else, after all, could just blip into existence like that?

But no, that was only a fantasy. Fold-ships made a violent entrance. If thousands of ships from Earth arrived this close they'd all be annihilated by the strange forces that flowed out of that maneuver, and anyway, Earth did not have even fifty ships that could fold space. Of those only one—now that the *Wildflower* was gone—could fold in close to a gravitational body. Gloria sat at the controls of that ship right now.

"It's . . . ," Xavi said, and even he had to pause to catch his breath. "It's the Builders."

The scope image came into focus. A long, seed-shaped vessel identical to the remnant that had sat above Darwin, Australia, so long ago. Then the image shifted to another. And another. And another. Every second it cycled as the armada of Builder ships arrived.

Instantly the swirling morass of the Scipio Swarm shifted. It broke like the unfolding arms of an octopus, one section remaining in pursuit of the *Lonesome* while many others branched and twisted away to address this newly arrived threat.

And a threat the Builders were. The ships opened fire as they came into range. Everything Gloria could see became awash with brilliant flashes and the spray of molten projectiles.

"It's Eve," Vanessa said abruptly. "She says . . . she says this is our moment."

Gloria felt a wide grin expand across her face. "Here we go, everyone. Hang on to something."

She twisted the *Lonesome* upward, parallel with the collapsing, wavy space elevator, and throttled the engines to maximum burn. An indicator in the corner of her screen began to tick upward toward escape velocity.

"Were you successful?" the familiar voice asked.

"Eve," Skyler whispered through a jaw clenched tight. The climber shifted like a large ship on a stormy sea, pulled one way and then on some great unseen curve lurched back in the other direction. Above, the cord had gone from a rail-straight line to an undulating ribbon, the curves becoming more and more pronounced as the whole thing was heaved upward. "Eve, not now."

They were dangling at one end. Skyler felt the icy air on his face growing colder and then painfully frigid. His nose had gone numb, and his breaths were now a mighty effort that made his lungs sting from the freezing temperatures.

"Sam, my visor," he managed to say.

She looked at him from her spot on the platform. They were all lying on it, holding on for dear life. She seemed confused for a second, and then realized his problem. "Shit," she said. "Tania, his visor is open. He's going to freeze to death."

Tania began to crawl her way to him.

"Skyler . . . ," Eve said.

"Not now!"

"Did you succeed?"

Tania was grabbing his arm and pulling him. His whole face hurt, and he had to close his eyes lest they freeze over. He could feel his spit freezing.

And then he was off the platform, and Skyler imagined himself tossed overboard, deadweight. This lasted half a second until his back slammed down onto the floor of the climber. The sounds of the rushing air vanished a second later with a dull click.

He waited, felt the warmth returning, and when he had the courage he opened his eyes. He was in a small room, Tania collapsed against the wall across from him, studying him.

"Are you okay?" she asked.

"Where . . . ," he began, and then he knew. The climber compartment. "Why didn't we get in here before?" he asked.

"Because it was full of soldiers before. We thought they were still inside and Prumble decided not to bother facing them unless they came out on their own." She narrowed her eyes. "Who were you talking to a second ago?"

"Eve," he said.

Her eyebrows rose. "What?!"

"Eve."

"She's not gone? But I thought—"

Skyler held up a hand. "Eve," he said. "I'm listening now." He bridged the comm channel so Tania could listen.

"Did you succeed?" the Builder intelligence asked.

"I . . . ," he started, and realized a strange truth. "I really don't know. I don't think so."

And then, quite bizarrely, his mouth moved of its own accord. Several incomprehensible sounds tumbled out. Then something like language.

Eve replied, in kind.

"What the hell was that?" Tania asked breathlessly.

Skyler waved her off. He felt for that moment like a passenger in his own body.

"Skyler," Eve said.

"I'm here now. What was that? What just happened?" He asked the question, though in his heart he already knew. He was not a passenger in his body, but he carried one.

"You hold our salvation within you," she replied. "We have come to help you get away."

"Have you been here this whole time?" he demanded. "Did you just decide to let us fumble about here?"

"No," the AI replied. "When I realized the *Chameleon* was doomed I sent you off on the best paths I could, and then I transmitted myself out, toward another of my kind. We gathered, and as one we decided to return if we saw signs that it would benefit you for us to do so. When the Swarm began to fall inward, we advanced, staying just out of range, watching—"

"Skyler!" Vanessa interrupted. "The Builders are here! In force!"

He inhaled shakily, aware of the dangers of hope but unable to stop the feeling from coursing through him. "Are you ready for us?" he asked.

"We'll find out," Vanessa replied.

26

THE *LONESOME*

The *Lonesome* dipped below the end of the elevator cable as Gloria pulled it from its free-fall dive into a vicious climb. The hull shook violently as the engines strained against the planet's gravity.

There was too much debris now for a human, no matter how skilled, to have control. Gloria ceded maneuvering thrust to the ship and turned her focus to the next task.

"Vanessa, Alex, ready down there?"

"As we'll ever be," the woman replied.

"Seal it up, then."

Seconds later the center chamber of the *Lonesome*'s interior became an airlock reception room, segregated from the compartments above and below.

"Xavi," Gloria queried.

"Go ahead."

"Don't take your damn eyes off that velocity reading. When it's right, we go, no matter what."

"Got it, boss," he said.

All her focus poured into the climber then. It was a blip on the screen, but growing fast. She dropped a marker on it, and had the computer calculate its path and figure out how to line up the *Lonesome* with it at the moment their velocities matched.

No solution came. The *Lonesome* was already going too fast.

She eased off the engines slightly. Then a bit more. A little more.

"Boss, we're slowing."

"No choice," she said. "Got to match them. No talking now."

He made no reply. Good lad. Gloria dialed the engines back another tick and—*yes!*—their path would meet the climber. The ship turned and twisted onto the new course.

Gloria Tsandi flipped on the PA. "This is your captain speaking," she said formally. "Prepare to take on passengers."

A celebratory holler went up from Xavi's bay, one floor below. Beth cheered into her mic, and Vanessa, a moment later, acknowledged on the comm.

"Swarmers inbound!" Xavi shouted.

Gloria glanced at the display. *They're on to us,* she thought. *They understand now.*

The blips were closing fast. She switched one screen to the rear view. Most of it was blotted out by the turbulent flare of the engines, but off to one side she could see the spherical body of a Scipio Swarm ship as it arced in toward the *Lonesome,* tentacles stretched forward to grab.

No, she realized, not to grab.

It was firing a weapon.

The *Lonesome* lurched and, for one horrifying second, Gloria thought they'd been punched by some missile. But it was only the evasive actions of the autopilot. A hail of rail gun projectiles tore through space mere centimeters from the hull.

And then the swarmer exploded. A dazzling fireball that whited out her screen and shook the *Lonesome* as expanding gases and debris slammed into her. Gloria saw a blurred streak lance through the remains of the enemy vessel only a heartbeat later. A Builder ship, at full acceleration, diving downward, had annihilated the enemy and kept going, straight down, to their home world. A place the Builders had not visited in centuries.

A ping from her console whipped her attention back. "We're okay! We're okay! Ten seconds!"

The ship began to wiggle as a thousand tiny course corrections occurred. *Too fast,* Gloria thought. *We're coming in way too fast.*

Then the climber snapped to one side, yanked by yet another perturbation of the ribbon to which it was attached as some station, hundreds of kilometers above, exploded and released its mass from the line.

The ship had expected this. Counted on it, in fact. Its calculations were perfect. The change in direction brought the climber straight toward the *Lonesome,* and her ship rolled to meet it at just the right angle, all at the very moment that the two objects were moving at an identical velocity away from Carthage.

A deep boom rocked the ship.

Skyler gulped and then covered his face with his arms. A pointless thing, but he couldn't just do nothing.

"Déjà vu," Tania said, one arm around him as she prepared to open the door.

"If you give me your air again this time I'll never forgive you." He made a little gap between his elbows to see through, and caught her smiling at him.

"When you reach the vacuum, exhale every bit of air in your lungs. Otherwise your chest will explode," she said, smile fading.

"That's . . . a visceral image. Thanks for the tip."

"Here they come!" Samantha shouted from outside.

It happened so fast he barely followed the series of events. A rush as the door opened and the air was sucked out into space. Tania's strong hands guiding him, her boots propelling them across the gap. He slammed into something. They'd missed. No, he felt arms, a squeezing embrace. Another slam, this time solid. A wall, maybe the outer hull of the other ship. They had missed!

Skyler kept his eyes clenched shut against the vacuum and felt the bizarre sensation of naked skin against the vast emptiness. A thousand pinpricks of pain. No sound whatsoever. His ears stung as if spikes of ice had been jabbed in there.

Then a hiss. High and strange, lilting and growing stronger, deeper. High-pitched voices, shouting. Cries that sounded inhuman, so thin and distant. It all crashed down into normality like a curtain falling. Not inhuman cries, he realized, but cheering. The arms around him tightened, and he felt a pounding hand against his back. "We made it! We made it!" Prumble roared.

Skyler pulled his arms away from his face. Vanessa stared at him, her arms around him. He grinned and embraced her with all his strength.

They had made it. They were aboard and the airlock had been sealed.

Tania joined the hug, a smile so wide on her face he found himself matching it reflexively. Sam and Vaughn were pressed together behind her and to the left, arms around each other, their helmets already off to allow the deepest kiss Skyler thought he'd ever seen. He saw Prumble, smiling like a fool in one corner, clasping hands with Alex Warthen, of all people.

A voice came over the PA. "Did we get them?"

"Captain Tsandi," Skyler replied. "Permission to come aboard?"

"Granted, Mr. Luiken," the voice replied.

Another cheer went up.

The captain shushed them. "No time for a welcoming party, I'm afraid. Get below and strap in. I fear that was the easy part."

A click at Skyler's feet as the interior door unsealed. Tania went first, pulling her own helmet off as she went. Skyler followed right behind toward a common area where the crew likely relaxed under normal circumstances. This was not, he realized suddenly, Gloria's ship. Too big by far. He'd ask later. Skyler found a harness chair that unfolded from the wall and heaved himself into it. The craft lurched suddenly and something boomed outside.

Everyone froze, looking around. A strange moment of helplessness as they waited to see if the vessel would crack open or, more likely, it would all just end before their minds could comprehend it. Vaporization by a direct hit. But nothing happened. Just a boom that rattled their bones and then the desperate flight continued.

Skyler buckled his harness and looked directly across the small chamber at Tania. She held his gaze, and he hers. The moment dredged up old memories of their flight to Hawaii, when he'd first met her, and they'd leapt out of the *Melville* together and into horrible danger. He smiled, and she returned it.

Prumble settled in beside her. Sam and Vaughn to Skyler's left.

The five of them sat in silence as passengers, unable to do anything but wait, and trust the skill of their new captain.

Gloria ramped the engines back to maximum burn, though she had no idea what she was going to do next. Ahead, at a distance that rapidly approached zero, loomed a cloud of debris so large and thick she could not see the stars beyond it. She added the maneuvering thrusters, also at full bleed, to try to push the *Lonesome* clear, but no amount of course correction would take them out of harm's way. Not unless she turned the ship and used the main engines to handle the task. She did not have the fuel for that. She could only go straight ahead, with minimal drift thanks to the tiny engines on the sides of the ship, and . . . and what?

The craft would be pulverized in that field of shrapnel. The space station there had come apart, or been blown apart. Now a billion tiny pieces of destroyed Scipio tech stood in her way. Not enemies bristling with weapons, not those terrifying orbs with their probing segmented tentacles. No, the enemy now was just bits. Chunks of space station no bigger than her hand or as large as a building, it didn't matter. She couldn't avoid either if they were going to reach escape velocity, and she couldn't reach escape velocity if the *Lonesome* was torn to shreds by all that flaming junk.

"Boss?" Xavi asked, an utterly foreign note of panic in his voice. "Are we really going through that?"

"No choice," she said.

"I know but—"

"No choice," Gloria repeated. "Sorry."

A silence stretched between them at the word, and she thought she'd lost him. She'd finally made a decision that even his sense of loyalty could not accommodate.

"You got us this far," he said then. "I'm with you. Always will be."

Gloria Tsandi fought back a sudden rush of emotions—regret, sorrow, love, it was all there in full force, but this was not the time. She snarled at the image before her, the debris field, as if by a sheer outpouring of anger she could make it go away.

Countless tiny explosions began to ripple through the field.

"Boss!" Xavi shouted. Excitement there. Triumph.

She glanced at her readouts and saw what he saw. A half-dozen Builder ships swooped in and pulled alongside the *Lonesome,* their guns roaring. The path before her did not clear, that would have been impossible, but the Builders reduced the obstacles in front of her to so much dust. Their numbers swelled as the forces converged around the one target that mattered. Builder ships tore in-system at monstrous speeds, becoming missiles themselves, slamming into space stations all around the belt of the world. Scipio ships and those of their clients began to flee, knowing the party had finally, after so many centuries, ended.

Gloria knew in that moment that this was not the final battle, though. There was no ending here, but a beginning. The start of a great war, but it would be a war out of spite. This place had been the source of the Scipios' power all this time, since their betrayal, and knowing that, she felt she understood that what she'd done, what they'd all done, was the only solution possible. This place needed to be razed to ever truly be wrenched from the Scipios' foul grip.

As the *Lonesome* reached the debris zone, speed climbing, engines thrumming, her hull was peppered by a million bits of microscopic flotsam and scoured down to the bare metal, but she made it through. A thousand warnings on the screen, Klaxons wailing, but they'd done it.

"Beth!" Gloria shouted. "It's all up to you now! Go for fold!"

"I'm ready!" the engineer replied.

"Someone kindly ask those Builder ships to get clear," she added. "They're not going to want to be anywhere near us when this thing goes off." After a second she added, "And please, thank them. For me. For all of us."

Skyler acknowledged.

"Now then," Gloria said, "Miss Lee? If you'd be so kind? Get us the fuck out of here."

From a launch tube on the *Lonesome*'s belly, a field cavitation imploder rocketed outward, straight ahead, and Gloria pushed the ship beyond all safety restrictions to catch it.

"It is we who thank you," Eve said to Skyler's relayed message. "You have undone a great injustice here."

"The price, though."

"We all knew the price," Eve replied. "We just couldn't pay it until we had what you now carry."

"What is it, Eve? Inside me."

This reply took longer, but judging by the intensity of the battle outside he could hardly blame her. The ship began to shake, far worse than earlier, worse than anything Skyler had ever known, even when he'd ditched his own beloved *Melville* over Australia. The *Lonesome* was going to shake itself apart, had to, no way it could keep this up.

He held on for all he was worth, Tania's hand clasped in his right, Vanessa's in his left. He screwed his eyes shut and waited for this implosion to occur, or for the ship to come to pieces by its own insane acceleration or simply because some swarmer out there happened to get a tentacle into its path.

"A great mind," Eve finally replied. "A Passenger now, a stranger. It does not know how to talk to you, how to make use of what you can offer it. But in time, it will."

"I . . . I think I understand."

"You must keep yourself safe, Skyler Luiken," Eve said. "It is the last of our Creators within you, and all the memories it was able to collect. A substantial trove."

He marveled that it could all fit. He was lucky to remember which shoe went on which foot, some mornings. And to stay safe! He did laugh aloud at that. "Eve, I cannot imagine a scenario less safe than the one I'm presently in."

"Then perhaps you should have a look outside," she replied.

To hammer that point home the *Lonesome* was rocked to its core. The lights went out, briefly, and Skyler heard the engine stutter.

"Hell!" he heard Gloria shout from several decks away. Her

voice came on the PA a second later. "Close one, but we're on target. Eighteen seconds.".

Just a little bit more, Gloria silently urged. *Give me a little more.*

The ship seemed to have nothing to give, though. The rate of acceleration did not increase. Gloria regretted her lie. That blast had left them off target, in truth. Too slow, and the *Lonesome* would not be able to make it up.

She could cancel the implosion. That was a terrible idea, though. She'd save all their lives, but give the Scipios the ultimate consolation prize as the fold device went inert and floated about the system, ready to be plucked by one of the fleeing ships.

No shortage of those, either. Gloria's radar looked more like an aquarium full of spooked fish. Ships were everywhere, going in every direction and at every speed. Shooting one another to pieces, slamming into things when their ammunition was spent or their courses could no longer be changed. It was a bloodbath, an orgy of wrath against desperation.

"And here comes the big finale," she whispered as the imploder neared its moment. She would not stop it. Could not. *At least,* she thought, *we'll all go together, and none the wiser.*

She felt a strange, small punch in her lower back. Familiar, except that she had not commanded it.

The *Lonesome* had found its nerve, and accelerated hard at the last possible moment. And then all at once everything went dark. Screens, displays, everything.

A hundred meters below her, unbeknownst to Gloria Tsandi, her engineer, Beth Lee, had *fiddled* with something. She'd recognized the dilemma and instead of pondering her legacy she'd found a solution. Later, much later, Gloria would thank her for that bit of initiative and clearheaded thinking. She couldn't just now because the ship had lost power. The ship had lost power because Beth Lee had taken it all and rammed it back into the engines for one . . .

. . . final . . .

Burst.

The imploder's core ignited.

JASON M. HOUGH

Space and time crashed inward in a blast powerful enough to ignite a star. Energies so titanic that the very fabric of the universe was turned violently inside out. Whatever Scipio infrastructure was left in that area all slammed inward, pinched together to an infinitely small point. It all collided in the center and rebounded outward like a supernova.

All except the one thing that had been close enough to ride the fold.

The *Lonesome* had vanished.

27

THE

The *Lonesome* did not reappear near Earth. Far from it, in fact.

Gloria, even in that hurried and frantic escape, remembered enough of her training not to point the Scipios right where they could go to find a new home world to conquer.

"No," Gloria said, "I'm afraid we're adrift in the middle of nothing, a billion miles from anything of note."

She noted the crestfallen expressions on their faces, save for that of Xavi and Beth, who knew the score. Gloria smiled, and let the other shoe drop. "Well, that's not exactly true. This is a staging point, one well known to the fleet. There's even a supply cache here, and a small space station where we can rest."

"Oh hell," Prumble boomed. "I like you." He turned to Vanessa, seated beside him. "I like her quite a lot."

"You like everyone," Vanessa said, laughing.

The big man laughed right along with her.

In the days that followed they rested, ate, and partied. They spent many hours recounting all that had happened, and mourning the two they'd left behind despite the circumstances of their deaths. Some of them made love, were even quite . . . spirited, in those endeavors. Samantha was not the sort of person one asked to keep it down.

Some merely lay in each other's arms.

Tania rested her palm over Skyler's heart and felt the rhythm of his pulse. Her cheek rested on his shoulder, allowing her to gaze past his strong chin and out the expansive window of the magnificently appointed outpost. She and Skyler did not make love. He couldn't, not yet. "I'm no longer just me, Tania. There's someone . . . something else . . . in here, and I can sense it observing through me. It's too strange. For now. I'm sorry."

She did not mind. It was enough for her simply to be in his company, and—though she felt rotten to admit it—without any competition or romantic politics to consider. They didn't talk about Tim, save a toast with the group to mourn his death. Prumble said kind words, as kind as could be found, at least. In the end the poor young man had been blinded by affection for her, and so she felt partly to blame in a strange way. She knew she should not, that this was a false line of thought of the worst sort, but there it was.

After sixteen days spent in recovery, conversation, and somber celebration, a blip appeared on the radar exactly one million kilometers away. Tania knew from Gloria's smile that this was not a pursuing Scipio warship, nor even Eve come to give a more proper and proportional thanks.

It was a ship from Earth. A beautiful, sleek thing. Tania sat beside Skyler and watched it approach, and it swelled her heart to know that humanity had made such a brilliant recovery since the plague had been eradicated.

An hour later they went aboard, Tania with one arm around Vanessa, grinning like she hadn't been able to do in a very long time. Another hour and space was folded over on itself once again, and this time they punched into a deep orbit out beyond Neptune and began the long, leisurely cruise toward Earth.

28

DARWIN, AUSTRALIA

10.DEC.3911

A summer shower did nothing to dampen the mood of those gathered.

They danced in a corner of Nightcliff normally serene and sparsely trafficked. A park of rolling green grass and meandering paths, where small plaques at regular intervals marked the locations of the many historic events that had taken place here. Along one edge ran the low "cliff" of the shoreline, and beyond waves flecked with the golden glitter of sunset bobbed and rolled.

Against the heat of that afternoon, and the downpour that followed, a great tent had been erected in the park. This had done its job during the wedding ceremony, but despite its vastness could not contain the party that followed.

"Sam's okay with this crowd?" Tania asked, one arm looped through Skyler's as they strolled along the shore, far enough from the revelers to have some quiet, but not so far as to be accused of ditching the event.

Skyler grinned. "Sam wanted a small affair. Vaughn wanted to invite the whole planet. This was the compromise."

"Uh-huh," Tania said, unconvinced, enjoying the distant sounds of laughter rolling across the park where the Platz mansion had once stood. In the middle distance the gleaming new elevator tower seemed to leap into the darkening sky. New to her, at any rate. A historical site already to those of Gloria Tsandi's Earth. "So strange," she whispered, the words all but lost on the breeze.

Skyler pulled her a little closer. "What is?"

"The contrast. Visiting this place twice in as many years, from our perspective. Seeing how it's changed."

"Some awful things happened here," he said.

"It's lovely now."

A climber, sparkling in the setting Sun, slid down the now-ancient elevator cord and disappeared into the top of the tower. Beyond, huge skyscrapers both old and new stretched from horizon to horizon.

"They're building a defense fleet," Skyler said, after a time.

"I heard. Not sure how I feel about it, but I can't blame them."

"I suppose not." Skyler took a seat on a bench on the edge of the path and she settled in next to him. A row of trees behind them rustled in the breeze, stirred by a natural rise in the wind.

It reminded her of another bench, a long time ago, on one of the farm platforms, where Neil had first told her that he'd hired a scavenger to find the data she'd needed. Some pilot named Skyler, but she wouldn't know that for some time.

"Do you think they'll come here? The Scipios?" she asked.

"I don't really want to think about it," he answered, his fatigue seeping into the words whether he'd intended it or not. "I feel like we've done our share."

"I won't argue with that."

Skyler took her hand and held it tight. "I'm more interested to know if the Builders will come. If they'll take this . . . whatever . . . out of my head, or at least tell me what the hell I'm supposed to do with it."

Tania kept her questions unvoiced. She had so many, but he wasn't ready. The Passenger mind within him had yet to manifest itself in any meaningful way, save for the occasional guttural snippets of speech voiced through Skyler's mouth as he slept beside her, late at night. In the cool evening air, as the summer rains fell outside the flat they'd been gifted, Tania would do her best to soothe the dreams he never remembered, and hopefully soothe the *other* as well. At least they knew it yet lived.

At some point, when he was ready, Skyler would ask for her help, and she had a plan prepared. She would teach the Passenger, via Skyler, as if it were a toddler. If her theory was true, that would help it mesh with the pathways inside the human brain that were still wholly alien to it.

A bright light caught her eye, off near the wedding tent. Several hovering camera drones buzzed around a lavishly dressed figure, who made sweeping gestures as he spoke to their lenses.

"Prumble's on the 'nets again," she said.

Skyler laughed and shook his head, amazed and amused in equal proportion. "The man, the myth, the legend."

The former smuggler lord of Darwin's post-apocalypse underworld had become a major celebrity in this post-post-apocalyptic version of their home. He'd even hinted at running for the OEA council. "Literally two thousand years of perspective," he joked his campaign slogan would be, saying the statement was perfectly honest by political standards. For now, at least, he was content to give almost daily interviews, broadcast all over the resettled world. In doing so he'd taken the spotlight, and the pressure, off the rest of the crew, and Tania suspected Prumble's love of the lens was, in truth, more of a sacrifice made for the benefit of his friends.

She loved him for that, and so much more. She loved all of them.

Except one. She held back a sigh at the thought of Tim.

"It's weird," Skyler said, after a silence.

"What is?" she asked.

"I can feel this thing sometimes, inside me. It's like it's . . . I don't know, groping around. Sizing things up. It's like . . . revisiting a place you once lived."

"I did that just recently," Tania said. "Anchor Station." She'd barely recognized any of it, so much had been replaced in the centuries gone by, but a few of the original rings remained, preserved as a kind of monument, and it had been one of the strangest experiences of her life. "I guess that's not really what you mean," she admitted.

Skyler waved her off, not unkindly. "It is, though. It's like visiting a place like that and getting that flood of memory that comes back. That nostalgia. And yet at the same time I have this sense that there's someone else with me, there for the first time and trying to make sense of it all, but I can't explain any of it."

"Don't take this the wrong way, but I'm fascinated by this. By you."

He grunted, amused and perhaps a little frustrated, too, for which she could hardly blame him. Skyler let go of her hand and stood, ready to walk again. After a few hundred meters they reached a part of the path that ran along the route of the original wall erected around Nightcliff to protect the Elevator's base. They followed it for a long time in silence, well away from the party now. The marvelous, impossibly modern city vaulted upward all around them. People ate in brightly colored restaurants along Wall's Path, as it was known. There was even a pub called Woon's Tavern, though Skyler had scoffed at that the first time they'd seen it, days ago.

Eventually they reached Ryland Square, where food riots had triggered so much of the strife that surrounded the days of the Builders' tests.

Skyler stood for a time and just looked at it all, and Tania said nothing, allowing him to remember, and perhaps also to forget. And maybe also to let the mind inside him see what he was seeing, so it might understand what befell this world just to save it.

He started to walk again. He said, "I suppose we're both trying to figure each other out. It needs me to experience the world, and I must find a way to . . . put up barriers, as bad as that sounds."

"No," she said. "It doesn't. I understand."

He smiled a bit sadly, and squeezed her shoulder. "I have to find a way to still be me, when I want to. I have to find a way to not let it talk through my mouth when I don't want it to."

She took his hand this time, and he let her. The sounds of the wedding celebration drifted to them again on the wind, growing a little louder with each step. It sounded quite raucous now.

She'd expected nothing less, considering the bride and groom.

"I just wish I knew what I was supposed to do with it," Skyler said, still embroiled in his thoughts.

She had no real answer for him. Theories, but nothing more.

He sensed her hesitation, shifted a little, put an arm around her. "Doesn't matter," he said. "We'll figure it out, or we won't. I don't see what we can do in the meantime, one way or the other, except live our lives."

"Perhaps," she said hesitantly, "the being inside you has the answers."

Now he did look at her, one eyebrow raised.

Encouraged, Tania went on. "I imagine it has a lot it could teach us, perhaps even help us find a way to move it from you to someone else, should that be . . ."

"If I'm on my deathbed or whatever."

"Well, yes. I mean you're not getting any younger." She pinched him.

Skyler let out a little gasp of artificial pain, then pulled her closer. "You're saying I should stay out of harm's way? Take care of myself? Perhaps even step into one of those time-slowed bubbles until the Builders return?"

"I do like the idea of you remaining safe and healthy, I admit," Tania replied. "But what I meant was, perhaps we can speed up the process of making it—that mind, I mean—a full-fledged citizen of the nation of Skyler."

"Meaning what, exactly?"

"Suppose you were to go sit in on a few language lessons with some six-year-old children for a few weeks."

"You can't be serious," he said, laughing.

"I am serious!"

He laughed harder, shaking his head, but she could tell he saw the wisdom in it. "I don't know . . . ," he said after the silence had returned. A sliver of the Sun was just visible now in the west, under a sky of glorious purples.

"Do you have a better idea?" she asked him, trying to put just the right amount of invitation in her words without pushing him too hard.

Skyler Luiken shrugged. "Play it safe . . . educate this mind . . .

keep it healthy. All very wise ideas, Tania Sharma."

"Or?" she prompted.

Then he turned to her. "Or," he said, "I had this thought that maybe you and I could jump out of an airplane over Hawaii."

ACKNOWLEDGMENTS

First and foremost I must thank my agent, Sara Megibow, and my editor, Michael Braff (plus everyone else at Del Rey who helps bring my books to life). I'm endlessly grateful for all the hard work that goes into a project like this.

Thanks be to the authors I'm so proud to call mentors, friends, and contemporaries: Chuck Wendig, Delilah Dawson, Peter Clines, K. C. Alexander, Kevin Hearne, Ramez Naam, Django Wexler, Kat Richardson, Scott Sigler, Robin Hobb, Shawn Speakman, Wes Chu, Sam Sykes, M. D. Waters, Alexandra Oliva, and on and on . . . If not for this wonderful community I don't know how I'd get by. You wonderful weirdos are amazing.

My extreme gratitude to Felicia Day, whose support, generosity, and encouragement have kept me motivated while writing these books. You'll get your sequel one of these days!

Thanks to my wife, Nancy, for her constant support. Love you, sugar!

And, last but not least, thank you for reading. In the end that's all that matters.

—*Jason M. Hough*
Seattle, 2017

ABOUT THE AUTHOR

Jason M. Hough is the *New York Times* bestselling author of the *Darwin Elevator* series and *Zero World*, published in the UK by Titan Books. He has been a 3D artist, animator, and game designer for *Metal Fatigue*, *Aliens vs. Predator*, and others.

THE DIRE EARTH CYCLE
JASON M. HOUGH

The automated alien ship came and built us a space elevator—an impervious thread connecting Darwin, Australia to the heavens. We took advantage of the Builders' gift and established orbital colonies along the cord. Then, years later, a plague almost completely obliterated the world's population...

BOOK ONE: THE DARWIN ELEVATOR

"A thrilling story right from the first page"
Ted Kosmatka, author of *The Games*

BOOK TWO: THE EXODUS TOWERS

"Doesn't spare you one moment to catch your breath once you start reading" The Book Plank

BOOK THREE: THE PLAGUE FORGE

"A powerful and rewarding end to a fast, tense and above all enjoyable series" SF Book

THE GENESIS FLEET
JACK CAMPBELL

Earth is no longer the centre of the universe. After the invention of the faster-than-light jump drive, humanity is rapidly establishing new colonies. But the vast distances of space mean that the protection of Earth's laws no longer exists. When a nearby world attacks, the new colony of Glenlyon turns to Robert Geary, a former junior fleet officer, and Mele Darcy, once an enlisted Marine. They must face down warships with nothing but improvised weapons and a few volunteers – or die trying.

The only hope for lasting peace lies with Carmen Ochoa, a "Red" from anarchic Mars, and Lochan Nakamura, a failed politician, and their plan for a mutual alliance. But if their efforts don't succeed, space could become a battlefield between the first interstellar empires...

VANGUARD
ASCENDANT (MAY 2018)
LIBERATOR (MAY 2019)

"Campbell's skillfully constructed tale keeps a riveting pace"
Publishers Weekly

"Strong characters, complex politics on multiple worlds, battles against impossible odds, this book has the whole package"
Elizabeth Moon, bestselling author of the *Vatta's War* series

TITANBOOKS.COM

THE LOST STARS
JACK CAMPBELL

For the first time, the story of the *Lost Fleet* universe is told through the eyes of citizens of the Syndicate Worlds as they deal with defeat in the war, threats from all sides, and the crumbling of the Syndicate empire. In the Midway Star System, leaders must decide whether to remain loyal to the old order or fight for something new.

TARNISHED KNIGHT
PERILOUS SHIELD
IMPERFECT SWORD
SHATTERED SPEAR

"Campbell maintains the military, political and even sexual tension with sure-handed proficiency... What emerges is a fascinating and vividly rendered character study, fully and expertly contextualized." *Kirkus Reviews*

"As can be expected in a Jack Campbell novel, the military battle sequences are very well done, with the land-based action adding a new dimension." SF Crowsnest

STARK'S WAR

JACK CAMPBELL (WRITING AS JOHN G. HEMRY)

The USA reigns over Earth as the last surviving superpower. To build a society free of American influence, foreign countries have inhabited the moon. Under orders from the US military, Sergeant Ethan Stark and his squadron must engage in a brutal battle to wrest control of Earth's satellite. Up against a desperate enemy in an airless atmosphere, ensuring his team's survival means choosing which orders to obey and which to ignore.

STARK'S WAR
STARK'S COMMAND
STARK'S CRUSADE

"High caliber military science fiction ... non-stop action and likable characters." *Midwest Book Review*

"A gripping tale of military science fiction, in the tradition of Heinlein's Starship Troopers and Haldeman's Forever War. It serves as both a cautionary fable and a science fiction adventure, doing dual purpose and succeeding on both levels."
Absolute Magnitude

"Hemry has a solid sense of military thinking and lunar fighting... I really liked this series." *Philadelphia Weekly Press*

JAG IN SPACE

JACK CAMPBELL (WRITING AS JOHN G. HEMRY)

Equipped with the latest weaponry, and carrying more than two hundred sailors, the orbiting warship, *USS Michaelson*, is armored against the hazards of space and the threats posed in the vast nothing between planets. But who will protect her from the threats within?

He is Ensign Paul Sinclair, assigned to the USS Michaelson as the ship's lone legal officer—a designation that carries grave consequences as he soon learns that the struggle for justice among the stars is a never-ending fight...

A JUST DETERMINATION
BURDEN OF PROOF
RULE OF EVIDENCE
AGAINST ALL ENEMIES

"First-rate military SF ... Hemry's series continues to offer outstanding suspense, realism and characterization." *Booklist*

"The legal aspects are brilliantly intertwined within a fantastic military science fiction drama." *Midwest Book Review*

"Hemry's decision to wed courtroom drama to military SF has captured lightning in a bottle. He builds the story's suspense expertly." SF Reviews

TITANBOOKS.COM

11/07/17

FOR MORE FANTASTIC FICTION, AUTHOR EVENTS, EXCLUSIVE EXCERPTS,
COMPETITIONS, LIMITED EDITIONS AND MORE

VISIT OUR WEBSITE
titanbooks.com

LIKE US ON FACEBOOK
facebook.com/titanbooks

FOLLOW US ON TWITTER
@TitanBooks

EMAIL US
readerfeedback@titanemail.com